The North Face of Shakespeare

How can teachers and workshop leaders use active and dramatic methods to make Shakespeare more accessible to their students?

Experiencing Shakespeare through active teaching methods gives children and students a sense of ownership and helps them to speak, read, understand, and work with the text.

This book is structured to appeal both to teachers and drama practitioners beginning to use practical techniques and to those who want to develop their practice in new ways. It includes over 200 activities, exercises and games, and is divided into two sections.

The first section presents the case for using active and dramatic methods and then addresses approaches to teaching language, narrative and character in Shakespeare's plays, showing how practical methods arise from critical consideration of these three central, formal aspects of the text. The second section focuses on the principles and organisation of practical work and drama workshops.

The ultimate aim of the book is to help those who wish to, to be able to take the drama workshop, and students' learning within the workshop, as far as possible towards the dramatic life and intensity of the stage.

This book will be a valuable resource for teachers of English, Drama and Performance Studies, whether in schools, colleges or universities – and for Theatre and Drama practitioners whose professional lives include organising and leading workshops.

> 'Whatever stage of teaching you are at, this book will provide a guide and a stimulus . . .'
>
> Cicely Berry

The North Face of Shakespeare

Activities for teaching the plays

James Stredder

With a Foreword by
Cicely Berry OBE, Hon DLit

First published 2004 by Wincot Press, 42 Maidenhead Road,
Stratford-Upon-Avon, Warwickshire, CV37 6XT

© 2004 James Stredder

Typeset by Exe Valley Dataset Ltd, Exeter, Devon
Printed and bound in Great Britain by Short Run Press Ltd, Exeter

British Library Cataloguing in Publication Data
A catalogue record for this book is available from the British Library

ISBN 0–9547407–0–X

Contents

Foreword

It gives me particular pleasure to write the Foreword for this book – for two reasons. First, because in it James Stredder brings the spoken language into the classroom: and by this I mean he validates the need for this heightened text to be experienced actively in order for it to be fully understood, so that it conveys something beyond the literal meaning on the page. And second, because the number and scope of the exercises he describes cover many aspects and levels of the teaching of Shakespeare in an accessible and practical way.

I have always believed that you do not understand Shakespeare fully, or indeed any other writer of plays or poetry, until you have spoken the text aloud or, in the case of the deaf speaker, until you have felt the language muscularly in the mouth. This is because there is something in the physicality of the language, i.e. how the consonants are disposed and whether voiced or unvoiced, and how they are juxtaposed with the variable lengths of the vowel sounds, which is not only an intrinsic part of the rhythm and form of the writing, but also of the underlying motive and reasoning of the characters involved. And I believe young people of whatever academic ability, and whatever dialectical variants they may have, given the right opportunity to speak the language, latch on to this in a remarkable way, and I know it excites them and makes them want more. For I firmly believe that the two areas should go on together – i.e. the academic exploration and the practical experience of the language itself. They each resource the other. For Shakespeare, like no other writer before or since, wrote the spoken word, and that is why it can still excite us when we speak it aloud.

Soon after I joined the RSC back in the early 1970s, I started, with the help of Maurice Daniels who was then in charge of all the scheduling, to do workshops in schools: sometimes I would take actors with me, but more often than not I would go in on my own. It was, I suppose, the first stage of our Education Department, now a large and highly organised operation. I did countless workshops in community centres, schools round Stratford, inner-city London schools – even in Brooklyn when the Company visited Brooklyn Academy, all with very different expectations and abilities. I would go into a classroom not knowing what to expect – inner-city teenagers, perhaps not very interested in Shakespeare, or sixth-formers studying for their A-Levels who knew it all! Each time it was both a challenge and a surprise. But my aim was always to get them to understand something new for themselves through the very speaking of the text out loud. And because of the very different responses which came back to me I had to think on my feet in order to clock into the right exercise which would make them respond positively to the play in hand. And always I found myself using physical means, sometimes quite rough, to open up their understanding to this heightened language: this of course had a surprise element for them which one used to advantage, but it very clearly deepened their awareness and sometimes their revelations were quite breathtakingly profound.

This work influenced me deeply, and has informed my work with actors ever since. For I believe actors today are faced with a real dilemma: i.e. how does he/she honour the often extravagant imagery and heightened language yet keep it sounding as if spoken and relevant for now. How do you excite the listener and make her/him enter that other world with those extreme feelings, yet keep truthful for today's world. So all the exercises I have since developed for actors stem from this work, for always they use physical means to help the actor reach for the scope and landscape of the play – and so excite the audience.

And we must keep this excitement alive: and in different ways I think James Stredder does just this, for all the work he lays out in this book is designed to provoke reactions from the class – reactions to the characters, to their predicaments, and to their world: and this in the end makes them involved in the story from their own personal viewpoint and experience – and so be committed to it and want to speak the words. I particularly like the inclusivity of the work – of everyone taking part and being equal: this to me is crucial, for so often those with perhaps a particularly heightened imaginative awareness are not able to express themselves fluently, and perhaps even have difficulty in reading. I think, for instance, dyslexia is something which is not taken anywhere near enough into consideration in our educational system – but that is another story: however, work like this can be of enormous help. I think what is important is to get these young people to experience a feeling of owning that language, of having the right to express it in their own way – and so feel part of it.

Now I know all teachers are very aware of these issues, and will have their own ways of dealing with them: but whatever stage of teaching you are at, this book will prove a guide and a stimulus. Crucially we need to keep the excitement of Shakespeare alive: for I think that business jargon and techno-speak are so taking over our lives that we could be in danger of losing the imaginative essence of our language. From a world perspective, what concerns me is the number of languages that are lost each year: now of course we will not lose the English language for it is the basic language of commerce – it is world currency at the moment – however just for that very reason the spoken language is losing some of its power – and we must not let this happen. The bottom line is this: we must keep Shakespeare alive and speaking in the classroom.

Cicely Berry OBE, Hon DLit

Acknowledgements

Parts of Section I of this book have appeared previously. Thanks to:

The Open University for allowing me to use 'The North Face of Shakespeare: Practical Approaches to Teaching Shakespeare's Narratives', which appeared in *Learners and Pedagogy*, ed. Jenny Leach and Bob Moon (London: Paul Chapman Publishing in association with the Open University, 1999), pp. 171-84. This book is the 'Reader' for O.U. course *E836, Learning, Curriculum and Assessment*, that is itself part of the Open University MA programme.

Birgit Bergmann for permission to use 'Teaching Character in Shakespeare', which was published in *Der Fremdsprachliche Unterricht Englisch* (2002) No. 56 *Shakespeare Kreativ*.

Patrick Spottiswoode, Director, Globe Education, for permission to use *The Enactment of Shakespeare's Language on Stage and in Education* (1995), first printed for the Globe Education Conference, 'within *this* wooden O', which was held at Shakespeare's Globe Theatre, London, in April 1995.

Thanks are also due to:

Cicely Berry, formerly Head of Voice at the RSC, and the inspirational figure to whom everyone working with active methods of teaching Shakespeare is indebted, directly or indirectly, consciously or not.

Rex Gibson, whose *Shakespeare in Schools Project* at the Cambridge Institute of Education has transformed, and is still transforming, the working practice of numerous teachers of Shakespeare, and has brought experience of the delights of 'Active Shakespeare' into the lives of countless children; and John Salway, the Project's Research Associate, and all the other teachers I worked with during my term with the Cambridge *Project*.

Rob Jeffcoate, for all I have learned from our teaching collaboration over many years, and for its pleasure and enrichment, and for his meticulous attention to, and invaluable comments on, the early drafts of this book.

All the students, especially the Drama and English students at the University of Wolverhampton and members of the Arena Theatre Summer School, which ran for ten years in Stratford-upon-Avon, who have helped so much, with their joyful energy, responsiveness and creativity, to forge the material in this book.

Colleagues in the Drama Department at the University of Wolverhampton and the staff of the Arena Theatre in Wolverhampton. I am particularly indebted to all those with whom I have shared teaching, for the fun and the inspiration of working with them, especially to those with whom I have taught courses on Shakespeare: Phil Tilstone, Cathy Macgregor, Andrew Jemmett and Peter Cann. Jeremy Brown, Kate Hale and David Allen for our shared work on the techniques of Drama teaching and Drama workshops, Ruth Shade for the enlivening influence of her work in other shared areas of the Drama curriculum and Judith Aston for her unfailing help and support over many years.

All those who have read and commented on this book, or particular chapters, in manuscript, especially a number of colleagues already mentioned above, Anna Clarkson (Routledge) and Eleanor Rivers, Andrew Pierce, Jon Dudley, Susan Dransfield, Tina Tilstone, Norbert Timm and Dick Leith. Malcolm Griffin for numerous valuable suggestions and modifications to do with safety issues.

Richard Willis, Colin Morgan and Bettina Newman (Swales & Willis), Roger Horton (Routledge), Jim Shaw (Librarian, The Shakespeare Institute, University of Birmingham), Gabrielle Byam-Grounds (English Serenata), Charlotte Allison and Nancy Williamson (Stratford-upon-Avon High School) and Perry Mills (King Edward the Sixth Grammar School, Stratford-upon-Avon).

Finally, Kathy and Sophie, whose sharing of the educational values and beliefs underlying this book, have helped so much to keep them 'burning bright' in my heart and mind.

Introduction

Using this book

Shakespeare remains the central pillar of the 'classical curriculum' in English Literature. The plays are taught throughout English-speaking schools and colleges and often, too, where English is taught as a Foreign Language, sometimes (as in the Gymnasien of Germany) with a depth and thoroughness which one might only expect to encounter in specialised, native-speaking courses. In Britain and beyond, the plays appear on syllabuses for English, Drama and Performance Studies and some children find themselves studying Shakespeare as early as the age of seven or eight. The common ground for those working in such a range of ways, in so many different cultures and educational institutions, is personal and academic involvement in the work of Shakespeare, and a shared intellectual and imaginative interest in the plays, whether they are teaching Shakespeare as English, as Drama or as Theatre or Performance Studies.[1]

This book is addressed to anyone working in any of these subjects, who wishes to develop or improve their teaching of Shakespeare's plays through active techniques, the pedagogy of 'Shakespeare shared'. It does not assume prior knowledge of drama teaching or any special expertise in acting or theatre arts, though anyone who becomes interested in using drama to teach Shakespeare will probably want to take opportunities to do for themselves, through the educational support offered by professional theatre companies, for example, what they want to ask their students to do.[2]

Those beginning to use practical work will find in this book an emphasis on starting-points and ways into the plays. The various teaching techniques, many of which are transferable to other kinds of literature and language work – and, very often, to the teaching of other subjects, are arranged in categories. In most cases, the play chosen to illustrate a particular technique, is unimportant. The emphasis is on the process of building up a repertoire of approaches and methods. For those already using active methods of teaching there are accounts of ways of developing techniques further. These should be used and adapted in whatever ways seem appropriate to the teacher in their own situation. This is the approach I have taken in my own work as a teacher of Shakespeare, work which has largely been in an urban 'new university'[3] in England, teaching on a modular degree and diploma scheme with large classes of students of varied ability. When I went on to hold workshops either exclusively for teachers or largely attended by teachers, I thought, at first, that I needed to be sure that particular methods and approaches would be suitable for the institutions in which workshop participants were teaching, or that I had evidence to show that such techniques would work in these institutions. I quickly learnt that this was the wrong approach. It is futile to spend time debating what might or not work in a particular environment, unless one is part of a team planning a programme of shared work. People need to make their own decisions about what will work for them in their circumstances. So, I changed the way I introduced my workshops, simply saying that we would ourselves be actively working through different methods of approaching and exploring Shakespearian texts. In evaluative discussions afterwards, people would often talk about their plans to use the material they had experienced, in their own teaching, or about work they had undertaken in their own work-place as a result of earlier sessions, but no one was concerned, any longer, to justify themselves if they felt that a particular activity was not for them, or not for their school or college. Working in this way is similar to the way that actors and theatre practitioners work in education. They offer their experience and expertise to participants in practical work, whether taking workshops with a community group, in a primary or secondary school, a college or university or in a drama school, modifying their approach and their mode of discussion depending on the group, but essentially dealing with the same substantive material. Also, like other English and Drama teachers, I have always been something of a jackdaw, appropriating ideas for teaching and modifying them for my own purposes. Many of the methods in this book have been collected and adapted in this way (from Charles Marowitz, Cicely Berry, Augusto Boal, Keith Johnstone and others) and may, in turn, be applied to the work of other playwrights, other genres of literature – even to other academic subjects. Practical work, like theatrical production, is always a mixture of the tried and tested and the experimental or the modified.

The great majority of the exercises and activities in this book may be used at any level. In general, practical methods have traditionally been excluded from the academic study of Literature, except for the very young, yet older students, including the highly educated, discover rich new insights, at both personal and theoretical levels, from even quite simple practical work. In claiming this kind of 'universal application' for practical work, it should be added that reflection at an appropriate level of sophistication (usually through class discussion of some kind) should take place. Whether this discussion takes place during or after the practical work, it will naturally return to the teacher's objectives for the class and to the substantive subject-matter that gave rise to the practical activities in the first place. Objectives must normally operate within the aims of syllabuses and intended outcomes mostly stipulated for us by others, and individual objectives may vary greatly, according to the experience and academic level of our students, but they all share the obvious need to be clear, relevant and realistic. The task of analysing the text, fixing teaching objectives and deciding on activities to meet those objectives, requires the same care, whatever the nature or ages of one's group – and when dealing with active and dramatic approaches, an essential consideration must always be safety.

Chapter 5 (pp. 122–8) gives more attention to safety issues, but from the outset, our responsibility, as teachers, for the physical and emotional safety of those we teach must always be uppermost in out minds. As part of our planning and active practice, each of us needs to take careful account of the particular circumstances and make-up of each and every group of students, of the physical conditions in which we are working and of our own competence and ability to supervise safely any given activity. As with any teaching activity in any subject, we need to identify hazards and assess associated risks. Teaching plans need to include the measures that we shall take to prevent harm or to reduce any potentially harmful effects to an acceptable level or to minimise the likelihood of harm's occurring in the first place. In the pages that follow, there are many activities that involve movement and contact (physical and, at times, emotional) between students. In choosing, planning and carrying out any activity, can we always demonstrate (if necessary with the aid of our syllabus and teaching notes) that we have exercised appropriate care and due regard for the safety of all involved, including ourselves? This is the question we must always be able to answer about any practical work we undertake with students. If necessary, exercises should be adapted, or others, with the same learning objectives but which present less risk to the group in question, should be substituted.

Practical work is not, of course, an end in itself. It is a way of approaching teaching – and to teach texts, one must first read them critically. To teach them using practical methods, that critical reading must examine the dramatic features of texts, and the origins of those features, for these give rise to the practical activities and endow them with potency. 'Critical reading' involves awareness of the ways in which meaning, tone, address, imagery, rhetorical devices and metrics operate, from the micro-level of the word or phrase, to the broader frameworks of narrative, convention and genre, and all this takes place in shifting cultural contexts, in which what is assumed to be agreed by readers, is always changing. In the late twentieth century these changes were sometimes spectacular, especially in readers' understanding of issues of race, colonialism, gender and sexuality, but small changes in the way texts are read and understood are always taking place, as the meanings of words evolve and as the significance of particular kinds of behaviour is felt to alter. It is through constantly returning to critical reading, and the changing issues which accompany it, that our work as teachers is energised and maintained.

Section I of the book deals with 'active and dramatic approaches to teaching the plays'. Here it is suggested that the most distinctive dramatic features of Shakespearian texts emanate from three central formal aspects of those texts: language, narrative (in which I include plot and scene construction) and character. A chapter is devoted to each. Each of these three chapters begins with a commentary on the aspect's distinctive kinds of action, excitement and pleasure, such as play, theatricality, rhetoric, imagery and musicality (in language); pattern, suspense and surprise (in narrative); and imitation, recognition, setting and mood (in character). All these qualities, brought into the social arena of the workshop, give dramatic life to the practical exercises. Ideas for active work on a given text emerge from theoretical consideration of its formal aspects and what we are trying to teach about them. Many of the practical ideas, of course, may be adapted for use in other contexts, but in tracing specific connections to

Shakespeare's language, narrative or character, I am trying to suggest how one can focus and sharpen the use of active techniques – which sometimes seem to surround us like a sea of useful, but chaotic, flotsam and jetsam. The book is primarily a handbook of practical techniques, but, particularly in the commentary sections, it aims to demonstrate the continuity of practice with theory – its dependency on theory, even. This means that the book is about Shakespeare, not just about teaching Shakespeare.

Each of the three main chapters on language, narrative and character, has three broadly 'graded' categories of suggested 'teaching approaches'. These generally increase in complexity and in the demands they make on teachers and students, although the divisions are not at all rigid and it is not suggested that these categories should be worked through systematically, in order. There are some activities in the third categories, for example, that teachers with no experience of teaching drama would be happy to use straight away. Suitable approaches may be selected from any category, depending on one's particular teaching objectives at a particular time. The approaches to language, in Chapter 2, move from 'Listen and speak', through 'Active reading', to 'Learn and act'. Teaching approaches to narrative, in Chapter 3, move from 'Structural', through 'Dynamic', to 'Investigative' and those in Chapter 4, on character, from 'Personal encounters with roles', through 'Roles in social settings' to 'Roles in action in the narrative'. These three chapters, together with Chapter 1, which presents arguments for the use of active methods of teaching the plays, make up Section I of the book.

Section II, 'General workshop activities and the Shakespeare workshop', is made up of four chapters. The first, Chapter 5, discusses general issues to do with practical work and is concerned with the planning and running of workshops. The warm-up and preparation exercises of Chapters 6, 7 and 8, dealing with group formation activities, games and drama exercises, are included as resources to be used, for the most part, in the opening stages of workshops. Each of these three chapters includes an overview of how their various kinds of practical and dramatic activity fit into practical work on Shakespeare. As well as being valuable as warm-ups and preparation for drama workshops, many of these activities may also be adapted to play a substantive role in workshops. Some ideas on how such adaptations can work for specific plays are provided. Throughout Section II, the particular concerns of 'the Shakespeare workshop' are never far away, but the whole section is of general applicability to drama teaching and to teaching other subjects through drama. Those who have come to drama teaching through their work on Shakespeare, may be able to use this section to further develop their expertise. But remember to always work within your expertise and to select activities that you assess as safe to use with your students.

Developing the use of drama to teach Shakespeare

This book is intended to be a contribution to the 'Active Shakespeare' movement (p. 5) and its particular goal is to also suggest ways in which active and practical work can make increased use of the specific practices of drama teaching.

The descriptive methodological terms 'active', 'practical' and 'dramatic' overlap in common usage and vary in their meaning according to context. Silent reading is nevertheless 'active' (responsive and creative on the part of the reader)[4] and learning has to be active in some sense in order to take place at all, while 'practical criticism', as developed by I.A. Richards and F.R. Leavis in the early part of the twentieth century actually refers to a particular tradition of, again sedentary, but highly engaged and alert critical analysis, which may be done in seminar discussion or alone.

My use of 'active' and 'practical', here, refer to ways of teaching which contrast with traditional methods of transmission, and I use 'active' as the more inclusive of the two terms. For example, if I am leading a seminar or standing before a class of students lecturing, with the students sitting taking notes, I would not consider either case to involve 'active' teaching methods. If I break off to set students discussion tasks, sitting in pairs, or if I ask for half a dozen to come up to the front to help me demonstrate the way a scene works, I would call these 'active methods'. At the other end of the scale, I would also call obviously 'dramatic' workshops on specialised techniques (mime, movement, voice or improvisation) 'active', i.e. the word includes a very wide spectrum of activities.

I use 'practical' for 'the next level up' in inclusivity, i.e. I would not describe the examples above of paired discussion and lecturer demonstration, as 'practical', but if the whole class were making an image of the social and political relationships of a play, or if students were working in groups on scenes, or rehearsing, or were taking part in one of the drama workshops mentioned above, then I would call those activities 'practical'.

The third term, 'dramatic', or 'using drama', is more specialised again, for now there is the implication that students are performing or using the idea of performative voices or roles or structures. Taking part in the practical activity of making a tableau or image is barely dramatic, but may rapidly become so as participants are invited to speak, relate, move or comment, in role as characters from the play. All teachers of Shakespeare will probably feel confident to use some dramatic methods, but not necessarily to teach specialized techniques. Many will be conscious that they know little of 'Drama', as a discipline in its own right, and that there is an enormous amount to learn, some of it only through training. I believe that all teachers of Shakespeare who wish to, can use all of the activities proposed in this book, but that everyone must go at their own pace in developing their drama-teaching skills and that some will decide certain activities will probably never be for them. In the theatre, actors with no special ability or training in song or dance, frequently sing and dance, unpretentiously, to great effect and approval – but this generalist development of a range of skills is very different from immodestly attempting to perform 'in a huge sphere, and not to be seen to move in't'. The same is true of developing one's ability to use drama in one's teaching,[5] and this is the ultimate aim of the book – to help those who wish to, to be able to take the drama workshop, and students' learning within the workshop, as far as possible towards the dramatic life and intensity of the stage, albeit without a discrete audience.

All the exercises and activities in this book are learning vehicles, often dramatic in their own right, but they are not to do with training students to perform and present work outside the workshop. Nevertheless, one of the rewards of teaching Shakespeare through drama is the scope it provides for the broad development of students, in skills, confidence and imagination, development that takes place as the substantive activities on Shakespearian texts are carried out. This 'development' can also benefit students by furnishing them with skills and qualities that can be taken into other contexts. Drama is skills-based, especially in the individual areas of listening, reading, speaking and performing and in the social skills of group-work: co-operating, discussing, communicating, valuing contributions, sharing, modifying, compromising and so on[6]. Because of the assumed difficulty of Shakespeare, achievements in repeating, reading, learning and performing the text, may have a markedly positive effect on students' confidence as well as competence. In terms of imagination, there are opportunities to speak musical, resonant poetry in the working context of an activity or exercise and to experience remote, mythological stories and characters through the immediacy of one's own faculties, mind and body.

The teacher's autonomy

In the chapters that follow, the role of teachers in presenting Shakespeare is mainly discussed through their participation and activity and their skill as facilitators and 'sharers', but, more fundamentally, shaping the work will be the particular enthusiasms, theoretical perspectives and knowledge of individuals. These are the vital energising properties of the teacher. We are teachers of Dramatic Literature in the first place because we want to share and debate our readings at the primary level of the text, so it is rewarding to explore one's own interest in the plays of Shakespeare, as one is working on them with a class. This happens, for example, when one stages a production or takes a class to a live performance. In the same way, the provision in Chapters 2, 3 and 4, of 'critical contexts' or commentaries, proposing direct links between formal aspects of Shakespeare's texts and active ways of teaching them, is intended to interest the reader as a fellow student of Shakespeare, whatever the age or composition of the group with which they are working. Similarly, the warm-up and preparation exercises of Section II are included, partly, in recognition of our need, as teachers, to take existing techniques and adapt them to our own purposes.

The book argues for the primacy of personal control, so whether we teach in colleges, schools or universities, it is the habit of making one's own connexions between critical analysis and teaching method that is central. In this, the experience of the teacher is parallel to that of the student. In the process of learning, our students also require a feeling of personal control, of being at the centre of their learning and the creation of meaning. When a practical class produces exciting, focused work, there is a particular pleasure and exhilaration shared by teacher and students. Active work may not be the only way to come by these things, but, as Chapter 1 argues, it is, with its visible engagement and its harnessing of the social power of the group, a vitally important way of learning.

Section 1

Active and dramatic approaches to teaching the plays

Chapter 1

Why use active methods to teach the plays?

The North Face of Shakespeare

The frontispiece to the First Folio edition of Shakespeare's plays pictures the playwright's forehead as a shining dome. Shakespeare's editors, the actors John Heminge and Henry Condell, who chose this memorial image, were consciously making the theatrical writings of their friend into a monumental literary work. Of the thirty-six plays published in this first 'Collected Works', seven years after his death, eighteen, including *Macbeth*, *Julius Caesar*, *Twelfth Night* and *The Tempest*, had never appeared in print before and, without the enterprise of Heminge and Condell, might have been lost forever.[1] The frontispiece image, which seems implacable and authoritative in that engraving of 1623, has been widely used in our culture, often as an advertiser's kite-mark of quality. I call this image 'Shakespeare's North Face' because Shakespeare and his plays, products of some twenty-five years of hectic theatrical activity, can seem as indifferent and unscaleable now as the icy north face of the Eiger.

This stony imagery of awe-inspiring monuments and icy Alpine precipes is intended, however, to suggest what our culture has made of Shakespeare and what approaching his work is like for many people, not the actual difficulty of the plays themselves. Elizabethan and Jacobean audiences might be surprised to find, after four hundred or so years, that that most popular of their playwrights, William Shakespeare, has such an intimidating reputation – and many teachers of Shakespeare, today, would agree about the potential accessibility of the plays, which those original audiences considered to be so theatrical and entertaining. It is not that the language and frames of reference of Shakespearian drama are easy, now, or do not require the labour of close study. It is rather that the feeling of being overwhelmed by the supposed difficulty and remoteness of Shakespeare from the outset, as though his works are an icy rock-face, will inevitably intimidate or alienate many learners. Yet, as with everything else in the world, where you happen to be situated, is crucial.

For some fortunate children and students today, Shakespeare's plays have been reclaimed from their reputation and history, so that they can experience them immediately and freshly, without trepidation, for themselves. In Britain, theatre companies, especially travelling companies like Northern Broadsides, Cheek by Jowl and Théâtre de Complicité and many Theatre in Education companies,[2] as well as touring operations from the Royal Shakespeare Company and the National Theatre, have been wonderfully successful with their Shakespeare productions and accompanying Shakespeare workshops, in school, college and community venues – and many full-scale productions in theatres throughout the land, from the RSC and Shakespeare's Globe to regional Repertory Theatres have left an indelible impression of energy, excitement and beauty in the minds of the children and students who have been lucky enough to be taken to them.[3] Some recent film versions, with Shakespeare almost seeming like just another contemporary screen-writer, have been widely enjoyed by young audiences too, and always there have been inspired individual teachers, who, whatever their style of teaching, have been able to establish a lasting, positive disposition towards the plays, in their students.[4] Most importantly of all, there has been a shift towards the use of active approaches to teaching Shakespeare in education, partly because of the active and creative ('progressive') direction taken by English teaching since the 1950s and 1960s and partly because of the increase in popularity of Drama itself, as an independent subject.

Drama, as it evolved in British schools, was particularly associated with the progressive developments of the 1960s. This was a period when the subject was re-invented, with a specific commitment to many of those developments – 're-invented', because, of course, dramatic methods of teaching literature go back at least as far as Henry Caldwell Cook and Harriet Finlay-Johnson in the early part of the twentieth century,[5] and active approaches to teaching Speech, Drama and English were widespread before and after the Second World War. In the 1950s Drama had been strengthened by Peter Slade's work, which included the provision of a theoretical grounding for the subject, in play and child development. When I started teaching in the late 1960s, my own practice was greatly affected by the excitement and educational potential of this relatively new school subject, as propounded by Slade and then by others such as Brian Way and Dorothy Heathcote. There were other powerful influences too, such as: the creative, personal and socially-aware emphases in David Holbrook's books on English teaching; the old tradition of 'choral speaking' which had been revived and re-energised by the 'live poetry' movement of the late 1950s and the 1960s; and the emergence of numerous courses and books on dramatic techniques, such as Viola Spolin's *Improvisation for the Theatre* (1973), and on 'gaming' and (pre-computer) simulation and role-playing, which were used widely in business training and in a range of subjects from English to Social Studies and Geography. Simulation and gaming, in particular, directed my attention to structural elements in plays and provided the stimulus for developing the kind of work which is described in Chapter 3 on Narrative.

All these developments in English and Drama also encouraged expansion in the educational work undertaken by theatres and theatre companies – and the creation of companies specialising in Theatre in Education. But the most influential specific initiative in Britain, in the last twenty years, has been Rex Gibson's 'Shakespeare in Schools Project' at the Cambridge Institute of Education. This started in the mid 1980s and was funded by the Gulbenkian Foundation. Seconded teachers worked together for a term at a time on 'Active Shakespeare', with Rex Gibson and John Salway, developing their own practice as teachers of Shakespeare and helping to generate material for the Project's publications.[6]

The Shakespeare in Schools Project provided a structure and way of working capable of reaching, resourcing, supporting, developing and, perhaps most importantly, exciting and challenging every teacher of Shakespeare in the land. It demonstrated that active methods can be adopted widely. This book hopes to add to that demonstration and, in particular, to encourage teachers of Shakespeare to develop further as teachers of Drama. There is a broad and sound basis for this. At the time the Shakespeare and Schools Project started, practical and dramatic approaches to teaching Shakespeare were already widespread, especially through the pioneering workshops and publications of Cicely Berry, then Head of Voice at the Royal Shakespeare Company and through workshops and education programmes taught by actors, directors and education officers from professional theatre companies of every kind – from the big national and regional companies to a host of small touring companies and Theatre in Education companies. For Drama teachers, crucial texts by theatre practitioners had appeared, and have continued to appear, especially those by Clive Barker (1977), Keith Johnstone (1981; 1999) and Augusto Boal (1979; 1992), all of which have greatly strengthened Drama teaching in all its manifestations. Every country in which Shakespeare is taught will have a different experience of these various educational developments, but reports from other areas of the world, from the United States, Canada, Germany, Italy and Australia, for instance, indicate that similar forces are at work there.

Although all these developments plainly indicate that it is by no means true for everyone, including those who have never taken an exam on a Shakespearian text, that 'Shakespeare was boring at school', the dominant reality of contact with Shakespeare in education is probably still, for most learners, a reality of problems and barriers: the weight and authority of academic tradition, the difficulty of language, allusion and plot and the complexity of subject-matter and theme. It is hard for teachers, in the context of the daily classroom round, to constantly stimulate and inspire and to imbue every hour of work with interest and involvement, yet as we all know, once learning activities achieve a certain momentum, the teacher no longer has to struggle and fight. At this point they can resource, observe, support, develop, respond – really teach, in fact.

The main argument for practical work on Shakespeare, the subject of this book, is that it is invaluable in meeting the challenges I have been discussing, not least because it offers every individual personal contact with the plays, in the context of the pleasure and support of social, creative activity. It also requires learners to be, and assumes they will be, responsible for the work that goes on in the classroom or workshop, and to become involved with it. Practical work is especially effective in motivating, 'empowering', and developing confidence. The point of a handbook of practical approaches, of teaching methods using drama, is to try to open up the texts as fields of play, and so of learning, so that students become, and feel, equal to the demands of that learning.[7] This chapter examines in greater detail the arguments for using active methods of teaching. Subsequent chapters deal with the principles of using practical work and drama workshops to teach the plays of Shakespeare. But first we need to look more closely at the question of reputation and how this can work as an obstacle in our culture and our educational institutions.

The problem of monumentalism

Shakespeare's intimidating reputation is likely to be encountered before his texts, but reputations represent what the world thinks and when we encounter them we probably want to find out for ourselves whether or not they are justified. With great cultural and historical monuments, this can seem presumptuous or futile: their reputations are so firmly established, their value so universally assumed and continuously re-affirmed. For those suspicious of received wisdom and tradition, iconoclasm may be tempting, but it is one thing to vandalise and quite another to mount arguments that will challenge received opinion. It is more effective and easier, perhaps, to claim revolutionary authority, moral and aesthetic, asserting that demolition of cultural monuments is a progressive duty that will benefit oppressed groups. This has sometimes been argued strongly in Britain and the United States over the last thirty or so years and many universities have given their curriculums complete overhauls, as a result of often bitter conflict. It is, of course, a feeble defence of the status quo to say 'we should go on doing this because we've always done it'. Such questions as 'what's the actual use of this?' and 'are our students positively represented, now, in what we have chosen to teach them?' must be answered.

In the case of Shakespeare, without even entering critical debate at the level of the historical text, supporters can point to two powerful, living aspects of his reputation. The first is that his plays, in modern times, have often been read and staged, not as the inevitable property of rulers and colonisers and the powerful, but as open, contemporary, even anti-establishment texts, sometimes, in the theatre, even presented in direct opposition to oppressive regimes and cultures. The second is that the plays continue to have a strikingly healthy after-life on film and in the theatre. The theatre, including its subsidised wing, requires commercial success, popularity, just as the cinema does. But my purpose here is to respond to the ubiquity of Shakespeare in our educational systems, and to add to the resources for teaching the plays. It is not to debate his reputation or the merits of teaching the plays, although I certainly believe it is rich and worthwhile for children and students to read and study them. Such as it is, the book's contribution to the critical defence of the study of Shakespeare depends less on criticism than on the broad argument that once one thinks of the classroom or workshop as a kind of dramatic or theatrical laboratory, with all the participants as equal players, study of the formal aspects of Shakespearian texts, their language, narratives and characters, will generate a stream of ideas for active work – and that use of these will deliver a peculiar abundance of creative, emotional, and intellectual or critical insights and stimulation, to those who work with them.

Nevertheless, Shakespeare's monumental reputation inevitably hangs over many as they embark on study of the plays. By 'monumentalism', I mean an aura bestowed by culture and history, a feeling of immoderate respect, that can make people snobbishly subservient or cowed and resentful. Monumentalism, in Shakespeare, as in the rest of the curriculum, entombs and mystifies the object of study. It can demoralise, and weaken the resolve of the learner. This book presents active teaching approaches as a way of overcoming the mental encrustation, the deadening effects, of monumentalism in Shakespeare, but it is written with general principles in mind and applies to the situation of learners wherever monumentalism positions them outside their field of study.

The greatest value of teaching Shakespeare actively is that it allows all the students participating to be included and to be successful. All those subject to the power of the classical curriculum should, I believe, through their education, reach a personal sense of equilibrium, a kind of ease, with that power. Students should feel secure in their own achievement[8] whatever its level. Systems of education often bring about exactly the opposite effect, leaving many humiliated by their encounter with cultural power, rather than proud of their own experience of using that power. Students who have been Hamlet, who have made, in a workshop, their own experience of 'To be or not to be . . .', will not be intimidated by the cultural power assigned to the play, whatever uses are made of it in the educational system, nor will they feel excluded if they have, themselves, moved into their own relationship of equilibrium with the play and its power – just as any Greek, standing in the theatre at Epidaurus, regardless of their personal knowledge or ignorance of their ancient culture, should feel a sense of equanimity before that massive cultural monument. And, like those native Greeks, our native citizens should not be told that access to their cultural tradition is restricted and that some are best to leave it well alone, so: 'To the monument!'

The teacher repositioned: 'Shakespeare shared'

The first question for the teacher[9] is how to draw learners into the field of study. It is easy, traditional even, for we as teachers to contribute further to the process of exclusion. At worst, our own success, enthusiasm and expertise become part of that exclusion, part of the cultural monument, yet it is not our brief to hide our skill, to leave students to their own devices or to fail to lead. We need to lead from within the learning group (we *are* within it, in the sense that it operates through a kind of collaborative, symbolic production) – just as parents are very obviously within the 'learning group' when participating in their child's acquisition of skills and knowledge; the pedagogical significance of the phrase *in loco parentis* is much overlooked. Teachers, like parents, are constantly mediating the world, acting like story-tellers to introduce new material and ideas, and remaining forever on the lookout for ways of cultivating independent exploration in their students, but, to present our 'teaching narratives', we have to move over, repositioning ourselves as tellers and involving the listeners in the telling of the tale.

When this happens, ownership becomes shared and it moves to the centre of the learning activity. This is obvious in the play-learning of young children. I was taking my daughter to see *A Midsummer Night's Dream*. How should we prepare for an experience which, first of all, I wanted her to enjoy? I would not risk turning it into 'a story out of my head', nor would I, as an introduction, read her the versions by Lamb or even Bernard Miles. My basic principle would be a basic teaching principle: facilitating ownership. Certainly this means involvement, active learning, participation, but with the aim of learners making the material their own, 'owning' it. She would need to make the characters of *A Midsummer Night's Dream* her own, as well as the story and some of the language. Her bedroom was full of soft toys. 'Who's to be the powerful Duke Theseus of Athens?' I began. 'Who's to be Hippolyta, Queen of the Amazons, the famous tribe of warrior women?' As I told her about each character, she selected whom she thought to be an appropriate player – from teddy-bears, Snoopy, Jemima Puddleduck, Mr. Punch, a monkey, dolls. I had written, names on self-adhesive labels, which she stuck on the toys, and as each was identified we discussed where in the room they should go (where would the wood near Athens actually be?) and to which group they might belong. Lysander's dowager aunt doesn't appear in the play but she has a house seven leagues from Athens and to get to it, when they elope, Lysander and Hermia must cross the wood outside the town. This characterising and locating, with the child moving the toys around as the story unfolds, is proprietorial: the child creates the scene, the people and the narrative. At the same time, without slowing down this process (and thereby taking it back from the child) I brought in fragments of original language, especially magical forest language[10] – 'Ill met by moonlight . . .', 'I know a bank . . .', 'You spotted snakes with double tongue . . .', 'What thou seest when thou dost wake . . .', 'Thou art transformed . . .'.

At another time, when we went to see Tchaikovsky's *Swan Lake*, we used a familiar, traditional device (the toy theatre) in the same sort of way. We made cut-out characters, coloured them with felt pens, stuck on large expressive faces, wrote names on them and moved them through the ballet on a cardboard-box stage.[11]

These preparatory readings are 'productions of the text', rather than responses to it. They are about making meanings with the text, an active process which is personal but not private. It is less 'my view' or 'my response' and more of a process like theatre production, taking up the text, experimenting with it, improvising imagery and meaning from what-ever materials and resources are to hand. In workshops, this becomes a group process, and for it to function well, it must not be exclusive, with a few in the limelight and the rest observing – like those old-fashioned elimination games at children's parties, in which an ever-increasing audience of 'knocked-out' competitors patiently watched the slow emer-gence of a final winner. There may be much in *Hamlet*, and educational tradition, to justify treating Shakespeare as an elimination game, but the workshop process with which we are dealing here, will mean that a session on Hamlet's soliloquys entails as many Hamlets as there are people taking part. Active Shakespeare means that all participants are active. Shakespeare is shared.

In practical work, the emphasis is thrown from the teacher on to the class, the 'co-owners' and 'doers', and this focuses minds, creating absorp-tion and, therefore, good conditions for learning. Practical work functions as ceremony and it proceeds through rituals (encounters, sharing, displaying), like those which maintain cohesiveness in the wider social world. It seems to reactivate participants as social beings with presence and validity. There is a place for the teacher as lecturer addressing rows of students, but in that situation there are opportunities for becoming non-players, rather like those at an auction not participating in the bidding. Practical work calls students back to themselves and utilises the different strengths of participants. It throws the focus on collaboration and it releases a whole range of modes of communication within groups. Furthermore, used thoughtfully, it is very efficient. Learners who are stimulated and interested are more likely to be motivated to read and to work independently. At the very least, practical work can dispose students to think well of the text they are about to study, while at best, in Perry Mills's phrase, it can 'turn on a light in the mind'.

Starting active work

All teachers must judge for themselves when and how to work actively with their classes. Those with no experience of drama might begin with a short piece of active work, without any special announcements or commitments to clearing away tables and chairs or elaborate plans for a full workshop. Five or ten minutes of such activity in the setting of a more traditional lesson, for example, may be much more rewarding than a more ambitious drama workshop, which you do not feel ready to handle. In starting to use active and practical approaches, it is essential to build up one's own style and self-confidence gradually, in one's own time. Begin with simple exercises which seem, to you, appealing and 'possible'. There are concentration exercises, for example, which involve the individual creating an imagined world in their own immediate space[12] and there are numerous ways of introducing controlled participation: a teacher explaining structural material, such as the background to the usurpation of Richard II by Bolingbroke, for example, can produce a new quality of interest by composing a living genealogical diagram, made up of people called up from the class, to illustrate the motivation and relationships of the characters. This technique was used very effectively in the theatre by Clive Wood when playing the Duke of York in the RSC 2000/01 production of *Henry VI, Part II*. In Act II, Scene ii, York explains his claim to the English crown, to Salisbury and Warwick. He begins 'Edward the Third, my lords, had seven sons' and goes on to detail the line from Edward's third son, the Duke of Clarence, through his daughter Philippa, who married a Mortimer, down to York's own mother, Anne. All this was very amusingly and clearly demonstrated (for the benefit of the audience, of course, as intended by Shakespeare) by York, with the aid of a bag of stones, which he spread all over the stage in representation of the numerous relatives named in the text. In such ways, a lecture can become a dramatic event, with a shared, physical learning zone created through the active involvement of the class.

The great advantage of this kind of teaching is that it nurtures concentration. Just as actors want to create complete absorption in their audiences, so do teachers want to see everyone in their class concentrating – absorbed in learning activity, which is the best foundation for the growth of interest and successful continuing work. Absorption is the first aim of teaching. While it may appear as a result of the charisma of the teacher, for absorption to be sustained, the learning activity itself must acquire its own dynamic. Too often, in education, this dynamic cannot develop or it is destroyed. The self-discipline of the learning activity breaks down and the teacher resorts to emergency measures and imposed discipline. When this happens, the importance of the social organisation of the learning environment is revealed all too clearly. In any group, social forces are immensely powerful. The way these forces are recognized, controlled or harnessed is all-important in educational situations. In the classroom without focus or discipline, these forces can be anarchic and destructive. Even in well-ordered post-graduate seminars, individuals can feel threatened, lost or too under confident to participate, when the activity is perceived as socially fragmented or exclusive. If all are to learn, there must be cohesiveness and absorption, which it is the responsibility of the teacher to create. Active methods are a very effective way of fulfilling that responsibility. Use them in a more sustained and structured way and the teaching session has become a workshop. Learning has become a shared event, and the workshop, a vital form of theatrical production.

Drama workshops

If Shakespeare in the theatre should be a dramatic delight, so, too, should be the collective dramatic performance, the theatrical production, of the drama workshop. Yet 'workshops' sometimes come under the sort of attack formerly reserved for 'progressive education',[13] so I shall restate their value here. The workshop is a truly participatory form and those taking part should be equally involved and active throughout; there should be opportunities to learn through the full range of participants' capabilities – intellectual, emotional, spiritual, moral, social, political, physical, imaginative. A good workshop is full of unfamiliar angles and challenges, of unexpected transformations of theory into image and feeling, and *vice versa*, of new, three-dimensional ways of understanding, communicating and creating with others: it should have the satisfaction and the dramatic delight of successful stage performance.

It is axiomatic in workshop theatrical production that the particular imaginative and dramatic forces of texts should be made available – whether those forces be in the revenge structure and final duelling of *Hamlet*, the storm of *King Lear*, the murders of *Macbeth*, the battles of *Henry V* or the humour of *As You Like It*. And if, in the plays, there are storms, duels, quandaries, murders, moments of exhilaration or recognition or despair, battles, songs or witchcraft, we should have their dramatic force, too, as best we are able, in our workshops. This sounds intimidating. How, with a whole class, can we possibly venture towards battles or murders without being shouted down or swept away ourselves? And what will be achieved unless the activity is grounded in the specificity of the text under consideration? We need to control, focus and structure the work, slowing it down without removing the tension, maintaining pace through disciplined sequences, rather than chaotic activity. In the chapters that follow, workshop techniques are suggested to make this possible.

Workshops conceived in this way, as communal, concretised zones of learning, develop a sense of ownership in participants. Much of the time, however, our competitive, grade-centred systems of education deliver the contrary message, 'this is not for you'. I was talking, once, to a man with an extraordinarily deft control of language and richness of vocabulary. Finally he asked me what I did for a living. When I told him I was a teacher he began to apologise and mumble, saying he had been no good at school, and, especially 'no good at English'. When we speculate that curiosity mysteriously deserts children at some critical age, we might also reflect that curiosity, the need to empower oneself intellectually, depends on the security of ownership.

The learner and the text at the centre

Although the experience of drama and speaking verse is, first of all, practical and physical, reflection and analysis emerging from that experience should always be integrated into the work (see pp. 136–8 on *Active discussion* and p. 131 on *Texts and note-books*). Critical discussion arises from practical work in many ways and at different levels. Take, for example, Hamlet's cry for vengeance on his uncle Claudius, the 'bloody, bawdy villain' – and what Literature teacher can resist a modest declamation of those words? In active Shakespeare, everyone tries them out. Comment might then involve the revenge tradition, a discussion of bombastic, pre-Shakespeare verse, actors' interpretations and so on, or it might simply focus on psychologising Hamlet's lines, referring to the text of the play, to discover ways of making them work dramatically.[14]

All practical work is, pre-eminently, production. This notion of producing or 'making' the characters or the narrative of a play is attractive both to progressive pedagogy (it is creative, stimulating, participatory, offers ownership) and to the rigours of modern critical theory (where meaning is actively produced by reader/audience and situation, rather than universal or inherent, and where the language and conventions of the text generate multiple meanings, rather than a single, harmonised perspective). Taken together, these progressive and critical emphases set up a learner-centred and text-centred base for active work, which is invaluable to teachers.

Along with 'active' and 'social', the terms 'learner-centred' and 'text-centred' are key aspects of the pedagogy, the theoretical basis and practical application, of teaching Shakespeare actively. This pedagogy combines traditional and progressive elements and underlies all the ideas for teaching to be found in this book. After years of ideological struggle, I believe we are now at a point where out of the old thesis of traditionalism and antithesis of progressivism, a synthesis has been forged, making a 'new progressivism' possible. Talk of 'child-centred' education,[15] for example, can still polarise educationists, throwing traditionalists and progressivists into conflict over old issues, but both will happily accept the 'learner-centred' notion of a child sitting alone with a computer carrying out an interactive programme, in control of their own learning resources and proceeding at their own pace. Information Technology, fortuitously at one level, but also inevitably in that the personal computer has been developed as an extension for our individual brains, has helped to retrieve the idea of child-centredness – so much so that parents find, in matters of modern electronic communication, that they are rearing, willingly or not, a new form of 'self-regulated child'. The economically-driven concept of students and parents as clients or consumers has also influenced thinking. In the climate of modern education, 'learner-centredness' is uncontroversial. In teaching Shakespeare actively, the teacher is present in a vital organising role, and technology is probably not involved significantly, but a similar 'learner-centredness' is nevertheless evident. Students are personally involved, enmeshed even, in a learning matrix in which they must actively manipulate resources and make individual decisions. There is a high level of autonomous activity and their learning is taking place independently, facilitated by a teacher, but owned and energised by the students themselves. The acid test, of course, is the effectiveness of teaching Shakespeare this way. My own experience of its effectiveness is the reason for writing this book.

The second key term of the pedagogy of active Shakepeare teaching, 'text-centred', also represents a synthesis, a 'new progressivism'. Traditionalists can welcome the principle that the original text is always used, while progressives know that the work is freed from the tyranny of authority and propriety. The text is treated as a script, a score for performance, a huge store of words to be taken out and used, a field for play and experiment. As Peter Brook has observed, whatever you do to a text in the theatre[16] or the workshop, there it is again after you have finished with it, pristine and whole once more.

In spite of the cultural changes discussed in the previous two paragraphs, which make it harder for institutions, subjects and teaching practices to preserve traditional approaches to education uncritically, how can a 'new progressivism' be established, when outcomes, targets, key-stages and testing seem to fill the day? It only has a chance of being established if it can be shown to work and that it is efficient – that, for example, half an hour of active Shakespeare improves children's general ability to listen and read and speak (I would claim it does), as well as their knowledge of a particular text. Even then, there is a systemic problem with the implementation and maintenance of progressivism and I believe that some of the difficulties Drama as a discipline has faced in the last forty years are down to certain fundamental characteristics it shares with progressivism. It is difficult, for example, to maintain the freshness and relevance of new methodologies while also establishing systems capable of reproducing and strengthening those methodologies. To survive they must eventually find ways of maintaining their growth and existence through settlement within the existing system, but it is the fate of many initiatives, which are positive and promising, to be viewed as unsustainable; we cannot see how they will work out in practice, so we distrust them.

Some would argue that, like social criticism inspired by religion or morality, it is the role of progressivism in education to be oppositional, that it should not expect, or desire, to achieve centrality. This book takes the opposite view. It is written in the belief that there is an innate, dramatic relationship between Shakespeare's texts and active teaching and that approaching Shakespeare this way, to whatever degree feels possible, is open to all teachers of his plays. New methods can be learned and can become established as vitally useful tools within one's teaching practice. Demonstrating this, was one of the great achievements of the 'Shakespeare in Schools Project', mentioned above (p. 5). So, this is a good moment for the active and practical teaching of Shakespeare and for development of the rather more performative and theatrical dramatic teaching of Shakespeare – or, 'teaching the plays through Drama'. In this respect, I also believe we need to capitalise further on the, currently uneven, but potentially very strong relationship between Drama as a method and a subject, and Theatre as a cultural industry (with some of its revenue coming from educational work, which is also an investment in future audiences). Each can vitally strengthen the role and purpose of the other.

Back to the art of teaching

For many teachers, the chance to stimulate, involve and motivate students, so that they leave classes collectively excited about reading and writing about their set text, is justification enough for practical work. For others, practical work can be a telling way of dealing with cognitive aims: how, and in what frame of mind, for example, does Hamlet first 'meet and greet' the other characters in the play? Practical work on this question would put every student through the various encounters. This is not only absorbing and creative; it is essentially efficient learning. When everyone plays Hamlet (and good workshop organisation means more or less constant activity for every participant), no one can day-dream or withdraw and everyone 'learns the way' through experiencing it personally. 'The way', in this example, is a sure and subtle understanding, and recollection, of Hamlet's position, at particular moments, within the web of people and relationships that make up the Danish court. Practical lessons call on learners to actually 'do' or enact the dramatic blueprint that is the text, and this is like walking a route, as opposed to studying it on a map.

Finally, teaching remains an art, practised through the teaching relationship. Active approaches remind us of this, because they begin with recognition of the situation of learners: teachers, with their resources and their power to develop or inhibit, must respond and relate to the learners and to the opportunities that arise, but this can only be done with art and with practice.

Chapter 2

Shakespeare's language

The aims of language work

'The language' is the feature of Shakespeare's drama most frequently cited as the biggest barrier to understanding and enjoyment. The fortunes of Shakespeare's language, the rich but essentially demotic language of the Globe Theatre, illustrate its common history with once-popular art forms that are now separated from popular experience. Language and forms of language that were once accessible are now perceived as obscure, no matter how many proverbial expressions and phrases we find in Shakespeare's language that are still current today, and no matter that all but a small percentage of the words are readily understood by contemporary English speakers today.[1] In spite of these things, there is no feeling of common ownership. Mastery of Shakespeare's language is now associated with cultural exclusivity, which is, in turn, associated with economic power, and as the power of class, symbolised in the rituals of speech and style, is mocked, in popular experience, through imitation and send-up, so is Shakespearian language mocked, albeit gently, for its high-falutin' assumption, its airs and graces. It is associated with privilege and is often seen as archaic and obscure. Like poetry, it can seem to be laying claim to feeling itself, to the discriminator of artistic sensitivity, and so has become a potential source of humiliation, avoided, or disdained, by those it appears to demote and exclude.

Those studying Shakespeare in cultures which are not English-speaking, may also experience a sense of exclusion when encountering Shakespeare's language. Familiarity with Shakespeare's language may be seen as proof of the academic success of the minority, which has not only mastered contemporary English, but the English of the Renaissance, its classical period, unfamiliar, even, to the majority of native-speakers.

My starting-point, with teachers of native and non-native speakers of English is, then, recognition of the frequent alienation and discomfort facing us, in tongue-tied students, especially older students, when we embark on working with Shakespeare's language. In these circumstances, it becomes especially important to find ways of teaching through success and achievement, utilising the positive strength of the learning group and eschewing the negative impact of ranking and competition. This is not to say that excellent individual work is not recognised and valued by students. On the contrary, students more freely admire and try to emulate such work when it is seen as connected to the efforts they have been making collectively, in practical work, rather than as simply illustrating standards they have failed to reach as individuals.

For devotees of Shakespeare, of course, this 'problematic' language is the most valued feature of Shakespearian drama. Using the qualities they appreciate, the language's playfulness and musicality, its strength of imagery, its style and sententiousness (all performable qualities), teachers of Shakespeare can find ways of outflanking the widespread alienation and sense of disempowerment. With the help of their own knowledge and powers of critical analysis to focus teaching objectives, they can reconnect students with the physical and performative pleasures of the language, engendering confidence and ownership and facilitating the reclamation of the plays as popular texts. Through speaking language, it becomes our own, and through speaking the language of the plays, the plays themselves, with their narratives and characters, their poetry and ideas and emotions, also become our own. This is why language work comes first. It gives access to everything else and it is crucial that students have confidence in using the language of the plays as their means of access. Without this confidence, they will remain outside the work of Shakespeare, victims of monumentalism, either resenting their exclusion or superstitiously respecting qualities they have not personally encountered. Active work on Shakespeare's language restores a sense of freedom of speech to students and gives them that sense of normality in the use of speech and language that they feel in their own contemporary usage. Beginning with translation or interpretation, on the other hand, may introduce a further level of debarment which, even if overcome, still leaves students with a sense that they are about to begin, instead of the feeling that they are already on the inside, engaging with the plays for themselves and with nothing before them that they might not reach. This is why it is a basic principle of the language enactment workshop that original language should be used, apart, of course, from the fact that something of the joyfulness, beauty and sublimity of Shakespeare's language will be experienced by, and may stay with, every participant.

Shakespeare's language gives 'the motive and the cue' for action

When language is used in social situations, we can call on numerous actions and gestures to help us define meaning or to ease the embarrassment of speaking out when a sense of relative status intervenes to inhibit communication. Speech and action are inextricably mixed and it is often hard to say when a gesture is prompted by a word or a word by a gesture. We may capitalise on these interconnections when teaching Shakespearian language, using actions to free words. More importantly, we may follow a line of thought frequently expounded by Shakespearian actors and directors: that Shakespeare's dramatic language, Renaissance blank verse drama in general, guides and helps the speaker. A highly artificial mode of language delivery, which developed within the working practices of the Elizabethan and Jacobean theatre, still seems, four hundred years after it was written, to be familiar and natural in use – to those willing and able to try it. Furthermore, the language seems to suggest and invite enactment. It holds 'the motive and the cue' for action. For the performer, this claim raises stylistic and methodological questions, which are relevant to 'active Shakespeare' too: quite what sorts of action are prompted; does Shakespearian language imply certain kinds of action rather than others and so give clues to Elizabethan and Jacobean performance styles;[2] and what are the implications for performers today?

For those taking active approaches to teaching, the claim that Shakespearian language suggests and invites enactment, means that work can be derived directly from the text and can directly illuminate the text. An obvious example of how language prompts action occurs in 'insulting' or 'flyting'. Gesture is almost intrinsic to the ritualised aggression of verbal insult: the language's motive and cue for action seems to flow directly into the speaker's face and body. There is an account below of ways of working with 'insult' passages, (see *Insults*, p. 49), but whatever linguistic formation is the subject of practical work, the same principles remain: that the teacher's analysis of the text, and their own teaching objectives, come first, and that the active method should bear a clear, structural relationship to the source text or material.

In language workshops, the starting-point is often direct conversion of the styles and registers of written language into what seems to be 'appropriate' action. Thus the colloquial language of the Nurse reminiscing about Juliet's childhood or Mistress Quickly recounting the death of Falstaff (*Henry V* II.iii), seem to infer naturalistic playing, while Lear's challenge to the storm, 'Blow, winds, and crack your cheeks! Rage, blow,/ You cataracts and hurricanoes' (*King Lear* III.ii.1–2) seems to call for a style of delivery which is inflated and rhetorical. In both rehearsals and workshops, however, the principles of experiment and discovery are important. Speech lives when it is spoken anew, as though for the first time, while rehearsed cadences can sound artificial or may be anticipated. Hence an opening exercise on this speech, rather than calling for the expected high volume delivery, might ask students to wrap themselves into tight balls, hunched against the skirting boards of the room, muttering the words to themselves, while transfixing the printed text as though it were itself the image of an ungrateful daughter. In this way they can discover the promptings of the rhetoric, but the actions through which they express their discoveries will be appropriate to the private, introverted context of the exercise.

Another example of text which seems to call for a particular kind of delivery occurs in the following extract from Act I of *The Taming of the Shrew*, in which the bombastic strength of the syllables and the metrical regularity of the lines may seem to discourage experiment. However, social context, or in theatrical terms, dramatic context, determine that volume and tone can never be fixed. Petruchio's self-conscious self-aggrandisement in Act I of *Shrew* continues to invite speakers to guy, with accompanying grimaces and gestures, the fustian style of out-dated, panto-mimic acting (the style of Bottom's 'The raging rocks/ And shivering shocks/ Shall break the locks/ Of prison-gates;' in I.ii of *A Midsummer Night's Dream*):

> *Petruchio:*   Why came I hither but to that intent?
> Think you a little din can daunt mine ears?
> Have I not in my time heard lions roar?
> Have I not heard the sea puffed up with winds,
> Rage like an angry boar chafed with sweat?
> Have I not heard great ordnance in the field,
> And heaven's artillery thunder in the skies?
>
> *The Taming of the Shrew* I.ii. 196–202

It is tempting to suppose that we have here a fossil record of acting matching a fossil record of language, but it is by no means clear that Petruchio is arriving like a blustering character out of Marlowe, an amorous Tamburlaine perhaps. Petruchio is a maverick, an outsider who seems to relish his assaults on social propriety – and can, therefore, be viewed more as Kate's ally, a strong, but finally gentle rescuer, worthy of her proud spirit, than as leading male oppressor. In these lines, Petruchio is speaking to Gremio and Hortensio, ineffectual and comic representatives of patriarchy, while his servant Grumio completes, and undercuts the final line of Petruchio's speech ('Tush, tush, fear boys with bugs!') with a cheeky 'For he fears none.' An Elizabethan actor might well have chosen an ironically sophisticated style of delivery at this point, rather than bellicose parody. We do not know. A modern actor, similarly, might choose to indicate incipient sensitivity in Petruchio by distancing himself from the rhetoric, as he speaks it. (Some Petruchios 'tame' Katherina by getting her to believe that she only has to join in the public game of wifely obedience and that she actually has all the freedom of their private love within which to live.)

The point still holds, however, that the lines prompt accompanying stylised gesture, whether or not one takes them and their invitation to action at face value or whether one questions, ironises or subverts them – perhaps with naturalism. These alternatives should be explored and dis-cussed. Gesture, though prompted by language and linguistic structure, should not be seen as inevitable or merely illustrative in the way that it is actualised. This is true of performance styles too. Different theatrical styles do not uniformly suit all venues, stage-spaces and events. Illustrative mime, in particular, may be both enlightening and dramatic in a workshop, but redundant on stage.

Although the link between written language and performance style often appears obvious, it is the objectives of the workshop (or the performance) that finally determine how the motives and cues for action are taken up. If workshop objectives are not clear and do not inform the activities, physical embarrassment will be added to mental confusion. When, for example, Cicely Berry uses her *Resistance* exercises, which involve blocking or jostling or overcoming obstacles of various kinds, they are in a context, which she articulates, of freeing actors and, in particular, of freeing the voice:

> All you do is come together in quite a close group, and as you speak the text, jostle one another. Although you know it is a kind of game which has been set up, you still feel a sense of irritation and annoyance at being pushed – a totally instinctive reaction. This quite unconsciously makes us feel that little bit aggressive and the language responds accordingly – the muscularity and energy of the language becomes apparent. But more than this, because we are moving quite vigorously, we cannot hold on to our voice in any way. It is being released from lower down and it stops being controlled and releases that innate but hidden strength, that primitive need to speak and not make our voice behave.
>
> (Berry 2001: 121)

In repeating or adapting such exercises in other teaching contexts (see p. 33), one must be clear about one's own teaching objectives and the ability of the group to work without putting one another at risk. Similarly, inviting students to deliver lines or speeches in a variety of different ways should be done with particular purposes in mind, or one may end up with students at a greater distance from the language than when they started. Drama games and exercises do 'work' – often like magic, but if teaching objectives are unclear, they may merely pass the time without facilitating engagement with the text.

To focus objectives for the language workshop, and the same is true if Shakespeare is to live on stage, it is necessary to return to the actual qualities and characteristics of Renaissance dramatic language.

Discourse and rhetoric as sources of dramatic energy and action

Plays are essentially speech utterances, but in the case of verse drama from around 1600, there is a special interest in the workings of speech utterances and interchanges. Writers, actors and audiences appear to have shared an acutely sensitive consciousness of language, especially language as a form of behaviour and a mark of quality and social competence. In many of Shakespeare's comedies, discourse, the specific range and play of language in a particular mode or context, becomes the drama's source of energy even, as Keir Elam says, in *Shakespeare's Universe of Discourse* its 'comic object' (Elam 1984: 2). He speculates that 'the principal mode of *praxis*' (action) in Shakespearean comedy, may lie in *lexis*, (spoken action), 'that is in direct acts of language rather than in some verbally decorated extra-linguistic substance' (Elam 1984: 6). Such direct acts of language are not confined to the comedies. They occur very widely throughout Shakespeare. Hamlet's soliloquies, 'the naturalistic convention of thinking aloud' (Gurr 1980: 101), Lear's invocation to the elements and Iago's subversion of Othello's love for Desdemona are striking examples from the tragedies.

In the educational workshop, practical work can be derived directly from the text and can directly illuminate the text. Cicely Berry's famous *Punctuation turns* (asking actors, walking as they read, to change direction on each punctuation mark) match the vagaries of thought – in Hamlet's introverted dialectics, for example; choral treatment of Lear's storm language can be backed with 'actor-generated' sound effects and actions and Macbeth's 'Is this a dagger' speech can be done in pairs, with one leading, as the dagger itself leads Macbeth (see *Reading on the move: hypnosis*, p. 37 below).

Inextricably linked to the idea of discourse as a direct source of dramatic energy and action, is the subject and practice of rhetoric. Rhetoric, the art of using language for persuasion, with its whole vocabulary of conventional gestures with which speakers could illustrate their arguments, is itself a kind of linguistically encoded action. Frank Kermode, discussing Shakespeare's use of a Senecan device (dividing single lines of verse into three) in Richard III's wooing of Lady Anne in I.ii of *Richard III*, describes the active and playful style in which Shakespeare continues the dialogue: 'shortly afterwards there is a volley of short lines, as if both players had advanced to the net (lines 196–206)' (Kermode 2000: 31). Consideration of the figures of rhetoric – Brian Vickers (1971) gives a useful outline of Shakespeare's use of rhetoric[3] – will immediately suggest various exercises to workshop practitioners. The same recognition, that the linguistically encoded action of rhetoric suggests appropriate kinds of formal enactment and movement, occurs when one considers twentieth-century linguistic analysis. A clear critical relationship can be established, for example, between Wittgenstein's *sprachspiel* or 'language game', a 'distinct form of language-use subject to its own rules and defined within a given behavioural context' (Elam 1984: 11) and Shakespearian dialogue. Wittgenstein's terminology plainly converts with ease to the workshop.

His list of 73 language-games, such as ordering (and obeying), describing, reporting or speculating about an event . . . asking, thanking, cursing, greeting, praying etc., is only indicative – there are many more. The crucial points for 'active Shakespeare' are the connections between linguistic theory and workshop practice and between language and its cues for action. Taking up the idea of language-games having their own rules, for instance, or realizing that a whole speech is actually about describing a particular event, can lead one directly into devising workshop activities, using the idea of the unspoken rules, or the techniques of description. At the most obvious level, actions or objects can be supplied to match the particular language-game – shaking hands every time thankfulness appears implicitly or explicitly in the text, or consulting a note-book when describing some event that is being recalled. Theatre productions often derive humour from such illustrations – the Archbishop of Canterbury, for example, consulting leather-bound law books in the first scene of *Henry V* and appearing to quote his arguments, justifying Henry's invasion of France, directly from them. Conversely, for exploratory purposes, we may impose a language game on a piece of text, regardless of the text's prompting, which is the basis of *Style shifts*, p. 42 below.

Public events, involving a number of characters and formal utterances, such as announcements, policy discussions, arguments, councils of war, declarations and so on, are also especially rich for workshop exploration. Such events depend on familiar language games, which simultaneously express the social situation. Heightened drama frequently follows from some variation or transgression of the familiar or anticipated 'play', as when Coriolanus, when asking for the people's 'voices', actually subverts the formal, required game of begging for support, or when Lear inappropriately introduces the private, and rather self-indulgent game of asking his daughters to say who loves him most, into the public arena of his court.

Another example of activities derived directly from the text, is drawn from *deixis*. In the Kingman Report (DES 1988), deictic expressions are defined as 'words and phrases whose interpretation requires a knowledge of who the speaker/writer is, and the time and place of the utterance' (quoted in Gibson 1988: 5). In *Deictic reading*, pronouns and possessive adjectives in a speech are glossed (aloud) with nouns, and students literally point to objects, places and to those actually playing the relevant roles. We need to understand the context in which words such as 'she', 'it', 'there', 'his' and so on, are uttered. This spelling out of the meaning acts as a form of simple clarification, but may also enhance the drama of the occasion – as does a similar linguistic ritual in the marriage service ('I, Jack, take thee, Jill . . .').

Those enacting Shakespeare on stage, or in education, can apply a kind of *deixis* to clarify or illuminate the text. This is quite frequently done on stage nowadays, as was the case in the RSC 2002 production of *The Tempest*. At the risk of pre-empting Miranda's wonderment on first seeing so 'many goodly creatures' in V.i, the characters of Alonso, Antonio, Gonzalo and others (but not Ferdinand) walked down-stage, as spirits or ciphers, as each was mentioned by Prospero in the story of the past he tells to Miranda, in I.ii.

Language ownership and familiarity through workshops

Students, like actors, can respond to cues for action in language, provided they feel they are using the language purposefully and are successful in their 'performed usage'. Physicalising language (as when we gesture or use vocal colouring) and developing language's potential creatively (as when speakers take up and respond to features within the speech of others), strengthen the sense of possession and control, allowing the language to be internalised before emerging freshly as the articulation of the speaker – ''Tis mine, 'tis thine'. Achieving this sort of familiarity with language can turn it from a hostile to a friendly thing. 'Ownership' of even a small number of lines can enable students to tolerate difficulty, and enjoy a play, to a greatly increased extent. In the descriptions of methods and exercises that follow, familiarity is the starting-point. There should be a kind of ease and an absence of exposure in doing the exercises. The work itself may be specific (as in identifying the caesura in a line of blank verse or the rhyming scheme of a sonnet or a particular image strand) or it may be open-ended, releasing students to discover through experiment. There are endless possibilities for meaning, as context changes (which is, of course, the essential premise for the theatrical mutation of classic texts). For students, as for actors, this open-ended work is liberating – and enlightening, provided discussion accompanies the exercises; but whether specific or open, the vital basis of familiarity, through personal and social connexion with the workshop, must be there. Actors and students, on stage and in workshops, each in their own form of collective theatrical production, can take up 'the motive and the cue' for action embodied in so much of Shakespeare's language.

TEACHING APPROACHES

The three sections of language teaching approaches that follow, mirror three basic language processes – learning to speak, learning to read and using language in a variety of social situations. All these processes result in accomplishments crucial to our future development. Similarly, if students are to understand Shakespeare's language, if they are to be in a position to notice its features and characteristics, and then analyse how it works, they will need to possess it, through speech, reading and activity, for themselves.

Almost all the teaching approaches listed can be used to work on any speeches, scenes or particular aspects of a play's language. While activities may be taken from any of the sections and used as desired, there is, broadly, an increase in the demands made on both teacher and students, as we move through the three levels.

Listen and speak

This is my starting-point for language work. The skills of listening, speaking – and imitating, are those we use when first learning to speak. In these exercises, language is 'given' directly to students by the teacher. Students are freed up, as there is no reading to master. The emphasis is on energy, immediate response and confidence-building through usage. Most of the work takes place collectively, with the pleasure and reassurance of whole-group activities uppermost.

Motto

This starter exercise, especially if done regularly, gives students a 'stake' in their play, as well as the pleasure of knowing some poetry by heart. Choose a few lines (one line is too short for the exercise), which have particular intensity and could be taken as a motto, emblematic of important aspects of the whole play. For example, take the following lines from *Macbeth*, III.iv:

> I am in blood
> Stepped in so far that, should I wade no more,
> Returning were as tedious as go o'er.

There are many ways of teaching these lines. Because it allows focus on the sound of the words, I like to form a circle, eyes closed, and then softly 'feed' the lines to the class, phrase by phrase. The class repeats the words, aloud, but just under their breath. Soon they will have them off by heart. Now I concentrate on rhythm and breathing, by devising a simple walking task (eyes open) to accompany the words. This might involve contracting and expanding the circle, or crossing it, or moving in and out of it in some way. For example, I might ask everyone to turn from the circle and walk towards the walls of the room, saying the first part with me: 'I am in blood/ Stepped in so far' (arrive at wall, turn back to face inwards, stand still, maintaining the momentum of the line, and say . . .), 'that should I wade no more/' (then walk back to your place in the circle, saying . . .) 'Returning were as tedious as go o'er' (arriving as you get to the last couple of words). This can be repeated a few times, all speaking together, by which time the teacher should no longer be leading, or even speaking the lines, and speech and action should be well co-ordinated. I do not tell the class where to breathe, as the actions take care of that, but to finish, I might ask them to take a good breath, fix their eyes on a point right across the room and slowly walk to it, avoiding and ignoring others, at the same time speaking the lines in one breath, and arriving at the point as they finish the lines. Achieving this gives students confidence – through having learnt the lines, and through having used breathing to control their delivery.

A simpler version of *Motto* keeps the idea of 'arriving', but uses just one line at a time. From the sides of the room, and watching out for one another as they go, the class can be asked to cross to the other side, or to a spot they have identified somewhere in the space, delivering the motto line as they go. You can vary the speed at which they move, from running to walking to slow motion, and you can introduce additional features, such as asking students to speak the last word of the line to someone near them (fun with a line such as 'O Romeo, Romeo, wherefore art thou Romeo?') or to add a particular gesture on a particular word. If you want a class to learn a few quotations, you can use this method.

A variation of *Motto*, when the words have been learnt, is Peter Brook's exercise, in which each person speaks just one word, concentrating on continuity, speaking as though with one voice. This can be done in a circle, or while moving around, each person cueing the next person simply by delivering their word straight to them. The motto can be repeated several times, so that everyone is included, all the time concentrating on the smoothness of take-up, aiming to create the feeling that we are hearing the voice of a single person.

Follow my leader speech

I remember the moment, in a workshop Cicely Berry was leading on *Macbeth*, when she asked all of us to repeat the Sergeant's sequence of three speeches (in I.ii) about the battle, phrase by phrase after her, moving freely as we spoke, adding our own illustrative actions. The effect was explosive. We used the whole space, different levels from the floor upwards and the other people in the workshop, to act out the violence and shifting fortunes of battle, described in the language. I have used this simple technique in a variety of ways and with many different plays and classes ever since.

Whereas Cicely Berry left it to us, a group of teachers, to do our own illustrative movement, workshop leaders can carry out 'explanatory actions' for their students to copy or use as a basis for their own responses. For those with a limited understanding of Shakespearian English, including native and non-native speakers, this copying activity is first of all an absorbing way into meaning, but for participants of all abilities and levels of experience, the technique offers a 'collective dramatic delight', using Shakespeare's language. This simple process of repeating the leader's speech and actions (generally in half-lines at a time to make repetition easy), but in an active, free-flowing mode, is a vital technique for teaching Shakespeare through drama. Apart from the immediate mastery of the spoken language and the excitement and freedom of the activity, there is general access to the enthusiasm of the teacher – a crucial aspect of teaching, but something from which many students feel routinely separated. Response and appreciation do not have to be registered (which would definitely not be things some would be seen admitting to), because unselfconscious response and appreciation are the essence of collective dramatic activity.

When leading *Follow my leader speech*, you do not have to plan your actions and gestures in detail. Check any words or phrases about which you are at all hesitant, and then improvise movement for the whole speech, with the class following you. In this way you will be able to vary your movement and actions, according to the way the group is responding.

A variation, excellent for listening skills, is for the class (instead of waiting for each line to be completed before speaking it) to follow the reader as closely as possible, so that they are virtually echoing every word, just after it has been spoken. In this variation, it's possible to speak 'by the line', rather than in short phrases.

A suitable way of 'warming up' for this work, is *Follow my leader down the room* (p. 147). When you move on to your Shakespeare speech, it is good to introduce a lot of variety into your movement and voice – turning, at appropriate moments, to individual students, whispering, chatting informally, declaiming to the whole group, varying the pace, doubling-back through the class, suddenly freezing, crouching, crawling, running, standing or stalking. I once used this technique with fifty students beginning work on *Henry V* in a large hall. We went straight into the Prologue to Act I. So many things emerged immediately – the exuberance and power of the dramatic imagination, a feeling for the spatial relations of the Globe Theatre, the charisma of Harry, the beautiful poise and skill of the address to the audience (the 'gentles all'), the shifting patterns of imagery (from accounting with figures and ciphers, to the splendour of monarchs and the dread of war). As soon as we had experienced the speech as a piece of collective theatrical production, in which we were ourselves actors and audience simultaneously, we sat down on the floor and discussed the working of the speech in detail.

I recall, on another occasion, introducing *King Lear* to an 'Access to Higher Education' class, all mature students preparing to apply for universities. Of the twenty-five students, none had either read or seen the play before. I began by saying we would first meet Edmund, a character who felt disrespect and alienation from the social order and then, using the *Follow my leader* method, invited the class to be him – 'Why bastard? Wherefore base?' They immediately tuned in to the seductive energy of Edmund and to the forensic power of his questioning of social injustice and hypocrisy. Starting with Edmund's perspective established a major concern and theme of the play: the testing of the idea that it is natural to follow one's own good, dispensing with social, including family, ties. Our half-day workshop aroused anticipation in the students about their visit that evening to the University of Wolverhampton's Arena Theatre to watch Kaboodle Theatre Company's travelling version of the play. When Edmund came down stage and began the speech, 'Thou, nature, art my goddess . . .' the whole class, dispersed through the audience, seemed to rise in their seats with recognition and excitement. How would this actor do *their* speech? This is a familiar reaction from those who have work-shopped a play before seeing it. Receptivity, appreciation and critical acumen are all enhanced greatly by successful practical work. There is also a generosity and acceptance of difference, in students who have experienced the chemistry, I'd even say alchemy, of actors (i.e. themselves as actors) mixing with the text in a dramatic space. This contrasts with the possessiveness and disappointment about particular actors' interpret-ations, sometimes felt by students who have worked only in a private and theoretical way.

If it is appropriate, the text may also be handed around the group, with members taking it in turns to read (still using a single copy of the text, of course) – and lead, but this is an advanced exercise for students to lead and anyone doing so must be absolutely on top of the meaning of every word and phrase. You might, if the class is familiar with the technique, allow time for everyone to study the speech and any accom-panying notes, and then suggest that, once the exercise is 'up and running', anyone who wishes to, may offer to take over the text from the current reader, without, of course, any pause in the flow of the work. Give people a chance for brief discussion at the end of the exercise, perhaps with everyone returning to their own copy of the text.

Paired follow my leader speech can be used when you're lucky enough to be team-teaching. One of you can lead one group of students as a particular character, and another, as another character, can lead another group. You can converse, confront, move towards or away from each other etc., all the time using the 'listen and speak' technique. If you are working on your own, depending on the nature of your class, you may be able to prime students to act as your colleague in this, and other suitable exercises.

Other variations of *Follow my leader speech* include, for example, Lady Macbeth reading the letter from Macbeth in I.v, followed by servants, and King Lear dividing up his kingdom (I.i), in the style of *Grandmother's footsteps* (p. 175) – all repeat his words, following him as he moves about the room, but whenever he turns, all must freeze – no one must be caught moving; and the next exercise, *The maze*, in which everyone in the class has a part in teaching lines to everyone else.

The maze

In this language-copying activity, everyone gets a phrase from a speech, which they learn and illustrate with an action – so it's a useful exercise if you want to look closely at a particular speech. If you have a large group, then work in pairs – for most classes, it's probably preferable to work in pairs in any case. Next, all are positioned in a zig-zag shape and each person takes it in turn to go 'through the maze', repeating the phrases and actions fed to them and so experiencing the whole speech. (When you get to your own position in the maze, you simply speak your own phrase.) I first used *The maze* with 'There's not a man I meet but doth salute me', Antipholus's speech from *The Comedy of Errors* IV.iii.1–11. The class was quite large, so we had two groups working separately and everyone also working in pairs (with the pairs agreeing on their action or gesture), which actually added to the quality of the work.

Feeding the language

This technique is described by Richard Hahlo and Peter Reynolds, using three 'shadows' who feed the text to three actors, who listen, take it in and then speak to the other actors, though I imagine it could be done with two, four, or even more shadows and players. In this way, scenes may be played, in their entirety, without the need for the learning of lines. As the actors do not themselves have texts, they are free 'to be totally in the moment with each line of language . . . Encourage the performers to take the line and let it drop down into them, before giving it out to their fellow actors in the scene' (Hahlo and Reynolds 2000: 174–5).

Language across the circle

Begin with the warm-up *It's not my fault* (p. 160), which involves students walking across the circle and addressing a given phrase or 'tag' to a person of their choosing, who then takes it to someone else. After a while, introduce tags selected from the workshop play. This usually surprises, and often delights, participants. They have moved, almost without realising it, into the world of the play. Here are some examples of language tags to use when working on King Lear:

Is not this your son, my lord ?

Nothing will come of nothing.

What paper were you reading?

Give me the letter, sir.

Do you bandy looks with me, you rascal?

You whoreson dog! You slave! You cur!

Dost thou call me fool, boy?

Dear daughter I confess that I am old. Age is unnecessary.

I will not trouble thee, my child.

I have no way and therefore want no eyes.
(*For this line, one person crosses the circle with eyes closed, finds someone by touch, and then speaks.*)

You do me wrong to take me out o' the grave.

Pray you now, forget and forgive.

If anyone gets the wording wrong, rehearse the whole class with the correct version. In fact it's good, with this sort of exercise in which only a few people are involved at any given moment, to bring in the whole class from time to time, e.g. 'everyone now crosses the circle together, turns back towards the centre and speaks the line altogether at the same time.'

Replies can be added, where appropriate. This creates a 'micro-drama', which is varied by students as it is repeated. The effect is to generate dramatic density and this is intriguing and imaginatively stimulating for participants. Viola's tag 'What country, friends, is this?', *Twelfth Night* I.i.1, for instance, can be answered 'This is Illyria, lady', though respondents must remember to revert to Viola's line, as they 'turn into' her to continue the exercise by themselves crossing the circle. It's worth rehearsing the whole class first, all together, when you're asking people to remember two lines in this way.

There are many variations on this basic game. My favourite is to devise a dramatic sequence, like the one that follows, *The king rises*, from *Hamlet* III.ii. Set a chair within the circle for Claudius at 'the play scene', and rehearse the class with the two lines of the micro-drama: 'The King rises' (Ophelia's line in the text), which they must deliver all together, as soon as Claudius stands up, and 'Give me some light. Away!', which individuals will speak if, and when, they play Claudius.

Now, demonstrate the sequence yourself. Let everyone stand in a circle for a moment, waiting for the entry of the king. Then, as Claudius, take the chair yourself and sit there a little while, as though watching the play, before suddenly rising to your feet, whereupon the whole group together comes in with their line 'The King rises!' As Claudius, you now say 'Give me some light. Away!' At this point, there are two ways of continuing. Either you stride towards someone in the circle, who now becomes the new Claudius and takes the empty chair, so the miniature drama can be repeated, or you ask everyone to move around, glancing at each other to see who will be the next Claudius. In this version, you leave it to the students to come forward to be Claudius, if they so wish. When a new Claudius takes the chair, everyone freezes, looking at the King and waiting for him to rise. In many classes, there will be no shortage of volunteers for Claudius. When people are more tentative about coming forward, there is more tension, but this quickly sags if the wait is too long – so have your eye open for a likely person to 'prompt' to take the chair, as a last resort. There is a surprising amount of drama in this little exercise.

Other 'whole group' sequences of a similar kind may be devised for the play on which you are working. Another *Hamlet* sequence (from V.i) starts with a crumpled ball of newspaper, Yorick's 'skull', placed in the middle of a circle of students who sit on the floor in a circle. One (the First Gravedigger) rises and picks up this make-shift skull. Then another (Hamlet) gets up and takes the skull from the Gravedigger, at the same time saying the lines 'Let me see. Alas, poor Yorick! I knew him, Horatio' (turning and walking towards another student in the circle, to whom he gives the skull). This person (Horatio) then receives the skull and walks to the centre of the circle, placing it back down on the floor and returning to their place. Then the whole micro-drama begins again. You can build in more tension and focus, by 'freezing' the Hamlet player, just before they speak their lines, and giving them the gist of the information about Yorick from Hamlet's reflective speech of reminiscence about the king's dead jester. Alternatively, give everyone in the circle a phrase from this speech, to deliver in order, while Hamlet revolves the skull in his hands (see *Choral distribution*, p. 44).

Another example, *Banquo's ghost*, from *Macbeth*, is taken from the banquet scene in III.iv. A 'loose' circle is formed by the whole class. One, 'Macbeth', comes out slowly from the circle and, turning round, still slowly and deliberately, surveys all the gaps in the circle, as though decid-ing where his place will be. As he does this, those behind his back close up the gaps in the circle, so there is finally nowhere for him to re-enter. (If you're working with a small group, you can use chairs: the teacher removes Macbeth's chair, so that there is nowhere for him to sit). At this point, Macbeth flares up:

Which of you have done this?

Everyone (the 'Lords' in the text) replies:

What, my good lord?

Macbeth then 'sees' one person in the assembled circle, as the Ghost of Banquo. He fixes his stare on them, saying the lines:

> Thou canst not say I did it: never shake
> Thy gory locks at me.

On these lines, he shrinks away, covering his face. You, as teacher playing Ross, then bring the micro drama to an end by speaking the line:

> Gentlemen, rise; his highness is not well.

Then the whole sequence is repeated again, with a different Macbeth emerging from the group. This exercise may be followed up by group work, in which students rehearse and stage their own version of the text.

Iambic pentameters

'Iambic pentameters' can be demonstrated by clapping out the rhythm together or by asking students to gently tap out five heart-beats (each with a light and a solid tap – *ti-tum*!) on their own chests, with a clenched fist or by using an exercise I like very much, which Rex Gibson noted when watching Teresa O'Connor work with children on an RSC tour: 'these (warm-ups) flow into poetic rhythm exercises as the children step out their five-beat "I am" using the full space of stage and seating – a vivid physical demonstration of iambic pentameters' (Gibson 1989a: 11) – and, I should guess, an excitingly affirmative way of getting the children to 'claim' and explore the whole working space. Imagine a whole class chanting 'I am! I am! I am! I am! I am!', as they go in every direction about the room! This is also a good way for students to internalise the length of the iambic line, for, as Gibson has pointed out, the iambic pentameter is actually not the most 'natural' line in English verse: 'For all speakers of English, tetrameter is the preferred traditional form, embedded in nursery rhymes and in most publicly encountered verse from the very earliest age' (Gibson 2000b: 156).

An 'iambic' activity that works in a similar way to *Language across the circle*, also uses movement. You can begin by demonstrating it yourself. Take five even paces across the circle, speaking the line 'How nice of you to come to tea today!' – a regular iambic pentameter – in a 'ti-tum, ti-tum' iambic rhythm, so that every other word, the stressed syllable of each metrical foot, starting with 'nice', is actually marked with a foot-step. When you arrive in front of the person you have been walking towards, making sure you stress '-day' to mark the end of the line, that person then carries the line across to someone else, again taking five paces. After a little while, ask the whole group to cross the circle all at the same time, in five paces, maintaining their awareness of others, so that they don't bump, and speaking the line. Then, if suitable for your class, get each individual carrying the line across the circle to change the line every time, improvising perfect iambic pentameters of their own. Next briefly explain that the iamb is the standard metrical foot of Elizabethan/Jacobean blank verse drama and that an iambic pentameter, the underlying pattern of blank verse, is a line with five feet, each foot made up of an unstressed and a stressed syllable. Now introduce a line from the play on which you are working, asking someone to read and mark the five stresses of the line with footsteps in the same way as before, as they cross the circle. You may find a perfect iambic pentameter ('Thou canst not speak of that thou dost not feel' from *Romeo and Juliet*, for example), but in all likelihood, the line will have to be forced into regularity. Now ask the next person to abandon the five paces rule and to take the line across the circle to someone else, moving slowly and naturally, as though thinking aloud as they speak, lightly stressing any words they wish, to make sense of the line. Repeat this alternating structure several times and then introduce a fresh line, treating it in the same way. It will quickly become apparent that there are actually very few regular iambic lines, although the underlying iambic structure, however uneven, is always strongly felt and seems to provide a sense of continuity and direction. It certainly makes the text easier to learn.

It's useful, during this exercise, to ask students to slap their thigh on the last word of each line (whether or not they are reading the line as a regular iambic pentameter, or naturalistically), as this maintains the sense of the underlying pattern of the verse.[4] I also teach students to 'peg out' the stressed words in their lines – literally asking them to mime fixing those words on a clothes-line with clothes-pegs. This helps them to keep the language alive and buoyant, right up to the end of the line.

You can introduce the idea of the caesura, the natural break[5] that occurs in every iambic pentameter, usually after the second or third foot, but sometimes after the first or fourth, by asking speakers to set out across the circle towards someone and then to change direction, at the caesura, so they arrive facing someone else. *Reading on the move in pairs* (p. 37) may be used to explore the caesura further, through a whole speech, with A reading up to the first caesura, with B following beside them, whereupon B takes over. B now strikes out in a new direction, silently accompanied by A, and reads to the end of the first line, pauses, and then continues walking and reading up to the caesura in the next line, and so on – all without any discussion or prompting.

If you wish, follow up these activities with detailed discussion of the metrical structure of a piece of text, perhaps using *Reading together* (next exercise below) as a way of launching the text – for this discussion, everyone needs to see the printed text. First, looking at the text in pairs, what are Shakespeare's departures from the regular iambic pattern, and second, maybe in a 'whole group discussion', what are the effects of these departures? The first four lines of 'To be or not to be' (*Hamlet* III.i), for example, have feminine (unstressed) endings ('quest-*ion*', 'suff-*er*', 'for-*tune*' and 'troub-*les*') while in the next six lines, there is only one more feminine ending ('consummat-*ion*') and this one is actually elided with the previous, stressed syllable, so that it does not give the effect of hesitancy found in the opening four lines. If students use an exercise such as *Language across the circle* (p. 28), which could be adapted so that speakers are asked to turn away from their chosen addressee on any line with a feminine ending, the class will collectively experience the effect of the metrical structure before discussion of its meaning takes place.

Active reading

The activities in this section mirror the process of learning to read, but learning to read actively, dramatically, bringing the internal animation of silent, private reading to life. Whether using fragments of language, or whole speeches or scenes, students are now reading, and working with the printed text. Individual, paired, small and whole group work are all used.

There will be times when the whole class can participate, in various 'Active reading' exercises, to give particular individuals or pairs a heightened sense of their vocal abilities. Some of the excellent *Resistance* exercises (see p. 20) devised by Cicely Berry for work with actors, for example, can be used. One such exercise (Berry 1987: 201) involves characters trying to reach a set point and being held back, while they speak – Lear, for example, in the storm in III.ii, 'Blow, winds, and crack your cheeks!' In another, *Restraining the actor* (Berry 2001: 210–11) a character with a strong need to communicate with, or reach, another, or two characters who want to reach each other, are physically held back so they cannot meet. A third is *Reaching across*: 'As the actor needs to get across to someone else, the rest of the cast should walk between them. It can be two actors wanting to get close, or it can be one actor needing to get to the other, and the rest of the cast should prevent it, not by physical restraint, but rather by getting in their way and making it impossible for them to reach each other' (Berry 2001: 211). Romeo and Juliet, for example, could each be given a speech to deliver, perhaps a couplet at a time, in turn, while each is boxed in by silent figures, the rest of the class, who prevent them from contacting each other. Othello could give his speech 'Yes: 'tis Emilia . . .' (V.ii) in a similar way, striving to get to the dead body of Desdemona. Another variation is Patsy Rodenburg's useful paired resistance exercise, which she calls *The rock* (Rodenburg 2002:

353). This involves using your partner, while you speak your lines, as a rock to be pushed about the room.

It's important that students do not lose their place when reading aloud, as this destroys the dramatic tension. A useful tip to avoid this, is for readers to keep a finger or thumb at their place in the text, so they can look up and 'engage' others while they are reading. In fact, it's excellent practice to do a reading exercise like this, so that you have to memorise short phrases before you speak them (you are not allowed to read, eyes down on the words, but must read a few words, or more if you can, memorise them and speak them to your audience). Trained actors do this so well, that they scarcely seem to be relying on the text at all. It's also a technique that seems to improve the reading capability of very tentative readers.

Reading together

This is the most basic 'active reading' technique to get a section of text 'launched' into the consciousness of a group, and although obvious and well-known, it, and variations on it, are indispensable. It is usually done standing in a circle, but may be done with students dispersed throughout the room. Instead of either the teacher, or chosen students, reading a speech or section of text aloud, everyone reads aloud together. In this way, there is no embarrassment over difficult patches, as the momentum of the group carries the reading forward, and everyone experiences for themselves, the feeling and pleasure of realising the printed text in speech. If you like, you can first read out, and very briefly gloss, any difficult words, but the emphasis should be on getting into the text through group performance. For classes unused to reading aloud collectively, it works well to ask everyone to read under their breath, keeping together, but in a just audible mutter. You can raise and lower the volume of the reading by indicating to the class to follow the level at which you yourself are speaking, or you can conduct the level with your hand. If you are working on a piece of dialogue, it is still a good idea for everyone to read all the lines, rather than having halves or groups reading just one of the parts. We are aiming for students to experience the whole sequence of the drama in a private and muted, though collective, way. Dividing the class into two or more to read separate parts, immediately brings in inter-active dramatisation and throws students' attention on to their part of the extract at the expense of the rest of it, and these are not the objectives at this point.

Reading round the circle

If you are working with a small group of good readers, you may want to simply read round the circle to get the text 'launched', each person taking it in turns to read a line, a section between punctuation marks or a whole speech, before their neighbour takes over.

With larger classes of confident readers, you can speed things up by *Doubling up*, pairing students with others diametrically opposite them in the circle, so that the exercise proceeds with two people reading their lines in unison. In this case, encourage students to 'engage' with their co-reader, in the manner described above in 'Active reading', so that their line emerges as though from a single voice. For less confident readers, you can do *Reading together* before going on to *Reading round the circle*, using the same piece of text.

It is useful to do exercises which teach students to pick up on cues, read 'run on' lines and generally develop their capability to handle the verse. A good exercise is *Chiming*: the last word or words of a cue are 'chimed' or overlapped, with speakers working to develop an absolutely smooth take-over. This is especially good for giving a sense of the importance of the line, and the ending of the line, in delivering blank verse. For example, ask students to come in towards the end of the line of the previous reader:

First Reader:	A terrible childbed hast ⎧ thou had, my dear;
Second Reader:	⎩ thou had, my dear;
	No light, no fire; ⎧ th'unfriendly elements
Third Reader:	⎩ th'unfriendly elements
	Forgot thee utterly. ⎧ Nor have I time
Fourth Reader:	⎩ Nor have I time
	To give thee hallowed to ⎧ thy grave, but straight
Fifth Reader:	⎩ thy grave, but straight
	Must cast thee, scarcely coffined, in the ooze . . .

Pericles III.i.56–60

This can be varied by overlapping the delivery of lines, so in the example above, the Second Reader would begin their line on the last word of the First Reader's line ('dear'), so that 'dear' and 'no' would sound together. At its most extreme the lines are 'fired', everyone speaking their words nearly, but not quite simultaneously, as soon as cued by their neighbour.

There are other ways of joining in on other people's lines, such as echoing or chiming with words which also appear in your own part or on words which are part of a particular image or vocabulary cluster. Collectively identifying such clusters, through active reading, will mean that students make choices for themselves about the themes and concerns of the text and can begin to follow their connections and trace how they work. Much of this kind of work is aimed at alertness and responsiveness to the nature of the language and its structures, but all the time it will also be building up students' familiarity and ease with Shakespearian language.

Reading on the move

Movement, and interaction through movement while reading or speaking, are liberating, making it easier to work with the language. Students are literally less pinned-down and so can be more experimental, more absorbed in the text. For whole groups, suddenly introducing general movement can galvanise interest – perhaps through asking a class dispersed throughout the room to move around, turning sharply, as they speak, from everyone they encounter, or to briefly engage with them and then part; or for a class in a circle to slowly contract and expand the circle as they speak. While reading aloud, but alone, all simultaneously in their own time (which I call *Reading on the move individually*), the same making and breaking of contact when meeting others, may be used, and the same sharp turns to mark structural features of the text (at punctuation marks, or units of sense, or elements of thought, or changes in the development of an argument). Cicely Berry, who first developed and popularised these ways of physically enacting the various structural characteristics of texts, has analysed the precise ways in which such exercises work – for example, here is part of a whole sequence of work on 'speech structures':

> Find your own space in the room. Speak one whole thought in one place, then immediately move to another part of the space and speak the next whole thought, and so on. What this does is make us aware of how each thought comes from a different part of one's awareness, and has a different energy and rhythm and texture. . . . Because you have moved to a different space for each thought, it makes you find the different quality of that thought, and how it has a different energy. It somehow makes you find it afresh.
>
> (Berry 2001: 163–4)

Later in the book, she describes asking actors to begin a speech crouching in one part of the room ('I like the crouching because it gives the actor a sense of belonging to that space and I think increases the urgency of the running . . .'), finish the first thought and then run to crouch in a different part of the room. She says that:

> The central reason for the exercise is this: because you are in one place for one thought, your mind stays on that one thought to its end – in other words, you do not pre-empt the next one. Then by moving to a fresh space for that next thought, you find it from a slightly different viewpoint and this gives you its shift in texture and rhythm.
>
> (Berry 2001: 223)

This physicalisation of thought seems to match our mental processes. As Patsy Rodenburg says, 'Thought is a movement or journey within the brain. In this way, thought is physical . . .' (Rodenburg 2002: 108).

Alternatively, when *Reading on the move individually*, but as a whole class working at the same time, students may be given a 'walking context', such as 'you're on a tightrope' or 'you're trying not to make the floor-boards creak' or 'you're absorbed in doing a cross-word puzzle in the paper as you walk through a crowded shopping-centre', etc.

With small, confident groups, try *Reading on the move: staggered starts*. Students stand evenly dispersed throughout the room. They begin reading the speech aloud, on the move, exploring the whole space, when you touch them on the shoulders, one by one. As soon as No.1 has spoken a line or so, start No. 2 off and so on. Encourage speakers to weave in and out of each other and, on their final word, to 'freeze' in a suitable pose. The 'diminuendo' effect at the end of the exercise can be very effective. The technique of 'arriving' (as explained in *Motto*, p. 24) may also be used in *Reading on the move*.

When doing *Reading on the move in pairs*, students can also reduce and expand the distance between each other, as they move and read – walking towards each other, halting and moving again by unspoken agreement, or parting and looking back or concentrating on their conversation while moving backwards slowly, and so on. It is exciting to maintain contact with your partner through speech and gesture across space, particularly if there are many others working in a similar way in the room. You can ask pairs, all working simultaneously, to experiment with the greatest distance over which they can maintain contact, combined with the softest delivery. Pairs can either speak alternate lines to each other, or they can speak in unison. A useful warm-up for *Reading on the move in pairs* is *Paired mime* (p. 197), e.g. carrying and using a long mimed plank together or starting close together with a mimed rope and then moving apart, keeping the tension in the rope and interacting with other pairs. Two specific variations of *Reading on the move in pairs*, follow.

Reading on the move: prompter technique

When performing speeches, pairs can use a 'prompter technique' (based on listening and speaking), with *A* following behind *B*, feeding 'whispered' text in short pieces, which *B* then speaks aloud.

Reading on the move: hypnosis

In another variation for pairs, *A* can go ahead of *B*, feeding the speech to them, while B, keeping a set distance between their face and *A*'s hand, maintains their focus on that hand and goes wherever it leads. To prepare for this, use Augusto Boal's *Hypnosis* game (p. 157), which is a silent activity. When going on to work with speech, I find it better to make the distance between face and hand a little more than in the original *Hypnosis* exercise – a foot, say. This technique works with any soliloquy, but 'Is this a dagger which I see before me . . .?' from *Macbeth* (II.i) is particularly apt. *A*'s up-turned palm (the dagger) leads *B*, while *A* feeds the speech quietly to *B*, who repeats each phrase while following the mesmeric hand.

The 'hypnosis' technique is effective in other contexts too. It would suit the two long sequences of dialogue in *Othello* (III.iii), for example, in which Iago manipulates Othello, almost like his puppet. Iago would speak not only his own lines (perhaps signifying this by first waving his hand at Othello, leaving Othello in a frozen position while he speaks as himself), but would also 'feed' Othello his own lines, using the 'hypnosis' technique. These two long 'temptation' sequences from *Othello* could profitably be split up among a whole class, working in pairs, with the brief to first carry out the exercise as outlined here, but then to refine and vary the physical interaction between Iago and Othello to draw out the particular qualities of each pair's section of text.

Words and images

(Please refer to the structural and dynamic teaching approaches in the next chapter, pp. 56–73, on ways of using 'images'.)

This is a way of involving students in the active reading of scenes, through the principle of giving a precise (and interesting) objective, e.g. 'find a fulcrum line, around the middle of the scene and show us an image of that' or 'in pairs or groups, find lines to make into a "fulcrum cluster" of lines, with a line for each character in the scene . . . show us an image of that, each of you speaking your own line . . . now move to the text before your fulcrum and repeat the process, showing us the "set-up" for your first scene . . . now move to the text after your fulcrum scene and repeat the process, showing us an "after image"'. The notion of fulcrum lines is similar to the idea of climax within dramatic units, whether scenes or acts or whole plays, but it is more accommodating and flexible. Students may find different lines about which a scene or section of dialogue seems to turn, and different choices can lead to valuable discussion after the exercise has been rehearsed and shown.

Dialogue using alternate lines

This is a variation on the speech exercise, in which everyone is given only one line with which to meet and converse with others in supplied or improvised contexts. Again, as it uses the line as the unit of speech, the exercise is good for 'honouring' the structure of blank verse. Give pairs a long speech and a co-operative context (e.g. hanging out clothes, shopper and shop assistant, taxi-driver receiving directions home from passenger) Then the conversation begins – in this example, using lines from *Hamlet* III.i:

A: To be, or not to be; that is the question:
B: Whether 'tis nobler in the mind to suffer
A: The slings and arrows of outrageous fortune,
B: Or to take arms against a sea of troubles . . .

A *variation* on this method is to ask *A* and *B* to read the speech antithetically, choosing their own moments to 'hand over' the argument. *A* might open with 'To be' or with 'To be, or not to be' or with the whole line. *B* then takes up where A left off, and so on, taking turns. Give a reflective or calculating context, such as two people drowning their sorrows in a pub, or trying to make some figures add up. Coach pace and pauses and levels of interest and involvement.

Any of the soliloquies, with their antithetical thought processes, will suggest similar dramatisations. One I have done with students is Gobbo's 'fiend' speech, 'Certainly my conscience will serve me . . .' (*Merchant*, II.ii.1–24). *A* saunters around, deliberating, as Gobbo, whether or not to leave Shylock and *B* darts from side to side behind *A*, speaking as the fiend from the left and as the conscience from the right.

Setting the scene in pairs

An evocative way for pairs to start a dialogue, is to 'set up' one person imaginatively in their own space and then have the second person entering that space – Calpurnia entering II.ii in *Julius Caesar*, for example, when Caesar (famously 'in his night-gown') is already established on-stage. This can be done quite simply, perhaps with actors being asked to begin with one action to establish their environment, or they can create their own environments more fully – the Caesars, for example, being asked to develop a sequence of three movements to indicate the dimensions and nature of the room they are imagining for the scene. Depending on the particular scene, one person can come near and observe their partner, silently, for a while, before entering their space. Shakespeare uses an approach rather like this in *Romeo and Juliet* (II.ii), when Romeo is observing Juliet at her bedroom window, though in this case, of course, he actually gives Romeo a commentary to speak on Juliet, who has the not undemanding task of remaining visible, but silent, unaware of Romeo, for 24 lines, before her first words 'Ay me!', after which she is still unaware of his presence.

Echoes and Clarification

I learnt these two exercises in Cicely Berry workshops. Detailed analysis of different applications of them can be found in her books. Both exercises are based on pairs taking it in turns to read and listen (listen without the text). For the reader, interest in the text seems to deepen as the reading proceeds, as a result of the 'feedback' or interventions of the listener, while for the listener, their brief promotes interest and involvement in the text. The exercises may be done 'on the move' or sitting facing each other, or sitting back to back, which is physically engaging, or in other relationships, such as the reader standing and the listener sitting on the floor beside them.

In the first, *Echoes*, the listener echoes any words that particularly catch their attention or interest, or any words to do with a chosen aspect or theme of a particular speech, e.g. words to do with night and darkness or words to do with love. In the second of these 'Listener' exercises, *Clarification*, the listener requests clarification from the speaker whenever they wish, and the speaker then repeats the word or phrase the listener has asked about. For example:

Speaker: Be innocent of the knowledge, dearest chuck,
Listener: *Be what?*
Speaker: . . . innocent of the knowledge, dearest chuck,
         Till thou applaud the deed.
Listener: *The what?*
Speaker: . . . the deed. Come seeling night,
         Scarf up the tender eye
Listener: *The what?*
Speaker: . . . the tender eye of pitiful day . . .

With *Clarification*, it is best for the teacher to first demonstrate the questioning process with a volunteer reader.

From text to improvisation

This activity is suitable for working on scenes, involving two or three characters, which have clear scenarios for action inscribed within them. Students first read through the scene aloud with the instruction that they should discover a possible sequence of actions for themselves to play. They then mime their sequences and, with large classes, play their work to other pairs or threes. The teacher then coaches their scenarios into greater clarity, using, for example, 'freeze frame' moments or coaching instructions such as 'show me that in miniature – very, very small; now take it up, make it much bigger . . . now just use your hands to show the action . . . or just your eyes.' Because this exercise is done with substantial sections of text, students are not expected to learn lines – after they have developed their sequences of actions, the text may be built back in again through 'active reading', if so desired.

An example of a scene in which Shakespeare has provided his own very clear instructions for (comic) action, which immediately 'fixes the mood' of the scene, occurs at the start of Act II of *The Taming of the Shrew*. Bianca enters with her hands tied, accompanied by Katherina, who tries to elicit from her sister the name of her preferred suitor:

Bianca:	Good sister, wrong me not, nor wrong yourself,
	To make a bondmaid and a slave of me.
	That I disdain. But for these other gauds,
	Unbind my hands, I'll pull them off myself,
	Yea, all my raiment, to my petticoat;
	Or what you will command me will I do,
	So well I know my duty to my elders.
Katherina:	Of all thy suitors, here I charge thee, tell
	Whom thou lovest best: see thou dissemble not. . .

After thirteen more lines, Bianca pleads to have her hands untied, only to be 'struck' by her sister, as their 'grieved' father comes in and tries to settle their escalating quarrel. In such active scenes, language and action gloss each other and, incidentally, students may seek information from the textual notes with interest (what are 'gauds' in the third line?), because of the objective of the work.

Having perfected a fluent set of actions, all of which have emerged directly from the text, you might ask students to up-date their roles and improvise the scene in their own language. Students can show, with confidence and vigour, just how the original has become their own. Improvisation has followed, rather than replaced the text and should benefit any further work on the scene in the original language, or any discussion of exactly what is happening in the scene and the play.

An example of a scene in which action, though not integral, is easily imagined, occurs at the start of *The Taming of the Shrew*, when the Hostess is quarrelling with Christopher Sly outside her alehouse, about the glasses he has 'burst'. For this activity, *Drunken Sly*, start with a line of drunken Slys down the centre of the room, with their backs to a line of Hostesses behind them. In pairs, the Slys lean back on the Hostesses. (Use *Bridges*, p. 171, as preparation if you like.) The shared objective is for the Slys to be ejected from the pub by the Hostesses, i.e. manoeuvred across to the wall, where the Slys slump to the floor. Pairs can practise this a few times, reversing roles too. Now pairs should take up their texts, perhaps having practised the language in unison and after checking word meanings, and play the scene (it's only about ten lines long) in their own space in the room and in their own way – with the proviso that the drunken Sly will need some support for some of the time. Having to hold up texts to read actually seems to help the physical comedy, though you could use *One word reductions* (p. 46) if you wanted students to dispense with texts. Encourage variety in the routines. Once again, students may now improvise their own contemporary versions of *Drunken Sly*, having absorbed the shape and humour of the original sequence.

Style shifts

This can be done as a whole group, all together, with everyone reading simultaneously, but in their own time, or it can be done as a performance exercise, in that one person at a time entertains everyone else in the class. Side-coach readers to concentrate on their address to their audience: ask them to believe that it is absolutely vital that every member of the audience is concentrating fully on what they are listening to. The class should be able readers, or familiar with the text chosen, which might be a short passage (repeated by a series of readers), a long speech (different readers taking up where the previous reader left off) or a number of different short passages, each with a different reader.

Sometimes I have introduced *Style shifts* spontaneously to stimulate interest, but it goes well, too, as a language warm-up. Each new reader is given a style in which to read, and act the passage of text. These styles may be given as verbs (flatter, seduce, command, threaten, order, etc.), as adverbs ('in the manner of the word' – charmingly, coldly, warmly, hesitantly, proudly, sadly, etc.) or they may be given as 'roles', as varied as a bookie on a race-course, sports commentators of different kinds, a salesman or saleswoman, weather or news announcers, someone feeling suicidal, a game-show compere, a rapper, a revivalist preacher, a station announcer, a Mafia boss, a doctor, a judge, a gossip in the hair-dressers.' Alternatively, you can leave it to the class to call out styles (students may want to call out the names of favourite soap-stars, which is alright for a short while, though the exercise is more revealing about the potential of the language and the nature of dramatic context if the emphasis is on the style of particular kinds of social usage). If you are using the single performer version, you may want to leave it to volunteers to enter the circle (either before or after the next 'delivery style' is announced), or if you use a 'tag system', in which the person leaving the lime-light hands over or 'tags' their successor, you can allow people to hand over to their successor as soon as they wish. As with other reading exercises, sometimes briefly doing the exercise all together, but not 'as one' (because individual interpretation and style are vital) will do much to banish inhibition. It's good to mix the 'whole group' and 'single performer' approaches.

This activity can be used, of course, for work on whole scenes or in other activities, e.g. *One word reductions* (p. 46). In this case, announcing a particular film, or genre of film, or TV show, will probably be enough to set students to work with enthusiasm.

Venetian market

This is an adaptation of the cumulative memory game, *Persian market*. I have used it to teach the vocabulary of economics and trade in *The Merchant of Venice*, though it could help to familiarise students with special vocabularies and systems of imagery in many of the plays. If you're teaching *The Merchant* regularly, you can make your own set of cards, one for each of the mercantile and commercial words and phrases in the play, including terms to do with wealth and property. You can put a note and translation on the back of each card, or just the textual reference so students can look up meanings and notes for themselves. This preparation is labour-intensive, though with advanced classes you could use the class to prepare the cards. Give pairs of students sections of text to search (if you give the same sections to several pairs, there is an added interest in seeing if anyone's found a word that no-one else has).

One student starts out with the formula, 'I came back from Venice with: . . .' (adding the item on their card) '. . . a bond'. The next person repeats that and adds the words on their own card, e.g. 'I came back from Venice with: a bond and three thousand ducats'. Further additions might be 'some argosies', 'a ring I had of Leah, when I was a bachelor' and 'a pound of flesh'. It is obviously desirable for students to know the meanings of any obscure words, and quizzes or team-tests can be used to reinforce their knowledge of these meanings.

Speech hurdles

This activity, treating speeches like races over hurdles, may be done all together or, competitively, in pairs or groups. A speech is prepared, which must be given absolutely crisply and clearly – any stumbling or faults count as hurdles knocked down. Pairs or teams are set off at the same time to race to the end of the speech. I have used this with Biondello's speech, 'Why Petruchio is coming . . .' at III.ii.41 of *The Taming of the Shrew* (describing Petruchio's bizarre dress and broken-down horse when he appears at his own wedding). It makes an excellent speech warm-up for advanced classes.

Learn and act

In this final section on teaching approaches, students read and learn small amounts of text. The exercises then call for language to be situated and used within more developed dramatic contexts derived from the plays. In this way, 'learn and act' exercises mirror the use of language in a variety of social situations.

Being able to write notes and under-line or circle words can be a useful part of the working process, so for some of these exercises, photocopied sheets are a helpful aid.

Choral distribution

A fundamental principle of Shakespearian language work, which goes back seventy or eighty years to the practice of 'choral speech' as a technique for speaking poetry, is 'distributing the text'. More recently, Cicely Berry's work, in particular, has popularised such work, and examples of classroom exercises devised by teachers may also be found in the 23 editions of *The Shakespeare and Schools Newsletter* (Gibson 1986–94). Many teachers might use *Choral distribution*, or a variation of it, as their opening language exercise on a new Shakespearian text.

In the most commonly used exercise, a long speech is split into suitable components (words, phrases, lines, depending on what you want your students to handle). The distribution may be done by simply reading round with everyone noting whom they follow (see pp. 34 and 132), or you can photocopy the text, highlighting the parts students are to learn and speak, or, more economically, make two or three copies of the speech, cut it up and give each student just their cue and their line (as in Elizabethan stage practice). If you do the latter, it's convenient to keep the speech together until the moment of distribution. Do this by cutting almost right across the sheet, but leave the last half-inch of margin holding the speech together until you come to tear off and distribute each 'part'. Students can be put into pairs to learn their short parts, check meanings and pronunciation and test each other, with the teacher quickly moving round, answering any questions. The process must not be slowed down.

It is then a good idea to rehearse a few times, all together, with every-one standing dispersed throughout the room, speaking simultaneously. Then, with parts learnt, and unencumbered by having to read, everyone is asked to move around and to experiment with 'live performance'. Once again, this is done simultaneously. Numerous ways of delivering the lines can be suggested, from singing them in a whole range of styles, from grand opera to rap, to whispering them as though plotting, shouting them for joy or as a football chant, saying them angrily, soothingly, tentatively, with laughter or scorn, or while sneezing or blowing one's nose, or with a nervous cough. Students can be asked to interact with each other using their lines – holding conversations, arguing, falling in love or discussing the weather. In terms of movement, you can ask the class to spread out, run around, close into a tight bunch, rush from side to side and end to end of the room, creep around the edges of the room, and so on.

The final stage, is to put the whole speech together and to perform it collectively. This can be done 'on the move', with everyone quickly clearing a space around, and focusing on, each new speaker; or it can be done in a circle, with speakers jumping forward to address everyone, gesturing as they speak, perhaps; or it can be done statically, everyone dispersed at random throughout the room, at one time, perhaps, hiding from each other and at another, maybe, calling to the previous speaker as though sharing news. However you choose to do it, ensure that people come in well on cue, and listen to each other throughout, so that the speech is delivered as though by one continuous voice. You can ask the group to speak very quietly but with very clear enunciation, or, depending on the speech being used, you can give a suitable context (e.g. as though intently trying to listen to words being spoken in the next room, and then repeating them for the group, or repeating words as though on the telephone, for the benefit of gathered listeners, or as though giving or repeating orders or instructions).

Further variations are to give certain lines to the whole group to speak – perhaps a 'rallying cry' phrase or line, if there is one, or maybe the first or last line of the piece. With a large class, you can give the same, or a different speech, to two groups. With one class I used 'Once more unto the breach . . .' from *Henry V* for *Choral distribution*. When lines had been learnt, we rehearsed in role as tired soldiers sitting around a camp-fire. Each soldier wearily said their line and everyone noted whom they followed. Then we jumped to our feet and, in the same order, each soldier performed an action for their line, without speaking, to be copied by everyone else. The final phase was an energetic, straight performance of the speech, with lines and actions spoken by each soldier in turn, and copied by the rest of the class. The last line, 'Cry "God for Harry, England, and Saint George"', which we had pre-rehearsed, was shouted by all as we rushed to the breach – in this case, the top row of raked seating in a lecture theatre.

An imaginative development of *Choral distribution* is to make an event or *Choral ceremony*, using the complete speech. I remember a beautiful ritual Peter Reynolds devised for a workshop he was leading on *Cymbeline*. In a darkened studio, with music playing, members of the workshop processed to Imogen's body, around which candles were burning, each in turn delivering their gesture as though it were a tribute or gift for Imogen, and at the same time speaking their fragment of the song 'Fear no more the heat o' the sun'. There are other detailed examples in *Practical Approaches to Teaching Shakespeare* (Reynolds 1991). The principle of devising an appropriate ritual or ceremony, with some kind of offering to accompany each individual's fragment of text, may be extended to numerous speeches from Shakespeare – not just to the more obvious ones, such as Mark Antony's tribute to Caesar over his bleeding corpse in *Julius Caesar*, or Gertrude's elegy to Ophelia in *Hamlet*, but also to a speech such as Mercutio's 'O, then, I see Queen Mab hath been with you' in I.iv of *Romeo and Juliet*. For this, appoint a dreamer to lie asleep, and have the class deliver their fragments of text as though they are strands of dreams, with accompanying actions on or about the sleeper, heavy enough to disturb their peace, but light enough not to waken them.

A simpler, but very effective, kind of ceremony arising out of *Choral distribution* has been described by Ralph Goldswain. Having prepared Claudio's speech 'Ay, but to die, and go we know not where' from *Measure for Measure*, with his 'A' level class, with students learning lines, exploring them in different ways and speaking the speech in order, Goldswain wanted a theatrical climax, though all he had at his disposal was a large classroom, with no blackout or lighting. He 'asked the students to lie on their backs with their heads touching and their bodies stretched out like the spokes of a wheel [and] told them to close their eyes and concentrate on their lines' (Goldswain 1990: 95). He then played, quite loudly, a recording of a Bach chorale on a cassette recorder, turning it down gradually after about half a minute and then quietly telling them to begin their collective speech. An extremely atmospheric 'event', invaluable imaginatively and in terms of alerting students to the potency of the language, had been created collectively and experienced by the class.

One word reductions

In this excellent activity, students study the text in order to enact it, but only a little learning of language is required. Pairs are given a piece of dialogue and instructed to reduce each speech to one word only and to accompany each word with an action. With those unused to practical work, I take exercises a step at a time, often demonstrating with chosen participants first and always avoiding complex instructions. In this case I might ask everyone to do only the first two speeches before viewing, checking and coaching their work. Dialogue which I have used with this technique includes Feste's proving Olivia a fool (*Twelfth Night*, I.v.63–79, 'Good madonna, give me leave to prove you a fool. . . . Take away the fool, gentlemen') and the 'sun and moon' dialogue between Katherina and Petruchio (*The Taming of the Shrew*, IV.v. 1–22, 'Come on, a God's name . . . it shall be so for Katherine'). Single speeches are also suitable for this technique, especially where the structure is antithetical. For close and active textual work, I have used in this way, Hamlet's 'O that this too, too solid flesh would melt . . .', photocopied together with textual notes, so students did not have to constantly turn to the back of their books for textual information.

An excellent 'warm-up' for *One word reductions* is Augusto Boal's exercise *Flowing pairs* (p. 156), which encourages students to use space and levels freely and to interact and link their actions, so their sequences become visual conversations, full of reaction and response.

One word reductions can be used as preliminary analysis, before students perform the full text, either reading or memorising their lines, but it is obviously a stylised exercise and the formal gestures or actions that accompany the single words each person delivers do not convert well into actions to accompany the speaking of the whole text, whether read or learnt. If you're taking students on to this stage, it's usually better that they use the actions just as memory-prompts, rather than trying to incorporate them into performance. Illustrative action and gesture, so commonplace in the language workshop, have, in any case, been controversial on stage, ever since Hamlet's instructions to the Players in III.ii: 'do not saw the air too much with your hand, thus; but use all gently'. (I sometimes feel this advice should be repeated to those actors who feel every *double-entendre* should be illustrated with a thrust of the forearm, as much to get an encouraging laugh from the audience as to gloss the text.) There are certainly times when a little explanatory gesturing is helpful, but it can easily be over-done and become ludicrous. At the other end of the acting spectrum, excess of naturalism has been associated with a disregard for verse-speaking, tending to make the language meaningless through the abandonment of rhythm and through inaudibility.[6]

Brief intense exchanges

This exercise, like *Language across the circle* (p. 28) is based on the idea of the miniature or 'micro-drama', but the little dramas that follow below are longer and are played in pairs. In rehearsal of a play, 'moving off the book', so that the actors are speaking from memory, rather than encumbered with texts, is accompanied by fresh levels of dramatic possibility. Where there is little time for students to learn lines, *Brief intense exchanges* permits this sense of freedom and dramatic possibility to enter students' work. Short passages are chosen which are relatively easy to commit to memory. Having discussed the dramatic weight of the immediate context (all the passages chosen are highly charged moments), students memorise and perform a short section of dialogue, searching for its conversational rhythm. It's efficient to teach the lines collectively, those playing each of the two roles standing on different sides of the room, before pairs begin their individual rehearsals. Stanislavskian questions (the Who? What? Where? Why? of the scene) may be combined with discussion, and performance, of actions and pauses. Some examples of passages that work well for this exercise, follow.

After the murder of Duncan

Macbeth:	I have done the deed. Didst thou not hear a noise?
Lady Macbeth:	I heard the owl scream and the cricket's cry.
	Did you not speak?
Macbeth:	When?
Lady Macbeth:	Now.
Macbeth:	As I descended?
Lady Macbeth:	Ay.
Macbeth:	Hark!
	Who lies i' the second chamber?
Lady Macbeth:	Donalbain.

Macbeth II.ii.15–20

You could ask the Lady Macbeths to begin the scene by waiting, sitting or standing, and the Macbeths to approach them from another part of the room, and you could ask pairs to include one or two pauses in ways that heighten tension.

Cassio is dead

Othello:	He hath confessed.
Desdemona:	What, my lord?
Othello:	That he hath used thee.
Desdemona:	How? Unlawfully?
Othello:	Ay.
Desdemona:	He will not say so.
Othello:	No, his mouth is stopped.

Othello V.ii.68–71

You could ask pairs to play this first at some distance from each other, and then to experiment with the amount of space between each other. Are there moments when one or other might back off or draw closer?

Say how much you love me

Lear:	Speak!
Cordelia:	Nothing, my lord.
Lear:	Nothing?
Cordelia:	Nothing.
Lear:	Nothing will come of nothing: speak again.
Cordelia:	Unhappy that I am, I cannot heave
	My heart into my mouth.

King Lear I.i.81–7

This exchange is good for exploring mood shifts. Anger may be expressed at full volume or in a menacing, quiet way or disguised with false pleasantness or humour. Where might pauses come and how do they alter the scene?

Family confrontation

Hamlet: Now, mother, what's the matter?
Queen: Hamlet, thou hast thy father much offended.
Hamlet: Mother, you have my father much offended.
Queen: Come, come, you answer with an idle tongue.
Hamlet: Go, go, you question with a wicked tongue.
Queen: Why, how now, Hamlet!
Hamlet: What's the matter now?
Queen: Have you forgot me ?
Hamlet: No, by the Rood, not so:
You are the Queen, your husband's brother's wife;
And, would it were not so, you are my mother.

Hamlet III.iv.8–16

This is not as difficult to learn as it looks. Hamlet has two lines that closely follow his mother's previous lines and his last speech may be learnt first, which makes these three lines seem less daunting. This is a good sequence for examining the body-language we use in arguments. Pairs can try the sequence with one trying to make, and the other trying to avoid, eye-contact, or with both holding eye-contact at first and then one or other looking away. Alternatively, either character can indulge in some 'displacement activity' – perhaps the Queen is brushing her hair and won't stop, or Hamlet flicks through a magazine or is absorbed with his mobile phone.

Insults

The class is assembled as two antagonistic characters in order to explore the richness of Shakespeare's language of conflict. The idea comes from Keith Johnstone's wonderful book *Impro* (1979: 53–5). Prepare two groups using Johnstone's game: two lines of, say, students and landords/ladies, football fans and rugby fans or Shakespeare-lovers and Shakepeare-haters, face each other, backs against their 'home' walls. (These 'warm-up' roles can be made to foreshadow the contest to follow – degenerate v. moralist, drinker v. teetotaller, chauvinist v. feminist, etc.). Group 1 comes up to the centre line and waits. Group 2 decides on a mild opening insult, comes up to the centre line and delivers its insult. Group 1 must repeat the insult in shocked disbelief and then fall back to its home wall to decide on a suitable rejoinder. (Rule: their response level must be pitched just 'above' the insult just received.) Group 2 remains at the centre line until it has received, and repeated in disbelief, Group 1's rejoinder; and so on . . .

Shakespearian characters I've used in the next phase include: Malvolio and Sir Toby Belch, Benedick and Beatrice and Petruchio and Katherina. One can either distribute all the insults to each group at the beginning, so that each group member has at least one (though the whole group, of course, speaks each insult in unison), or one can have a 'clerk' at the home wall, who feeds the insults to the group each time it falls back for 'ammunition'. Group members can take it in turns to lead the attack, adding rude gestures for their group to follow, if they wish. Stress that there must be no pushing, jostling or physical contact of any kind: the activity is about gesture and language, not contact. The important thing is to insist on the strict delivery/response structure of the game. The formality of 'flyting' (which is a contest of invective in a kind of high-stakes, linguistic game) accounts for its humour. It is plain how *lexis* works as *praxis* on such occasions!

Follow-up discussion based on such a stimulus, should be lively and involved. There are also opportunities for taking the polarities further in paired improvisations. Here are some examples of insults used:

From *Twelfth Night*:

Malvolio: Tinkers. Coziers. Go off, I discard you. Minx. Go hang your-selves all. You are shallow things. I am not of your element.
Sir Toby: Puritan. Time-pleaser. Affectioned Ass. Sheep-biter. Turkey-cock. Scab.

From *The Taming of the Shrew* (with the twist of Petruchio's irony):

Petruchio: Good morrow, Kate. Bonny Kate. The prettiest Kate in Christendom. Super-dainty Kate. Slow-winged turtle. Pleasant Kate. Gamesome Kate. Passing courteous Kate.
Katherina: Katherine! Moveable. Joint-stool. Ass. Jade. Buzzard. Fool. Mad-cap Ruffian.

Translations

This is a development of *Insults*. In *Translations*, for which I have used Benedick and Beatrice (*Much Ado* I.i) and Petruchio and Katherina (*Shrew* II.i), Group 2 decides on a modern, colloquial 'translation' of its first line of text, which it then takes up to the centre line of the room, where Group 1 is waiting. After delivery, Group 1 repeats the last few words, or any odd words they recall from the translation, in shock, and retires. The game is played just like *Insults*.

Chapter 3

Narrative in Shakespeare

Harnessing the power of narrative's theatricality

'Once upon a time': the telling of the tale, the invitation to listen, the casting of the speaker as storyteller and the listener as audience – the devices are primal and irresistible. Narrative is fundamental. Through the licence of its pretence, it immediately structures groups, speech and experience. We present so much material, whether it be literary, historical, scientific, mathematical, sociological, as narrative: surely monumentalism will succumb to its charm and none will feel alienated or intimidated? Our culture, however, is fragmented. Communication is uneven and unequal. The narrator, the teacher, is under suspicion and may not command attention. The problem is common to all disciplines and subjects, 'they just won't listen'. In discussing narrative in Shakespeare, and suggesting ways of teaching it actively rather than telling it passively, we shall be dealing with matters and methods which apply both to other areas of Literature and Drama, and to the curriculum in general, from French and History to Chemistry and Mathematics. What is particular about the teaching of narrative in Shakespeare, of course, is paralleled by what is particular about teaching narrative elsewhere: analysis of the specific nature and structure of one's material, of the stories it is telling, will lead to ideas for active pedagogy. Ask anyone to teach fractions to a child and it will probably not be long before they, or better still their pupil, will be cutting up apples or dividing pies into slices and then telling the story of the reintegration of their parts, of how they become one again.

In turning to Shakespeare's narratives, there are several features which immediately suggest classroom or workshop activity, just as the intrinsic features of 'fractions' suggest appropriate educational activity, and a kind of narrative.

First, Shakespearian casts are relatively large, with at least fourteen or fifteen speaking parts and sometimes as many as forty or so, as in *Henry V*, for example. Whether your class is small, so that you have your cast with no more ado, or whether it is large, in which case you can have two or more duplicated groups, there are welcome opportunities to conjure up, in flesh and blood, the people of the play, using the students you have before you as their habitation – remember that this is for narrative work, so small and large parts are equally important in creating a sense of the world of the play.

Second, the social groupings of Shakespearian texts are delineated with enticing clarity – families, especially parents and children, generations, lovers, men and women, masters and servants, nations, factions and ethnic groups. Their differences and their individual interests and expectations immediately become the stuff of the drama. Once again, the possibility of dramatic activity seems to push itself forward, so we feel eager to begin, like Bottom, when he hears Peter Quince reading over the descriptions of the parts in *Pyramus and Thisbe* and wants to play both the lovers and the lion as well. It is revealing, and fortunate too, that our culture does not see the social worlds of Shakespeare as disconnected from its own, contemporary concerns (witness, in the last few years, the popular film versions of *Romeo and Juliet* and *Hamlet* set in contemporary USA, as well as Kenneth Branagh's no less popular, but more traditionally situated screen treatments of *Henry V, Hamlet, Much Ado About Nothing* and *Love's Labour's Lost*). It is self-evident that the traditional social structures of Shakespeare's plays are strongly hierarchical, with almost every play located in the worlds of emperors, kings or dukes (for both Tolstoy and Walt Whitman, this meant that Shakespearian drama was fundamentally undemocratic), but, like the kings and queens of fairy-tales, Shakespeare's rulers are mythologised, their spheres of power and the legitimacy of their rule both constantly treated, not as set values, but rather as the live conditions of an archetypical kind of drama – which is why Hamlet is probably imagined first as a young man beset by a sea of troubles and second, emblematically (that is, without superstitious respect) as a prince.

Third, the dynamics of Shakespearian narratives invite analytical depiction, whether through the interaction of main plot and sub-plot, or in the movement from court to 'green world' and back, in some of the Comedies, or in the epic journeys of the Romances or in the events and geographies of the Roman plays, the Histories and the Tragedies. Of course, this dynamism applies to other plays of the period and outside the period too, but the deftness and pace with which Shakespeare's narratives unfold are unerring, partly because of the tried popularity and interest of the narratives and partly because of Shakespeare's skill as a working actor/dramatist in knowing what and how, in these narratives, to develop and vary, contrast and inter-cut, enlarge, diminish and, even, abandon. It is true that Shakespearian narratives are often complex and that audiences may not, when the play is over, be able to recall all the turns of the plot, but in the writing, the narrative tension is constantly maintained. Theatrical production, of course, may obscure the narrative, as well as other things in the play. Key information needs, in the theatre, not only to be spoken with complete clarity, but to be presented, where necessary, as a series of shaping moments. Good productions, whether or not their stage imagery is chaste or extravagant, always seem absolutely clear. Mike Alfreds's production of *Cymbeline* at Shakespeare's Globe in London in 2001 achieved this, using a handful of actors playing all the parts and, in Shared Experience's familiar style, without relying on the distinguishing effects of costume and scenery. The crystal presentation of the drama was entirely achieved by the skills of the direction and the preparation and skill of the actors. Adrian Noble's final Shakespeare production for the RSC, in 2002, a richly costumed, lit and staged *Pericles* with an extensive musical score, was just as strikingly clear, and as beautifully acted, although, like *Cymbeline*, it cannot be said that the plot of *Pericles* is simple and obvious.

We can realise these features of Shakespeare's narratives, in all their social and dramatic strength, in the workshop's 'empty space'. Here we may analyse, collectively, the structures of the narratives and create them afresh, through and in, action.

'Action!' The characters who have been standing around in costume, possibly improvising and conversing jocularly 'in character' while waiting for that call to action, which brings an expectant quietness, now begin to suggest their story as the camera rolls. Films and plays are enacted stories and the settling of audiences before the empty playing space is like a dampening down of the pressure of time, marking the onset of a completely new kind of time, the playing time of the narrative. The social experience of living through a theatrical event and the imaginative experience of following the narrative, are charged experiences. Live performance is not like running a film or video – it is like life, in that the unexpected may happen, the actors may not be able to sustain the event, the audience (whom, John Gielgud said, must be 'tamed' anew at each performance) may not co-operate in the illusion. They might not believe it or they might rebel or leave. All this makes live performance tense and dangerous, though the pay-off is that it naturally offers involvement and the possibility of strong collective focus, a kind of trance. In teaching narrative actively, there are the same sort of expectations, the same shared understanding of procedures and the same opportunities for concentrated social and imaginative experience as there are in the theatre though with rather less of the danger: the class is its own audience. If, as teachers, we recognise and take up this theatricality, we have a structure for learning with its own discipline and codes of social behaviour and its own open invitations to each private mind. Our students, deeply and instinctively familiar with the situation, will be inclined, like a theatre audience, to indulge us for a little while and give us time to convince them with what follows. To convince them, we first need to discover, in detail, the structures, conventions and workings of the narrative we are teaching, so that we can harness its latent energy. Harnessing that energy means, when active teaching approaches are used, that the participants perform the narrative, as actors do, but selectively and critically, using the special focus of the exercise chosen for their collective exploration.

The nature of Shakespeare's narratives

Shakespeare's narratives are, for the most part, complicated. Some, like those of *Cymbeline* or *The Winter's Tale*, may seem to over-burden the action of the final acts or leave some matters unresolved. Such features are partly explicable in terms of the variety and complexity of the source material, but although there is a general, and obvious dependency on that source material, Shakespeare also leaves it behind, developing new emphases in his own dramatic narratives and seeming less concerned with the details of connection to the original or with complete coherence. There is an absence of monolithic authority in the use of this diverse narrative source material. In a similar way, the development of Shakespeare's genius, apparently so effortlessly and 'inexplicably' fertile, actually owes much to the working conditions of the theatre of his day. This theatre, of course, depended on the work of numerous writers who collectively developed the playwright's craft, no doubt prompting each other, through new plays, to explore fresh ideas, subjects and styles, and new possibilities for language, poetry and dramatic art. In *The Genius of Shakespeare*, Jonathan Bate places special emphasis on the influence of Christopher Marlowe on Shakespeare's own development as a writer, tracing how a kind of rivalry operated up until, and beyond the date of Marlowe's death in 1593, but finally reminding us, too, of Shakespeare's extraordinary creativity:

> The origins of Shakespeare's art are to be found in the rhetorical training he received at school, in his reading, his reshaping of inherited materials and traditions, above all in his theatrical environment, his creative engagement with the tragedies of Marlowe and the comedies of John Lyly. But to explain the origins of his art cannot fully account for his genius.
>
> (Bate 1997: 157)

Theatre companies were in competition for audiences and the demand for new plays, taking the drama into fresh areas, was voracious. In the mid-1590s, a time of amalgamation among the theatre companies, Shakespeare's company, the Chamberlain's Men, was playing at The Theatre and their rivals, the Admiral's Men, were at the Rose. Andrew Gurr notes that in the 1594–95 season, the Admiral's Men 'performing six days a week, offered their audiences, a total of thirty-eight plays, of which twenty-one were new to the repertory, added at more or less fortnightly intervals' (Gurr 1980: 102).

There seemed to be no direction barred to the writer, whether in 'tragedy, comedy, history, pastoral . . .' (*Hamlet* III.2.396), and for writers, like the sea captains exploring the oceans, no theatrical voyage they might not undertake. Shakespeare's extraordinarily rapid and inventive development of the genres of drama, driven by the needs of the theatre of his day, would not have been possible without the mass of source material, which he used extensively and freely – material such as the historical works of Raphael Holinshed, Edward Halle, John Stow, Samuel Daniel, Belleforest, Foxe, Saxo Grammaticus and Camden; Sir Thomas North's translation of a French version of Plutarch's biographies of famous Greeks and Romans; tales from the Italian (Boccaccio's *Decameron*, Cinthio's *Hecatommithi*); prose romances by Robert Greene and Thomas Lodge; the plays of Plautus and others, many from unknown authors; the poetry of Homer, Ovid, Robert Henryson, Gower, Chaucer, Spenser, Arthur Brooke and Sir Philip Sydney; Ariosto's *Orlando Furioso*, *The Mirrour for Magistrates* of John Higgins, Reginald Scott's *Discoverie of Witchcraft* and much more.

This rich and diverse repository of traditional tales and plots and characters, together with Shakespeare's own developments and innovations, mean that the plays' narratives are especially suitable for active work. (For similar reasons, many of the narratives continue to be popular today, with film and television adaptations[1] devoid of Shakespearian language, still acknowledging Shakespeare as their source and inspiration). Following the principle that we should take 'the motive and the cue' for action from the material itself, leads to our devising active teaching strategies directly from critical analysis. This does not mean we are necessarily concerned with summarising events in some way, though this may be the objective on a particular occasion. As the range of methods that follows indicates, there are many aspects of narrative which we may want to teach, from considering the way the interactions of a family, or particular groups, shape events, to looking at a play as the personal odyssey of a particular character, or as, initially, a puzzle or enigma that requires solution through the disclosures of the plot. One also needs to do, or work through, the analysis for oneself and make plans to suit one's own situation, teaching objectives and way of working. Even when taking over a particular teaching strategy which is ready-made and seems perfectly appropriate, one needs to re-create and modify the suggested method for oneself, for all of us, as teachers, need the same active involvement in devising our strategies, as our students do in working them through.

TEACHING APPROACHES

A number of the teaching approaches in this chapter, especially in the first group (structural approaches) are teacher-directed, so care must be taken that they do not become teacher-centred. Also, in teaching narrative, one is sometimes dealing with sequences of events as facts, as, for example, in *Movement scenarios* (p. 62) and *Dance scenarios* (p. 64). Students' creativity is involved, however, in the way these scenarios are rehearsed and played.

As with Chapters 2 and 4, the teaching approaches that follow are grouped into three sections. Any of the activities may be selected and used as desired, although there is, broadly, an increase in the demands made on both teacher and students, as we move through the three levels.

Structural approaches

Structural approaches to teaching narrative use the still image as the main teaching device. In different ways, students enter narrative 'frames' and take up dramatised roles. Although the focus of the work is essentially static and analytic, active participation is very much required and the approaches form a useful starting-point for those new to dramatic methods of teaching.

Structural approaches to teaching narrative are the most familiar and the easiest to use, as my examples from *Henry VI Part II*, *Richard II* and *A Midsummer Night's Dream* in Chapter 1 (pp. 8–10) demonstrate. The old 'tableau' technique, beloved of producers of children's Nativity plays, in which costumed children form a motionless, or so it is intended, illustration of text read aloud by a narrator, is structural, as are 'still images' or 'photographs' or 'freeze frames'. For those beginning to use active methods, these devices are inherently disciplined and controllable, but one must be careful to keep them active and involving for participants. Distributing sticky labels or name cards on elastic necklaces (the latter can be re-used) speeds up the work and brings everyone in straight away. The whole class experiences the pleasure of identifying and meeting the play's characters, and of being those characters.

To familiarise students with the names, relationships and functioning of characters, you can use many of the activities described in 'Introductions' (pp. 162–6) and 'Names' (pp. 166–9) in Chapter 6. Some pointers to ways of introducing additional language and information, using these activities as a framework or basis, are also given.

Selected lines from the characters' parts or additional 'briefing' information, may be used for developing the work further. Here are some examples of 'name cards' from *Hamlet*:

Hamlet, the Prince   'Denmark's a prison.'   (II.ii.42)
Your father is dead and his brother, your uncle, has married your
mother and become King of Denmark. You not only despise this new
'King', but also suspect that he is the murderer of your father. You
once loved Ophelia, but then you rejected her. You feel trapped.

Gertrude, the Queen   'O Hamlet, thou hast cleft my heart in twain.'
(III.iv.152)
You are the mother of Hamlet. Very soon after the death of your
husband, King Hamlet, you married his brother, Claudius, who is
now king. Your son, Hamlet, is full of resentment.

Claudius, the King   'O, my offence is rank, it smells to heaven.'
(III.iii.37)
Soon after secretly murdering your own brother, King Hamlet, you
married his widow, your sister-in-law, Gertrude, and became King of
Denmark. You fear that Hamlet knows what you have done and you
plan to have him murdered.

Polonius   'Behind the arras I'll convey myself
                To hear the process.'   (III.iii.27)
You are an elderly, punctilious member of the King's Council. You spy
for the King, spy on your daughter, Ophelia, and set a servant to watch
your son, Laertes, in Paris.

Laertes   'A minist'ring angel shall my sister be.'   (V.i.231)
Your father, Polonius, is an adviser to the King and your beloved sister,
Ophelia, is loved by Prince Hamlet. You're worried by this, as you do
not trust Hamlet.

Ophelia   'Good night, ladies. Good night, sweet ladies, good night,
good night.'   (IV.v.70)
Hamlet, who once loved you, rejects you and then accidentally kills
your father, Polonius. You are driven mad by these events.

The kind of information we have above may be used, for example, as in
Variations on sculptor forms the image, which is described below, in which
there is no overall sculptor, but the characters may themselves 'sculpt'
others as they enter the tableau. The information they have on their own
card, and that they see on others' cards, allows them to do this, without
knowing the play. The language tags may be learnt (perhaps with
characters 'meeting and greeting' each other as they move around the
room for a few minutes – see p. 101 below) and, when it has been formed,
the tableau may be 'activated' by being asked to speak. For example, the
teacher can use the tableau to explain aspects of the play and its narra-

tive, but can also touch each character in turn as a signal for that person to 'unfreeze' and speak their line to a suitable person in the group, or to everyone as a whole. If you're doing this, it's useful to keep a 'master sheet' to refer to yourself, with all the characters and information and quotes on it. Chapter 4 has suggestions for developing the use of name cards further, in work on 'Character' (p. 99).

One can also, for example, write on each name card two relationship instructions (e.g. 'get close to X, who's your sister and avoid Y who lives in another town'), and then ask the class to give you a 'photo' image of the play.

The game *The bears are coming* (p. 176) or the old game of *Statues* can be useful as preparation (move around in character until the music stops – or at a hand-clap if you're not able to have music – then freeze immediately; or freeze into your character's shape; or make the picture when the music stops). If you want the whole class to work in groups focusing on one set of characters in the play (lovers and parents, for example), you can write more detailed information on the cards (e.g. 'you long for X, but your father wants you to marry Y; meanwhile, Z won't leave you alone'). Further ways of using the still image follow.

Teacher-constructed image

After everyone has received their label or name card, you might begin: 'Who's the most powerful person here?' The King or Duke moves forward. 'Servants – where are the servants? Get him a chair. King, have them place it where you wish and prepare yourself to receive the Ambassador. Now, who feels close to the King? . . . Take up your position, then. Using only the expression on your face, show us your feelings about the King. Excellent! Who feels distant from the King? Where will you stand? Should anyone join him?'

Go with what is produced, taking advantage of the opportunities for involvement and discussion. For example, if two Kings from the play come forward, then allow both: the class will be intrigued to see who is the greater, as the exercise is worked through, but a learning opportunity will be missed if the teacher simply announces the right answer.

Variations on teacher-constructed image

Instead of calling for 'the most powerful', you might ask for 'the least important' or 'most isolated person' and instead of the situation of receiving the ambassador, it might be having a portrait painted, or judging an accused person.

The teacher might begin with a more informative approach: 'You, . . . you're the most important woman in the play, but you are lost at the start of the play, separated from your brother, shipwrecked . . . show us how you feel, become a statue of how you feel . . . Good, now everyone be that woman; decide how you would feel and show that . . . when I say "freeze", show me how you'd be. Now, slowly change back into your own characters.'

Next the teacher addresses the Sea Captain: 'You come across the lost woman; take a close look . . . who is she ? . . . where will you stand . . . can she see you?' One at a time, everyone is brought into the photo. Where does everyone fit? If the class is big, make *Twin pictures*, one at each end of the room: students can identify their 'picture twin.'

I once used this *Twin pictures* device to start a session on Dickens's *Hard Times*, for over fifty mature students, making use of a curtain fortuitously hung across one end of the hall. The discussion and excitement before each photo was revealed, was intense, and these were adults meeting for the first time. There was also much comment on the actual choices made, some of it, from those who knew the text well, critically very sophisticated. It felt good too, to be pointing, rearranging, arguing, moving around, laughing, in a free-flowing manner, with the focus on the task, not on one's own anxieties about speaking or on the personalities (and status and 'clever-ness') of those who did speak. Some excellent comments were made, some at considerable length, and these were especially appreciated by the class, I believe, because everyone had contributed to the making of the images.

Sculptor forms the image

'We need someone to shape us into a picture.' A volunteer comes forward. 'Right, you may bring the characters into your sculpture in any order.' No one may speak and the characters must be physically loose and pliable. The sculptor moulds them into the image placing them in the group, curling a little finger here, tilting a head there, turning down the corner of one character's mouth.

A preparation activity might be sculpting given words, such as 'fear' or 'pride', in pairs or threes, or Augusto Boal's *Hypnosis* game (p. 157), which encourages students to feel relaxed and responsive (as does the familiar *Mirrors* game, p. 157), but initial demonstration, a 'slow build-up' and coaching co-operation and an increasing degree of experimentation, once the work is trusting and focused, are all vital.

Variations on sculptor forms the image

No sculptor is chosen, but as the characters enter the tableau, one at a time, they may 'sculpt' any alterations they may wish to make to those already assembled. Again, there must be no spoken instructions or requests; everything must be sculpted, but if you wish, the sculpting character going in may be invited to 'thought-track' as modifications are made', e.g. 'Well . . . I'm your brother, but you're jealous of me, so I think I'm going to move you over here and turn your head like so . . . You. Let's see, I'm your child. I'm going to put your hand on my arm, like . . . this. Fine. I've settled into the image.' In a similar way, the teacher can 'feed' all the information everyone requires: 'Once, in Verona, in Italy, there were two families who had hated each other for many years . . . Romeo, one of the Montague family (the student goes into the picture) turns from loving Rosaline (she takes up her position) . . ., to loving Juliet, who is a Capulet, etc.' A preparation activity for this variation, might be *The machine game* (p. 158).

Further developments of all these structural approaches to teaching narrative described above will depend on the particularity of one's teaching objectives. One might ask students to go off to make a *Prequel image* from before the start of the play (for *Hamlet* for example) or images for imaginary *Desired endings* (e.g. Edmund's ideal ending contrasted with Albany's in *King Lear*) or, in *Contrasting images*, representations of what characters are feeling in the middle of the play, contrasted with what they're feeling at the beginning (*Othello*).

Jane Coles has described an excellent use of tableaux in '"A" Level Workshops' and has also given a timely reminder that 'Too many teacher-directed activities can become tedious. Students are most excited by the challenge of imaginative, open-ended explorations.' Her tableaux activity is one such open-ended exploration. In it, she sends students off in pairs or threes with their texts 'to choose a significant quotation, possibly one containing a metaphor. After careful discussion about the line, they must find a physical way of presenting it to the rest of the group who will try to guess the actual quotation.' Students must be able to hold their pose for a minute or so and she notes that photos of the work, with captions beneath, can be made into a revision display for the classroom (Coles 1990: 90–1).

Students can also be asked to do some preparation in sub-groups. For plays such as *Hamlet*, *King Lear* or *Romeo and Juliet*, they can be asked to work in small groups to prepare *Family photos*, before combining to make a *Court photo*. In the case of *Romeo and Juliet*, this might be based on the appearance of Escalus, the Prince of Verona in I.1, when he threatens death 'If ever you disturb our streets again'. Rex Gibson describes a very similar approach, which he calls *Critical incidents* – climactic episodes, such as the appearance of Banquo's Ghost, Ophelia's madness or Claudius's rising from his seat at the play. How do characters speak their lines at such key moments and how does everyone on stage react? Who looks at whom and how are they all positioned? Students take on roles in groups and prepare a 'showing': 'Some students have prepared a mime unfolding in slow motion, but the most favoured method is to present a tableau' (Gibson 1998: 143). All of this work should offer plentiful opportunities for discussion – and for turning back to the text for evidence.

To think more deeply about how and why this image work should be developed, I would recommend readers to Augusto Boal's accounts of his 'Image Theatre'.[2] Boal calls his theatre participants 'spect-actors', active spectators who take part in the theatrical action in some way, for Boal's whole 'Theatre of the Oppressed' project is to use theatre as a participatory, critical and democratic form. The politics of his theatre share much with the politics of the active pedagogy which I am recommending in this book.

Dynamic approaches

Dynamic approaches to teaching narrative use the scenario, or outline of actions, as the main teaching device and focus on methods to do with transition, progression and unfolding. Dynamic approaches develop naturally from the still images and 'photos' of structural work and scenarios are frameworks derived from the basic narrative material. As scenarios emerge from that material, they often seem to 'cue the action', that is, suggest appropriate activities.

The important thing now, is to achieve movement and momentum, to find the rhythm of the work. Enactment, or 'doing', is the original meaning of 'drama'. Devices such as mimed, speeded-up or slowed-down 'run-throughs' should be introduced, depending on the need. *Style shifts* (p. 42) – 'play your scene as cool gangsters, as Tom and Jerry, as supermarket gossips, etc.' – may be useful to free the actors in their search for the shape and the rhythm of the narrative that they are experiencing.

In Shakespeare's theatre, a 'platt' or plot of the play's sequence of stage directions (entries, exits and actions) would have been posted backstage, as a guide to the cast.[3] Such plots or scenarios separate movement from language, but in doing so make it easy to clarify the narrative: it is easier to keep the flow of a sequence of movement going, than it is to tell the story in words or dialogue. If required, words can then be simply added back into a sequence of silent actions.

The section on Roles in Action in the Narrative in Chapter 4, especially the activity *Journeys* (p. 113), takes a similar approach to the activities that follow now, but there the emphasis is on character.

Transitions

If a group makes an image of the characters' relationships at the start of *King Lear*, for example, a card outlining what relationships are like in Act III can then be given, with the instruction to make the second image and then work out a *Transition* sequence in slow-motion, showing how the narrative transforms the first image into the second. A card for Act V might be given and used in the same way. Students can be directed to particular passages of text to help them work out their presentations. Where there is recapitulation actually in the plot (as in the two weddings in Act II and Act IV of *Much Ado*, or in the court scenes of *Hamlet*), close textual study is easier still to integrate.

Transitions in slow motion is excellent for focus and control and reassuringly simple to use for those with no movement training. It may be preceded by a *Paired mime* (p. 197) in slow-motion as a preparation activity (e.g. 'Tom falls through the ice and Sarah tries to save him' or *The action and reaction fight*, p. 195). Encourage the students to achieve clear definition and clarity with their movements (see *Definition*, p. 196 below). Another device useful in moving from the static to the dynamic, is percussion accompaniment provided by some of the group, or using hand-clapping rhythms or *Beating the floor* (p. 156).

Movement scenarios

Analysis of the narrative of the lovers in *A Midsummer Night's Dream* reveals an intricate pattern of attraction, repulsion, flight and chase and clearly demonstrates how a *Movement scenario* functions. The initial social structure, as is typical in Shakespearean comedy, is unstable, full of tensions, repressions and conflicts; in the body of the play (typically, this takes place in the liberating and unconventional 'green worlds' of forests, islands or countryside), rearrangements and confusions take place, before there is a social restructuring into new relationships at the end of the play. When written as a scenario, a series of 'set pieces' emerges (the first, a formal confrontation between parents and children, authority and subjects, and the next three, 'awakenings') with rather frantic sequences of movement in between. This converts into four 'pictures', with three 'movements' in-between. The whole sequence is a 'Dance of the Heart' or *Fond pageant*. Students can work in groups of four (just the lovers), five (four lovers and Egeus/Puck/Oberon) or six (four lovers and Egeus/Puck/Oberon plus a choreographer's role).

First picture: chains
Egeus is trying to force his daughter Hermia to marry Demetrius, though Hermia loves Lysander, and he loves her. Helena longs for Demetrius, who once led her to believe that he loved her, but now wants only Hermia.

First movement: chasing Hermia
Hermia and Lysander set off into the woods, to go to Lysander's aunt's house (where they can marry). Demetrius goes looking for them, followed by Helena, doting on him. Oberon watches. Hermia

and Lysander eventually lie down to sleep. Puck mistakenly squeezes 'Love-in-Idleness' flower juice onto Lysander's eyes. Demetrius shakes off Helena, who's left alone, near Lysander and Hermia.

Second picture: Lysander and Hermia wake up
Lysander, awaking, falls for Helena, who thinks he's making fun of her; Hermia wakes up from a nightmare and finds herself alone; Demetrius continues to long for Hermia.

Second movement: wrong partners
Helena runs away from Lysander, who follows her. Hermia unsuccessfully searches for Lysander. Demetrius chases Hermia, who continues to reject him and thinks he's killed Lysander. Hermia runs away from Demetrius. Demetrius, weary, sleeps. Oberon squeezes juice onto Demetrius's eyes. Lysander still chases Helena.

Third picture: Demetrius wakes up
Demetrius awakes and falls for Helena, who thinks he's making fun of her, just as Lysander seems to be doing. Both men love Helena and Lysander rejects Hermia. Helena thinks Hermia's joining in against her, with the men, to make fun of her. Hermia can't believe Lysander is rejecting her.

Third movement: chasing Helena
Helena feels mocked by everyone and runs away, with the two men after her. Hermia chases after Lysander, who continues to spurn her. The pace hots up. Helena turns on Hermia. They quarrel. Demetrius and Lysander quarrel. Hermia clings to Lysander to stop him fighting Demetrius. Helena and Hermia quarrel more. Hermia tries to attack Helena, who runs away. Demetrius and Lysander agree to fight. Puck intervenes, pretending to Lysander to be Demetrius and *vice versa*, so misleading each about the whereabouts of their opponent. Both men, exhausted by the chase, sleep. Helena wanders back, sleeps. Hermia wanders back, sleeps. Puck squeezes juice onto Lysander's eyes.

Fourth picture: harmony
The lovers wake up once more. Demetrius still loves Helena, and Lysander, now, loves Hermia again.

There are many ways of workshopping this scenario,[4] but as the sequence is based on chasing, a *Tag* warm-up is relevant. The one that follows, I call *Lovers' tag*.

Divide the class into groups of four, with a Hermia, Lysander, Helena and Demetrius in each group. Now select one, two or more of the groups to play the game, while everyone else stands still, spaced evenly about the room, acting as trees in 'the wood near Athens', around which the lovers will dodge. Phase 1 begins with this instruction: 'Hermia and Lysander hold hands and run away, Demetrius chases them and Helena chases Demetrius. Go!' There is an extra rule, however, which applies throughout the four phases of the game. Those being chased can spin round on their chasers, whenever they're actually caught, and shout 'Stop it!', whereupon the chasers must let go, freeze and count '1, 2, 3' aloud before resuming the chase. Phase 2 continues: 'Helena runs away, Lysander chases Helena, Hermia chases Lysander and Demetrius chases Hermia. Go!' Phase 3 is 'Helena runs away, Lysander and Demetrius both chase her, also trying to stop their rival from catching her, and Hermia chases Lysander. Go!' Phase 4 is brief and humorous: 'Hermia chases Lysander, Demetrius chases Helena, Lysander chases Hermia, and Helena chases Demetrius. Go!' All the groups should have a turn at this sequence and you can decide how many groups you are comfortable to have 'on the go' at once. It's possible, of course, to have everyone 'on' and no 'trees' at all, but there are advantages in everyone spending some time as audience/ trees, watching how the lovers interact.

After the *Lovers' tag* warm-up, work on *Fond pageant* should be much more free and inventive, but it's still prudent to begin slowly, with each group trying just the first picture, which can be shown to (exchanged with) one other group or shown to the whole class, before going on to the first movement, i.e. do a bit at a time, accompanied by discussion and analysis, leading, finally, to a complete action run-through. I have used overhead transparencies for this work, as they free students from poring over bits of paper and so remaining inactive. When groups have completed their version of *Fond pageant*, a good way of taking attention back to the text is to ask groups to find short language tags to add to the action. It's best if lines are learnt, but not everyone has to speak in every section. You could ask for a minimum of two lines from two different characters, for each section, and tags can be very short, e.g. 'By your side no bedroom me deny/ Gentle Hermia!/ I love thee not/ I am sick when I look on thee!/ I'll leave thee to the mercy of wild beasts./Thy lips, those kissing cherries./ Helen, goddess!/ Get you gone, you dwarf!/ Hang off, thou cat!' etc. Good theatrical productions of the play integrate the humour and fine balance of the dialogue with fluent ensemble movement, perfectly co-ordinated and rehearsed, and students, too, will enjoy, and benefit from, polishing their performances. They might also be asked to choose some music to bring in to the class, to accompany their work.

Dance scenarios

In working on the narratives of comedies, dance (after the reconciliations and denouements, a dance is often comedy's finale) frequently provides scenarios for practical work. Examples are an Eightsome Reel for *As You Like It* or an Excuse Me Dance for *Twelfth Night*. Both exercises will lead to a deeper understanding (critical and personal) of the plays' narratives, as well as generating amusement at the level of the actual comic concerns of the texts. *Dance scenarios* probably work best with quite advanced classes, capable of taking up the ideas proffered and carrying out some of the work independently. They should be rehearsed and polished for 'showing' to the other groups.

The 'eightsome' with which *As You Like It* ends, is made up of Rosalind and Orlando, Celia and Oliver, Silvius and Phebe and Touchstone and Audrey (whose 'loving voyage is but for two months victuall'd'):

> Here's eight that must take hands
> To join in Hymen's bands.
>   (V.iv.125)

Consideration of the way the love of these pairs develops through the play, points to the very different proportions of the strands of the narrative, differences that emerge from Shakespeare's free adaptation of the prose romance which is the source text. Rosalind and Orlando's meeting and courtship is a rich, detailed and curious mixture of touching innocence, theatrical frisson and philosophical meditation on love, while Silvius and Phebe play out a passionate, pastoral morality scene. Touchstone and Audrey's encounters mix, wittily but painfully, urbanity and cynicism with 'country pleasures' and a certain freedom of spirit and desire, and Celia and Oliver's union has a formal strength, deriving from a daring structural decision by Shakespeare. True their relationship is not dramatised in the play, but by Act V, the audience can smile and welcome the announcement of their instant love – at the start of V.2, Orlando says to Oliver: 'Is it possible that on so little acquaintance you should like her? that but seeing you should like her? and loving woo? And, wooing, she should grant? And will you persever to enjoy her?' With this love, almost at first sight, comes a complete change of heart for the formerly villainous elder brother of Orlando. When he settles his father's house and wealth on Orlando, and announces he will 'live and die a shepherd' in the forest with Celia, central moral and pastoral values are boldly declared in a kind of emblematic epilogue fitting to the underlying genre and spirit of the play. A similar marriage of thematic and philosophical convenience takes place, to the amusement, usually, of modern audiences, at the end of *The Winter's Tale*, when Leontes instructs Camillo to take Paulina 'by the hand'.

Working towards an *As You Like It* Eightsome Reel, through exploration of the contrasting narrative strands of the four pairs of lovers, reveals the narrative through its themes – which is important in other plays too, such as *A Midsummer Night's Dream* or *The Tempest*, where the action also appears somewhat circular and inconsequential, compared to the thematic deepening and contrasting that occur within the 'removed' (semi-pastoral) world of the text. To prepare for the reel,[5] each pair of lovers can be asked to research their parts in the text, select a few key phrases or lines and then produce a short sequence of, say, four or five appropriate dance movements, finishing up with a movement to image their marriage. The first step could be to ask each pair to make an opening 'address' to each other. This does not have to be from their actual first meeting – for Rosalind and Orlando, it might be 'O excellent young man!' and 'I cannot speak to her', accompanied by an opening movement. Once everyone has their opening, pairs can go on to develop their sequences of three or four more moves, accompanied by language. In groups of eight, these sequences can then be shown and enjoyed, before the final stage of the activity, which is to combine the sequences, with or without their accompanying language, into an 'eightsome'. Clapping and 'singing along' will be necessary, probably inevitable, as the dance shapes up. In a traditional Eightsome Reel, as with most reels, partners salute each other, dance together (simultaneously or in turn with other pairs), part, meet and dance with others and engage in movements involving the whole group. If you know the structure of the Eightsome Reel, you can teach the movements (and, perhaps, obtain appropriate music), but if you don't, several easy movements can still be incorporated – such as making a 'star' (four people go into the centre of the circle, right hands raised and clasping each other while they take four paces to the left, then they all turn, change to left hands clasped high, while taking four paces to the right); carrying out a 'chain' (partners face each other standing in their circle of four pairs, link right arms at the elbow and set off in opposite directions round the circle, alternating linked elbows as they meet each new person, so you link left elbows with the second person you meet and swing round, and so on back to your own partner, whom you swing round fully); and a 'general gallop' (all eight join hands in their circle and skip sideways eight paces round to the left, before turning and skipping back eight paces to the right).

Having practised a few of these movements, the groups of eight can be given a fairly open brief to use their own ideas, along the lines of partners dancing together, swapping with other pairs (all the time keeping their individually rehearsed moves, of course) and carrying out some corporate moves, including a finale.

The *Twelfth Night* Excuse Me Dance is simpler, though it, too, takes its form from the particular features of the narrative – in which, in this case, lovers are often isolated, alone and unrequited. First, each of the six characters involved, Olivia, Orsino, Viola/Cesario, Aguecheek, Malvolio and Sebastian, is given, or prepares from researching the text, their own

Love monologue, made up of language from their lines in the play. Malvolio's might be:

> To be Count Malvolio . . . having come from a day-bed where I have left Olivia sleeping . . . I will wash off gross acquaintance . . . my lady loves me, She did commend my yellow stockings of late, she did praise my leg being cross-gartered . . . Jove I thank thee: I will smile; I will do everything that thou wilt have me . . . To bed! Ay, sweetheart, and I'll come to thee . . . Some are born great . . . Some achieve greatness . . . And some have greatness thrust upon them . . . Madam, you have done me wrong, Notorious wrong.

These 'love monologues' can first be read aloud 'on the move' (p. 36), but in a completely self-absorbed way. Preparatory character work can also be done. This might include some miming, e.g. talking the class through waking up and getting dressed in character and then taking a stroll, and saluting or greeting the other characters as they go – each actor, having decided which part of the body will lead their character – Orsino by his heart? Malvolio by his nose or chin? Viola by her eye-brows? Now combine reading the text, with an appropriate individual dance sequence, devised by each character on their own.

Next, in their groups of six, the characters come together for the *Twelfth Night* Excuse Me Dance. Viola and Sebastian, who sits out of Phase 1, are given the same sort of hat to wear, to signify that they are identical twins. A humorous sticky label moustache or goatee beard for Viola/Cesario is also quite in keeping with the nature of the exercise. Each character has a different briefing card:

> **Olivia** wants to dance only with Cesario, but he eludes her. She thinks Malvolio's invitations are a joke and then gets rather alarmed by him as he persists, doesn't even notice Aguecheek's desire to ask her to dance and refuses Orsino's invitations flat.

> **Orsino** wants to dance only with Olivia, but is refused flat.

> **Malvolio** wants to dance only with Olivia. Although she refuses, he persists in asking.

> **Aguecheek** wants to dance only with Olivia, but is too embarrassed and awkward to ask, and anyway can't get near enough. He gets increasingly irritated by the attentions Olivia pays to Cesario.

> **Viola/Cesario** wants to dance only with Orsino, but is disguised as a man and can't ask him. With embarrassment she eludes the attentions of Olivia, who doesn't know that she's a woman.

Phase 1 of the dance begins with everyone reading their 'love monologues' aloud, but to themselves, while dancing alone and eyeing up those with whom they wish to dance. Soft, slow music can be played. When the words 'Excuse me!' are announced by the workshop leader, everyone may make their invitations, as on their briefing cards. Sebastian sits out for the whole of this phase.

Phase 2 of the dance begins when the leader sends Sebastian into the dance, at the same time giving out these additional briefing cards:

To Sebastian – When Aguecheek assaults you (but wait for it!), you are astounded, but quickly retaliate and put him in his place. When Olivia asks you to dance, you immediately accept her.

To Viola/Cesario – When Orsino asks you to dance, you accept gladly.

To Olivia – Wait until you see Aguecheek assault Sebastian. Then you ask Sebastian to dance, thinking he's Cesario. To your surprise, he accepts.

To Orsino – Wait until you see Olivia amd Sebastian dancing. Then you happily ask Viola to dance and she accepts.

To Malvolio – You follow Olivia, at a distance, but when you see her dancing with Sebastian, you drop out of the dance and sit down in despair.

To Aguecheek – You follow Sebastian around a bit and then (feebly) assault him. To your surprise he completely overwhelms you and you drop out in fear and pain.

Phase 2 does not last long, but the role of Sebastian in bringing about a solution to the dead-lock of the play, is clearly and entertainingly apparent.

Scenarios for improvisation

Certain scenarios may be improvised. The fifth act of *The Merchant of Venice*, for example, may be understood, partly, as formal play or celebration after the threat of the courtroom, and partly as a comic defusing of anxieties about monogamous marriage. It is helpful to experience what these things mean through groups devising ways of enacting a *Scenario for improvisation*, using their own words, along the lines of: *A* gives *B* a ring, which *B* swears to keep but then, as a reward for some service done by *A*, gives back to *A*, who is in disguise and so is not recognised by *B*; then *A*, no longer disguised, asks for the ring back. . . . Devise your own ending!

Mime scenarios

The Comedy of Errors, with its two pairs of identical twins, has two interwoven incidents which actually bring in almost all the action of the play. These are to do with the 'Gold Chain' (Antipholus of Ephesus orders this precious chain, but it is given to his brother by mistake) and 'Calling in to Dinner' (which involves marital expectations and servants delivering messages). Scenarios outlining what actually happens in these two strands of the plot, can be devised and simply given out for groups to work up into mimed sequences. Groups work on one or the other of the two scenarios. The comic potential of such scenarios is very strong, as with the lazzi of Commedia dell'Arte, and I know of no better way of bringing students inside the comic structure of the play and fixing its intricacies in their minds. These examples from *The Comedy of Errors* may also be improvised, with students using their own words or a mixture of their own words and the language of the play.

Units and actions

Texts, like tasks, can be handled more effectively if they are broken down into smaller units, but for learning to take place, we must do the analysis ourselves and do it actively. The analysis involved in *Units and actions* is laborious and the occasion on which to use this activity should be chosen carefully, but, because it involves the whole company or class as a single team, it bestows an unrivalled collective depth of understanding on groups which follow it through. You do not get such involvement through listening to a brilliant director or teacher expound, nor do you get it in a conventional play-reading, when you inevitably plan, and then come alive for, your own bits of text and, possibly, coast through the rest. Real shared understanding, invaluable for a class of students or a company of actors, can only come from a rigorous process of close collective analysis, such as that involved in *Units and actions* – some professional companies spend many hours, prior to starting rehearsals, in a form of traditional seminar discussion and analysis of the whole text.

Units and action is best used when following the intricacies of particular complex scenes, e.g. the Angelo/Isabella encounters in *Measure for Measure* or those of Iago and Othello in *Othello* – or, turning to quite different material, the events of the battles in *Antony and Cleopatra*, or the Greek and Trojan councils of war in *Troilus and Cressida*. The method is good for occasional use with a whole class, when students are actually preparing to act or improvise their own versions of such selected scenes, or as a small-group class exercise on a particular section of text.

The idea of 'units', and of 'creative objectives' for characters within those units, is derived from Stanislavski (1937), but the variation below[6] is only concerned with understanding the developing narrative of the text, its direction or dynamic, and not with the individual perspectives of actors. This is why it can be useful for students – because it deals with the story's primary level of meaning, stripped of interpretation and opinion. In the classroom, the method may be used as a basis for developing dramatic work or as an end in itself, for, used properly, it can bring with it: group discussion and the creative use of language; understanding of mood, motivation and character interaction; attention to meaning and context, including 'editorial notes'; grasp of narrative and structure.

The method by which *Units and actions* proceeds, should be adhered to closely. It is as follows:

1   The group sits in a circle, with copies of the text. *A* (the teacher to begin with) begins reading aloud, without dramatising the text, including all stage directions and taking all the parts. Members have been told to say 'unit' as soon as they sense a change of mood or subject or direction in the text. *A* chairs the discussion. The group must agree by compromise, not by voting or conflict. If the group does not agree that a unit should be declared at this point, *A* reads on until someone again says 'unit'. When agreement is reached on the unit, a line is drawn after the appropriate word, clearly indicating the end of that unit and the start of the next. (If texts may not be marked or a photocopy is not available, the units can be shown on the board or even on a large sheet of paper.) It sometimes takes groups a little while to grasp the point that they can only move on when they have all agreed – but that this does not mean abandoning positions just for the sake of unity. Agreement needs to be genuine. There may be a number of short units. Stanislavski, in fact, discouraged the creation of too many units, because he was after a broad understanding of the whole narrative,[7] but our method has no such objective. We are after detailed understanding, line by line. It is not our intention to perform the whole play, as a theatre company would.

2   The group agrees a title for the unit. This must not be interpretative or evaluative (e.g. 'Evil King cheats stupid subjects') but it should be concise and pertinent, encapsulating the main sense of the unit in a memorable way.[8] Good titles often sound like newspaper headlines or advertising slogans. Again, discussion should proceed until there is genuine agreement in the group.

3   Now the process continues, with the Chair doing all the reading until the next unit is declared. While the group is learning the method, the teacher will probably continue to read and to chair the discussion, but as soon as possible these functions should be passed on to *B*. Having pushed the group to agree a unit title, which is then clearly written in, responsibility for reading and chairing the next unit, passes to the next person in the circle.

4   Having 'united' the piece of text, the group may simply review their work in the wider terms of the play ('what have we discovered about structure/character, interaction/narrative, development/themes, etc.') or they may go on to use the units more actively.
5   Units may be used, for example, in improvising sections of text. The group memorises its list of unit titles (there might be ten or twelve for a particular scene), by chanting them together, in order. Having cast the scene, splitting up into extra groups if there are not enough parts to go round, the actors can next decide on an 'action' (i.e. a simple, clear gesture or movement by one or more of them), appropriate to each unit. Now the sequence of actions can be played, repeated and memorised.
6   There are several ways on from here. The whole piece may be mimed, with the actions giving structure and coherence; one line or a pair of lines, from the text may be added to each action; dialogue may be improvised, first around the actions and then between them, so the scene connects up; the actions may be used as ways into, or out of, tableaux.

At this stage, for the work to become fluid, the analytical frame of units and actions needs to sink from view – otherwise the stylised nature of the actions will inevitably make the work wooden. Natural movement will start to appear as continuous, motivated action takes over. Students should also be encouraged to return to the text, especially if their work is prompt-ing theatrical questions of staging and interpretation.

Points of view

For this exercise, you need a detailed summary of the play, preferably photocopied. Small groups are each allocated a character. They must trace their character's presence and role in the play, using the summary and the text to prepare a first-person, two-minute narrative of the play's action, specifically from their character's point of view. Groups then take it in turns to present their narrative to the rest of the class. You can also ask students to work in two or three representative or typical phrases spoken by their character. When groups narrate their version of the play, everyone in that group should be involved in speaking, using 'we' to tell their character's tale and taking over the narrative from each other and sharing it around as much as possible. Ask groups to narrate as though all members need help, confirmation and support from the rest of their group, as the narrative unfolds. If you wish, give groups a specific, and in some way appropriate situation for telling the events of the play, from their point of view, e.g. pupils called into the Head's study to explain their behaviour; gossips sitting on a bus; old men reminiscing in a pub;

women working on a line in a food factory. Do not tell the rest of the class what these situations actually are.

This exercise works well with any play, but *Julius Caesar* and *Henry V*, with their involvement of many characters in the moral issues of 'justifiable assassination' or the 'just war', are particularly suitable, as are plays with a focus on the allocation of responsibility for events, such as *Romeo and Juliet*, *The Merchant of Venice* or *Hamlet*.

The shortened play

This is a kind of 'text scenario', which I first came across in Buzz Goodbody's rehearsals of *Hamlet*, with Ben Kingsley as the Prince, for the RSC, in 1975.

Each scene is stripped to the central action, and, normally, the main characters, and any character included in a shortened scene has only one speech of a line or two in that scene. Each scene is delivered as a 'speaking tableau'. Depending on the size of your class, *The shortened play* may be carried out in small groups, with the whole class working through all the scenes and characters and, perhaps, the teacher selecting some episodes for comment or discussion. Alternatively, each student (with, maybe, two people sharing some roles if your class size demands it) can keep one role for the whole sequence, so you have a 'whole class' short version of the play. Shortened plays are quite time-consuming to prepare, but are an invaluable resource for plays one teaches regularly – and however well-done other people's shortened plays are, one never feels quite as confident when using them in one's teaching, as when using one's own version. Editing down is a creative function and in the case of preparing a shortened play, the nature of the result will be linked to what, whom and how one is teaching. Students may be set to make their own versions of shortened scenes, as a precursor to discussion of what the main concerns and impulses of particular scenes are.

The example that follows is Act I, Scene i from a shortened version of *A Midsummer Night's Dream*. It sticks to the rule of characters speaking only once during the whole scene (without conflating speeches, which would mean students learning a non-existent speech), though there is no reason why this opening scene should not be split into three or four scenes, if you are following the main divisions in the narrative.

Scene One (seven actors):
Theseus, Hippolyta, Egeus, Hermia, Lysander, Demetrius and Helena

Theseus:	Now, fair Hippolyta, our nuptial hour
	Draws on apace.
Hippolyta:	Four days will quickly steep themselves in night;
	Four nights will quickly dream away the time.

Egeus:	Full of vexation come I, with complaint
	Against my child, my daughter Hermia.
Demetrius:	Relent, sweet Hermia; and, Lysander, yield
	Thy crazed title to my certain right.
Lysander:	Demetrius, I'll avouch it to his head,
	Made love to Nedar's daughter, Helena,
	And won her soul.
Hermia:	In that same place thou hast appointed me,
	Tomorrow truly will I meet with thee. (*Spoken to Lysander*)
Helena:	I will go tell him of fair Hermia's flight: ('*him*', *said of Demetrius*)
	Then to the wood will he, tomorrow night,
	Pursue her.

An interesting variant of *The shortened play*, called *A beginning*, was given in *Shakespeare and Schools Newsletter No.2*, as part of 'Focus on *Macbeth* . . . a page of ideas for teachers – by teachers':

> Glue complete text of play to computer paper.[9] Display across floor of drama space. On text number single lines, selected to give outline of plot.
> Pupils allocated all the numbers of lines (we selected about 60, so each had three). Pupils sent in search of their lines; they write them down. Returning to their places in circle, pupils read lines of the play *in order*. Aim: pupils should feel they are constructing the story from 'their' lines (and to give points of contact when text encountered in full). Pupils working by torchlight in darkened space adds effectiveness.
> (Finch and Marston 1987: 15)

Shortened scenes

Students can also be asked to prepare short scenes, in order to explore the narrative. A good way in, is to ask groups to find the pivotal line of a particular scene, then 'image' the characters around that line, provide each character with a line to speak and then 'move' the scene – by asking the actors, depending on whether their own line comes before or after the pivotal line, to work towards or away from the pivot. The next phase is to do the same thing for the beginning and the end of the section of text allocated and use *Transitions* (p. 61) to connect them dynamically.

Investigative approaches

Investigative approaches to teaching narrative use the enigma as the main teaching device and focus on exploration and enquiry. These approaches to teaching narrative, unlike structural and dynamic approaches with their physical starting-points, lead with an intriguing mental challenge or enigma. As the work develops, any of the teaching methods already discussed in this chapter may be used, but the enigma must remain alive and challenging. Any teaching approach which does not disclose the play's ending, or uses gradual disclosure of the events of the play, or works with 'what happens next', is able to nurture, and draw very powerfully on, students' involvement and curiosity. (see *What will happen?* p. 80 below). A very ingenious investigative approach to narrative, a kind of *Cluedo*, is written up by Ralph Goldswain in 'Two Lessons on *Measure for Measure*: Sixth Form Shakespeare.' Goldswain took eleven short statements made about Angelo by various characters in the play.[10] Individuals learned their lines and then performed a simple ceremony in which they came up to 'the dead body of Angelo' (teacher in role lying on the floor!) and delivered their lines in turn. Knowing nothing of Angelo or of the play, and without texts to refer to, they then went on to construct or discover the plot of the play, with only the spoken clues of their group to help them. Goldswain reports that:

> Each time (they speak their allocated lines) everyone listens carefully for more clues to help them. It is then that accusations like 'hypocrite' and 'virgin violater' strike them vividly and become more significant. They are enjoying themselves and are absorbed in the exercise. Within half an hour they will have found the basic plot and most of them will be eager to get on and read the play.
>
> (Goldswain 1990: 93)

One of the key aspects of this exercise is that the language itself is crucial in debating and solving the 'puzzle' of the story.

A similar, but more open and performative approach to launching a play's narrative, is used by Perry Mills. He calls this activity *Kaleidoscope*. He chooses, at random, about forty resonant lines from the text his students are about to study, and then gives them free rein, in small groups, to devise short scenes, each of which must include some twelve to fifteen of the selected lines – without any additional speech of their own. The students then reflect on their scenes: what do they notice? What underlying ideas, patterns, themes and recurrent situations do they notice? This, like other textual exercises, generates a feeling of ownership of the play and an openness about the possibilities of the text. Later, when the lines are encountered by the class as they work through the play in detail, they also act as 'coat-hooks' on which to hang discussion of themes and issues arising from the text. It is also, of course, a highly student-centred activity, giving a lot of space for imagination and creativity.

If one is working with the episodes of a play in order, a whole sequence of 'investigative' work can be based on selected episodes, with the class experiencing a growing sense of excitement, as does an audience, about the resolution of the narrative, as well as a deepening knowledge of the themes, issues, characters and language of the text. Rob Jeffcoate has given a fascinating and revealing account (Jeffcoate 1992: 193–202) of how this operated for a vertically grouped class of 7–10-year-olds in a Liverpool primary school, when he and class teacher Susan Dransfield taught *Hamlet* in four afternoon sessions of two hours, mostly devoted to drama. They concentrated on the two families in the play and organised their sessions thus:

Session 1   Hamlet and the Ghost
Session 2   Hamlet and Ophelia
Session 3   The dumb show; the death of Ophelia
Session 4   Hamlet and the Gravedigger; the fencing match; Judgement
            Day

A brief look at the opening session, will give some idea of how the children became involved during the first episode. This opening session included the following activities: familiarisation with the characters, using *Names across the circle* (p. 166) with the children having name cards from the play; 'Drilling' and 'Changing the Guard' in the play-ground and paired work on Francisco and Barnardo's opening dialogue; the entrance of the Ghost (teacher in role), with the children sitting back-to- back, reaching out to try and touch the Ghost as he passed, and speaking bits of text they had learnt, such as 'Speak to me'; slow motion 'blocking' work with language tags, as Hamlet tries to follow the Ghost; the Ghost telling the children the story of his murder and an (extra-textual, but dramatic) 'swearing ritual' in which the children were invited to swear, on a toy sword prop, to avenge the Ghost's murder. Jeffcoate comments:

> They became engrossed in this situation – several of the younger ones seemed even overawed by it – and raised heartfelt doubts: 'What will happen if I don't?' 'What if Claudius isn't guilty?' 'What if he kills me first?' 'How should I kill him?' 'Shall I kill the Queen too?' Eventually, however, they all swore on the sword.
>
> The role-play finished at this point. As teacher I asked the class how they thought the story might develop, drawing their attention in particular to the characters called Players and Gravediggers. How might they come in? The class got very close to the truth on the first and narrowed the latter down to the burial of Hamlet, Claudius or Ophelia. This concluding discussion revealed that they already had a good grasp of the initial dramatic situation and the relationship between the characters.
>
> (Jeffcoate 1992: 195)

Could there be a better way of 'inserting' the children into the drama, the world of the play, and, I feel, bringing out the force of the role of the Ghost, that voice from beyond the grave – often such a difficult matter for contemporary productions in the theatre? The children's realisation of the implications of various actions, almost seeming to constitute an additional moral dimension to the experience of the play – and their commitment to this imaginative and truly educational mode of dramatic enquiry, continues to be felt in Jeffcoate's account of the remaining sessions. The final activity of the sequence, a 'hot-seating' role-play on the Day of Judgement, which had a particular force for these young Catholic children, brings us to the next set of activities in this chapter, *Trials, tribunals and enquiries*.

Trials, tribunals and enquiries

An intriguing enigma is presented at the end of *Twelfth Night*, when Malvolio turns to Olivia, puzzled that he has been done such 'notorious wrong'. However suave our critical explanations of the humiliation of Malvolio, the self-deluded, kill-joy antithesis of the play's comic spirit, audiences are often still left with a sense of guilt and pity that they must collude in his rejection and expulsion from the social world of Illyria:

> Why have you suffered me to be imprisoned,
> Kept in a dark house, visited by the priest,
> And made the most notorious geck and gull
> That e'er invention play'd on? Tell me, why?
> (V.i.340–3)

Olivia replies that Malvolio shall be both plaintiff and judge in his own cause, though the case is never heard in the play and it is left to critics and audiences to debate the enigma of his persecution, ever afterwards. Taking up this cue for a trial or enquiry, I once prepared briefs for a class, in the form of work sheets to be used in *Malvolio's enquiry*. Characters were asked to study certain sections of text, which were also studied by three prosecutors, who then cross-examined the characters in a tribunal. The characters also had to prepare certain pieces of evidence (the crucial learning element for students!), which would then be enacted during the course of the trial – the 'lighter people' were asked to be prepared to sing, in court, the catch that they sang in the middle of the night, that so upset Malvolio; Feste was asked to demonstrate how he proved Olivia a fool; Malvolio to read Maria's letter again; Viola to speak of true love, and so on. The more familiar a class is with a text, the more such investigative work can rely on their preparation, though the teacher will still organise the overall structure of the activity. Background information can be taken from the Internet and many theatre companies, notably the RSC and the NT, produce useful programmes or teaching packs. This exploratory way of working seems to encourage openness. Students remain intrigued. The text can become a permanent web of possibilities, suspended in their minds – as it is for actors and director.

There are other plays which may be approached in this way. Othello asks of Iago, at the end of the play:

> Will you, I pray, demand that demi-devil
> Why he hath thus ensnared my soul and body?
> *Othello* V.ii.298–9

The enigma concerns the hatred and racism at the heart of the play which, in some way, destroys Othello and Desdemona. Although the *Tribunal* is often the best dramatic device for investigative approaches to narrative (the group of three will prove to be effective in keeping the analysis and the action moving forward), consider other forms in order to teach different aspects of the text. A *Jury* format might be suitable for *The Merchant of Venice*, for example (at IV.i.89, Shylock asks 'What judgement shall I dread, doing no wrong?') with the panel of jurors representing different perspectives or positions on the racism, and commercial liberalism, of Venice. An arbitrary judge, like Azdak in Brecht's *The Caucasian Chalk Circle*, might be entertaining, as well as revealing, especially if played by a female student, if called to investigate *Katherine's complaint* in *The Taming of the Shrew*, while *The trial of Edmund*, with Prosecution and Defence lawyers or teams of lawyers (Edmund's would specialise in 'standing up for bastards') would be a good way to investigate the intricacies of the plot of *King Lear*.

Brenda Pinder has written of her use of 'Inquests and Inquiries: Trials and Tribunals' referring especially to her inquest into the deaths of Romeo and Juliet, which involved 'everyone in active exploration of the play'. Who carries the greatest responsibility for their deaths? Her three volunteer coroners drew up questions to ask the witnesses and five groups of students each prepared cases against a particular character or characters (Romeo and Juliet themselves; the Capulets; Friar Laurence; Mercutio; Tybalt), using any methods they liked, from the calling of witnesses to the presentation of 'flashbacks' in the form of dumbshow or freeze frames (Pinder 1991: 15).

Hot seating

A less ambitious kind of teaching narrative through enigma, is the personal challenge 'in role'. Here the emphasis is more on character, so my example, *Hot seating Jessica*, in which Shylock's daughter defends her desertion of her father, is included in the next chapter (p. 118).

What would you do?

In *The caskets*, the Belmont section of the narrative of *The Merchant of Venice* is taught through placing students in role before the three caskets of gold, silver and lead, one of which contains Portia's picture. Who chooses that casket, wins Portia. As music plays, students wander from casket to casket, reading and mulling over the riddle inscriptions, quoted by Morocco in II.vii:

> The first, of gold, who this inscription bears,
> 'Who chooseth me shall gain what many men desire;'
> The second, silver, which this promise carries,
> 'Who chooseth me shall get as much as he deserves;'
> This third, dull lead, with warning all as blunt,
> 'Who chooseth me must give and hazard all he hath.'

Regardless of whether they know the true answer, they are asked to reflect on their true, personal reaction to the challenges of the inscriptions. Which casket would they actually choose? Then, anyone who wishes to, may 'thought-track' aloud in front of each casket in turn. Chalked marks on the floor in front of each casket will help to heighten the drama and prevent the clumsiness of two people starting to speak together (as soon as anyone is standing on any of the three marks, the class can be asked to freeze and to listen as they reflect on the three choices). I have done this exercise with 15-year-olds and with undergraduates and the work was equally focused and atmospheric with both. Imaginative deepening of this kind is very rewarding as a stimulus for further work, and can be developed through whole group work, in pairs or singly. *What would you do?* exercises can usefully be derived from any situation where a character's judgement or decision is not obviously or easily acceptable to a contemporary reader or audience. Examples are Hal's rejection of Falstaff at the end of *Henry IV, Part II*, Henry's prosecution of the war in France at the start of *Henry V* or Brutus's decision to join the conspiracy to kill Caesar in *Julius Caesar*.

How to succeed

Some enigmas may be more mechanical, like knots which it is hard for the characters to untie, but focusing on them may still lead to the helpful consideration of essential questions about the play. In *The Taming of the Shrew*, there are two rudimentary *How to succeed* puzzles for the men: *How to win Bianca for a wife*, in which most of the men are interested, and *How to tame Katherina*, the shrew, in which only Petruchio is interested.

For *How to win Bianca*, an initial tableau of the characters in the play can be set up, positioning Bianca as unobtainable until her elder sister,

Katherina, has been 'removed' through marriage. Both women are within the bourgeois stronghold of their rich father's family, ringed round by sets of (male) servants and male suitors. Having begun with this familiar structural device, which clearly shows status and social position, the enigma of how to penetrate the family stronghold and win Bianca, can be addressed through the improvised approaches of those who think they have a solution. Acting out these ideas for solutions is actually just like Boal's 'Forum Theatre' (Boal 1979) and may be conducted in the same way, through the naturalistic improvisation of scenes. Finally, the complicated disguising that Lucentio, Tranio and Hortensio actually use in the play, can be acted out, in groups. For this, set students the task of discovering from the text, all the moves actually made by the characters and then formalise them into a comic, mimed routine.

In the case of *How to tame Katherina*, improvised solutions are tried out (perhaps with gender roles reversed), before the whole class. A good structure here, is to have an actor playing Katherina standing in the middle of a circle made up of everyone else – the 'Petruchios'. Individuals from the Petruchio circle then say, at random, to Katherina, what they would do to tame her. She must turn to the speaker and deliver a 'put-down' response; if the speaker feels it's a pretty good response, he or she must drop down on the floor. This can go on for as long as the teacher judges it to be working. Sometimes such exercises should be terminated after five minutes or so, so that they do not flag, while at other times, if they've achieved their own life and momentum, they can be allowed to run through to the end. 'The end', in this example, might be just Katherina and one Petruchio left standing, battling it out. It's important, in all improvisation, that students understand how to co-operate (see pp. 103 and 199): although this is a competitive improvisation, it's vital that good 'put-downs' from Katherina are rewarded. To encourage this, give the Petruchios the fun of hamming their defeats, i.e. 'if you feel she's scored in her response to you, wither and die in an appropriate way!' Another point: allow Katherina to leave the circle when 'she' (you might or might not stick to actual female Katherinas) has had enough, either with her 'tagging' the next person to go in or, better still, leaving it to anyone who wishes to, to fill the gap. This may be followed by work in pairs, in which the objective is to invent, co-operatively, a comic scene, with or without language, to present a taming strategy.

Lastly, Petruchio's actual scheme is revealed, from the time of his arrival home with Kate in IV.i. The scenario may be provided on prompt cards, or the class can be enlisted to help make out the scenario collectively, starting, perhaps, with:

1   Shout at servants for failing in their duties.
2   Attack Grumio for not bringing out the other sevants to meet you, etc.

In threes (adding in, as Shakespeare does, the further bullying dimension of the complicity of a second male, the servant Grumio), play through the scenario, using a particular performance convention, e.g. while the Petruchios/Grumios may speak as much as they like, the Katherinas may only reply, and then only with a single word on each occasion. The formal brutalities and structural inequalities of the text's patriarchy become very apparent, but so does the farce and the nature of the men and their motivation, especially if one uses *Style shifts* (p. 42), asking the Petruchios/ Grumios to play their scenes as rule-obsessed lawyers charged with carrying out the taming, or as theory-bound therapists etc.

What will happen?

When students do not know 'what happens next' in a play, groups can make their own proposals (through tableaux or improvisation), or dis- closure of the next stage in the narrative can be managed by the teacher within the framework of a contemporarised scenario. One does not, of course, try to stop anyone finding out about what happens – it's just that the emphasis is on the next event, not the end of the play. One example of this kind of investigative teaching picks up on the strange and episodic nature of the narratives of the Romances sometimes used by Shakepeare as his source material. In association with Lighthouse Cinema, I once made a Holiday Project video with some Wolverhampton children aged from about twelve to sixteen. It was a contemporary version of *Pericles*. This fantastic story, with its broken and re-united families, its ship-wrecks and deadly intrigues, its rulers, politicians and military, and its exotic setting in different sea-ports around the Mediterranean, lent itself well to updating as a popular serialised drama for television. I converted the narrative into a film scenario, which we improvised our way through, filming as we completed each section. As this was a holiday video project with the focus on making a film out of a good story-line, I didn't announce at first that we were working on Shakespeare, only that the main character, Prince, had many adventures, but ended up depressed and isolated, refusing to cut his hair or wash or talk to anyone. Would he be able to come out of this state? This man was the enigma that kept the children intrigued. At the end of the project, they were keen to see Shakespeare's version, playfully doubting that it could be better than their own! I felt the children had, quite naturally, been scrambling on 'the North Face of Shakespeare', without realising how perilous it is imagined to be.

Chapter 4

Character in Shakespeare

Changing ideas about character in drama

Meeting, and becoming involved with characters, is a fundamental part of experiencing and enjoying plays, but what seems direct and unsystematic in the theatre (particular actors *are* their characters for the duration of the show) is far from straightforward in the context of education. Literary education's traditional staple activity, character analysis, has always been linked closely to the illustrative and instructive purposes of critics and teachers. These purposes, usually assumed to be uncontroversial, taking the natural way to look at the play, are actually historically and ideologically specific. Simon Forman, after seeing a performance of *The Winter's Tale* at the Globe on 15 May 1611 noted down that he should 'beware of trusting feigned beggars or fawning fellows' such as Autolycus. Samuel Johnson wrote of Falstaff, in notes to his eight volume edition of *Shakespeare* in 1765, 'The moral to be drawn from this representation is, that no man is more dangerous than he that with a will to corrupt, hath the power to please; and that neither wit nor honesty ought to think themselves safe with such a companion when they see Henry seduced by Falstaff' – sound advice, but, no doubt, inadmissible as comment in a modern essay on Falstaff's character. Mary Cowden Clarke in her three volume work, *The Girlhood of Shakespeare's Heroines* (1851–52) pictured characters from the plays as real people, whose childhoods could be reconstructed from the evidence of the text – and very instructive some of the heroines' lives turn out to be. In the 1950s and 1960s we were asked, in school, to write character studies from a moral point of view, weighing up the good and bad points of the dramatis personae, searching for Aristotelian 'fatal flaws' leading to tragic downfalls, identifying qualities of leadership, responsibility and patriotism worthy of imitation. Sometimes, visits to the theatre seemed counter-productive: bad characters could be made to appear sympathetic, good characters, sanctimonious or hypocritical, contrary to the established readings of the classroom or the published exam. guides. What these approaches have in common, is a sense that people have stepped from the actual world into the world of the play, and that characters, like people, are fixed and can be known. This idea of character in dramatic literature has little critical currency now, yet we are faced with the paradox that we rely on our 'common sense' understanding of fixed character, as we see it expressed on the stage, construct it in the pleasure of private reading and judge it, for our own convenience and survival, in real life. But to teach character in Shakespeare actively, we first need to take account of changes in the way contemporary criticism perceives the idea of character and also, I'd suggest, emphasise the concept of 'role', i.e. the 'part' or raw material out of which characters are made.

Critical Theory has adopted the scepticism of the Social Sciences and Philosophy about the whole notion of the stable character or individual – a notion which derives from a universalising habit of mind, whose values are assumed. In Literature, as well as in life, people have increasingly been seen as the subjects of discourse, without that highly valued sense of stable individuality and capacity for independent action that was once traditional. Politically and morally, the idea of character as an essence, producing authentic acts of self-expression has lost ground to the notion of the socially constructed subject. We are perceived to behave as subjects of the discourses of power, of class, race, culture and religion, of gender and sexuality, and must live, in part, in the ways these discourses define us. 'Character' is also seen as subject to time and context, and cannot be summarised without reference to their mutability. In dramatic criticism, these changes of perspective appear in the way attention has been directed towards the literary origins of character. Psychological explanations and realisations of character, searching for coherent ways of unifying it and its utterances, rounding out and filling in with the commenting meta-language of the realist novelist – all have diminished in importance before contemporary, linguistically-based forms of analysis. Literary genres and their 'characters' are seen as artificially constructed, obeying their own rules and conventions, offering particular, historically-derived ways of seeing the world. Characters are analysed as made up from different registers of language and modes of discourse, rather than as rounded and set entities, exhibiting an identifiable range of personal qualities and character traits. Classroom discussion of 'character' once tended to work towards consensus about what a particular character 'is', through tussling over the meaning and significance of what is said (and having established what characters 'are', inferences could then be made about how they had behaved, or might behave). Now discussion is more likely to be severally related to role (a distinction between character and role is suggested below), function and position within the narrative, interactions with others and the characterising effects of different registers of language.

Workshops on character must take account of all these developments in critical theory, though, like theatre, practical approaches seem to mirror the diversity of contemporary critical theory and to resist the monolithic and universal. In the drama workshop, versions of the characters under consideration proliferate and diversify, springing out in all directions, even as the actors speak, interact and invent the action – but the task is how to use this in teaching about character. Practical work may avoid fixed and polarised versions of characterisation, but must still declare its own substantive aims and recognise its own assumptions and values. The most important of these aims, in the discussion of approaches to teaching character that follows, is to approach character through language and to see the speeches set down for characters, as roles.

Characters and their speech utterances

Characters in a play emerge from speech utterances, which, in Shakespeare, are often highly rhetorical. The performance of these utterances is experienced as widely variable: performer-personality, tone, inflection and gesture can all transmit modifications, even reversals, of apparent textual meaning. In addition to these variables, making and playing the characters in the drama workshop, through the formal qualities of the language, can mean that sophisticated critical objectives about the relationship of language to the idea of character, which can be elusive in sedentary discussion, become attainable. Take, for example, the well-known difficulty of Prince Hal's apparent duplicity in the first act of *King Henry IV Part I*. Veronica O'Brien has put the problem for the class-room teacher succinctly:

> At first hearing, the soliloquy 'I know you all . . .' usually evokes blank condemnation. A way of countering prejudice is to suggest that we are watching Hal in the process of learning what it means to be a future King, of finding for himself a right way of behaving.
>
> (O'Brien 1982: 52)

This quotation from the 1980s illustrates the traditional tendency to explain dramatic characters in terms of 'essence'. Hal is 'in the process of learning' and 'of finding for himself a right way of behaving'. This is unobjectionable at one level, for it is probably how we characterise the moral effort and struggle of our own lives, and of those around us, but it is not an analysis of the Prince's speech utterances. It is actually more akin to the sort of explanation an actor might give of his approach to 'finding' the character of Hal, perfect perhaps for creating a stage performance or 'reading' of the role, but not for exploring the elements making up, and the scope of, the complete role.

If we set out to explain the issues of 'I know you all . . .', either through a teacher-monologue or a dialogue with the more forthcoming members of the class, it may still be difficult to develop any historical or generic understanding. The children's general view may be established already – that they don't much like the Prince's turncoat behaviour and that the artificial imagery of the speech is, in any case, removed and alienating. Character improvisation, finding motivation in parallel experience from one's own life, may not help, for it is the category of character itself that is the problem. As a moment of character revelation, the speech shows an unsympathetic and contradictory speaker: an actor may be able to psychologise his performance, supplying naturalistic motivation to allow him to deal with the speech, but one actually needs to try to go beyond our habitually limited way of looking at the individual as, in Jonathon Dollimore's words, the origin and focus of meaning – an individuated essence which precedes and – in idealist philosophy – 'transcends history and society' (Dollimore 1984: 250). Looking for the 'pre-social essence' of Hal with his own 'quasi-spiritual autonomy' will only half explain the soliloquy. Hal seems to be the mouth-piece for future regal responsibilities he must bear (he is being 'spoken' by the discourse of kingship, in that he is its subject). In an active learning structure, students can feel the language of the Tudor doctrine of the 'King's Two Bodies' in the lines – the sun and gold imagery of the immortal role of kingship, with its power of redemption and reformation, set against the 'loose behaviour' of the fallible and temporary 'private body' of the King, as a man. There is an abstract, conventional quality to the language, which direct speech work can explore in an exciting and illuminating way, perhaps through *Dialogue using alternate lines* (p. 38) or *Echoes* and *Clarification* (p. 40) or by adapting Bertolt Brecht's technique of writing first person speeches in the third person, or asking his actors to describe their own actions in the third person. Ask everyone to start by reading the first thirteen lines of the speech all together (see *Reading together*, p. 34), perhaps as an official announcement. Then, split into pairs and ask everyone to read the last ten lines in the third person, changing 'I' to 'he' and 'my' to 'his' and using *Dialogue using alternate lines*, but as two friends making a plan, each 'topping' the suggestion of their fellow. As *Third person speech*, it would, therefore, start thus (the original words changed are in brackets):

A:　So when this loose behaviour he (I) throws (throw) off
B:　And pays (pay) the debt he (I) never promised,
A:　By how much better than his (my) word he (I) is (am),
B:　By so much shall he (I) falsify men's hopes.

Further work on the speech, and on the issue, might involve working in pairs on *Falstaff's dream*: Falstaff, drunkenly asleep in a chair, an empty tankard in his hand, is dreaming Hal's words (which Hal actually speaks softly to him, as though openly telling him the truth of what is to happen).

As he listens, his reactions to the words show in the way his face and limbs twitch, like a dog lying in front of a fire, dreaming of chasing rabbits. In exercises of this kind, students produce 'Hal' for themselves through performance of the complex rhetoric of his utterances. They can become aware of the qualities of the language out of which readers, actors and audiences conjure living characters and may be asked, in discussion, using the experience of their practical work, to articulate that awareness.

Hal, like all dramatic characters, seems to change as the narrative unravels. In traditional criticism, such change is seen as development, often towards maturity or self-knowledge or self-destruction, and the critic only faces a problem when there seems to be error or oversight on the part of the author. How, for instance, can Othello believe Desdemona to be unfaithful, when she has had no opportunity to be alone with Cassio? Some are irritated by blatant inconsistency here, while others are untroubled, perhaps invoking the concept of dramatic credibility: we, the audience, are convinced of the psychological realism of the action, or we suspend our normal, linear, experience of time in accordance with poetry's imaginative conflation of time's usual dimensions. Some see no problem, in any case: if people, their 'characters', are created by situation and discourse, then memory is unimportant and we should not expect consistency between, for example, the 'characters' of those brutalised in wars and subsequently humanised in peace-time. In the theatre, however, we perceive consistency, whether it is there or not, because we see the same, physical, person carrying their role through the different scenes of the play, all in a single evening. Nevertheless, Shakespeare's drama is rhetorical and dialectical and this means that we experience arguments that convince, move and sway us while we are listening to them, only to find them soon replaced by alternatives. In *Richard II*, the King speaks like a fine lawyer in his own defence, though we have seen the effects of his irresponsibility, and in *Richard III*, the King pleads speciously and seductively for his murderous and cruel ambitions. We can experience these things, while suspending judgement and the impulse to moralise. Later, the moralistic forms of the two narratives will bear down on both kings and our initial experience of their characters will be inverted. We become estranged from Richard III, having been coaxed, originally, into his mind, and we become intimate with Richard II, having viewed the opening acts of the play as his subjects.

Role differentiated from character

'Characters' are delivered in some way, whether in performance, private reading ('the theatre of the mind') or in discussion, and are, in this sense, completed and defined, fictional people, whereas roles are not pre-formed. They do not have to be analysed and mastered before they can

be acted, in workshops. Roles are for exploration and out of them performers and critics alike construct and conjure characters. This distinction
between role and character is important because it means, for instance,
that a particular way of playing some lines cannot be ruled out as 'unlike
the actual character' – though if, of course, this way of playing or seeing
the character is to be sustained through a whole performance or a complete critical reading, there will be numerous implications to take into
account and many questions to answer.

In working with roles, there are no set comic or tragic styles or concep-
tualisations to be represented. We suspend our ideas about the probable
effects of genre on characterisation: there are no expectations about how
one must act to suggest the murderer Macbeth, the lover Orlando or the
spirit Ariel. At one level, roles are simply 'parts', the actual words and
speeches set down for actors to play, but roles are also invisible fields of
power in which one immerses oneself – as oneself. Workshop participants
are not, of course, preparing to perform: they are performing, immediately and instinctively, and the reason that this happens, and is often such
an exciting revelation for participants, is that the structure and the rules
of the exercise or activity insert them directly into roles. Stanislavski
taught, albeit in the context of his theory of acting based on 'emotional
recall', that 'no matter how much you act, how many parts you take, you
should never allow yourself any exception to the rule of using your own
feelings. To break that rule is the equivalent of killing the person you are
portraying, because you deprive him of a palpitating, living, human soul,
which is the real source of life for a part' (Stanislavski 1937: 177). In
'active Shakespeare workshops', we are a world away from the painstaking
preparation of Stanislavskian theatre, but our practice depends, nevertheless, on the same rule – that the life and integrity of the work comes
from the living feelings and personalities of the participants. Character
activities and exercises work with the brief unity of performer and text
temporarily fusing into character, before they separate out again, the
performer becoming reflective critic and the text a source of information
about roles, rather than a resource for personal speech. If something like
this fusion is to occur, students will need to see characters, from ancient
plays, as real and feel them to be real, but how can they carry the
necessary conviction for them to seem real in the workshop?

In thinking of naturalism and realism today, film and television drama
immediately come to mind. In these media, popular perceptions of
realism and naturalism work with the idea that there is seamless continuity between fiction and reality, leaving it to academic criticism to
demonstrate that all fictions are constructed using particular conventions
and codes, which are prioritised and which vary, depending on the genres
and sub-genres concerned. The 'common sense' perception of the
seamless continuity, however, has its own critical integrity bound up with
another notion of what is 'realistic', which is to do with what is imagin-

atively convincing and this realism is as apparent in theatre, as it is in film and TV. The active principle here, as it is for actors in naturalistic work, is emotional truth, 'felt reality'. Those made to feel strong emotion, may judge a fiction to be 'realistic', whatever its formal aesthetic properties or visual codes. Elizabethan and Jacobean accounts of acting 'to the life', may be describing this phenomenon. 'Imitations of life' are measured, perhaps more frequently than we realise, against the 'felt reality' of emotional response evoked in performers and audiences, rather than against life itself. 'It was so real', a student once said to me, speaking of twenty lines of 400-year-old iambic pentameter, containing a dozen kinds of imagery and rhetoric. The lines had been spoken and acted with utter conviction, so that the emotion of the passage seemed to be transferred directly from the text through the actor to the audience. Similar connections may be experienced by students in practical work on roles, as set out in original text, and there will be an endless variety of expressions of those roles. In workshops, characters can never settle into a static essence or be confined to a single reading of their speech utterances. The drama workshop, like the stage performance, explores and experiments in order to discover which intrinsic qualities of the text might or should be brought into fresh conjunction with which of the myriad contingencies that make up ourselves and our world.

Character and setting

In memory, dramatic characters become welded into particular settings. Pictorial images of characters from Shakespeare often display emblems of their identity (Prospero's staff, Hamlet with Yorick's skull, Lear with his coronet of flowers, Macbeth with the daggers, Falstaff with a pint-pot or wearing antlers) and they are invariably situated in familiar surroundings. John Boydell's 'Shakespeare Gallery' project, which involved the establishment of a gallery and commissioning all England's most notable artists to paint Shakespearian scenes, led to Boydell's famous series of Shakespearian engravings, which appeared in an edition of the plays edited by George Steevens, between 1791 and 1805; many characters appear in such typical settings. Writing of Boydell's 'Shakespeare Gallery', Paul Lewis notes the pervasiveness of particular images. Before Boydell, eighteenth-century illustrations of the 'bedroom' scene of *Hamlet* (III.iv), in which, following his killing of Polonius, Hamlet harangues his mother and the Ghost of his father appears, contained traditional iconography:

> This scene has lent itself to illustration several times earlier in the century. It appeared as frontispiece to *Hamlet* in the first illustrated edition of Shakespeare, edited by Nicholas Rowe and published in 1709 by Jacob Tonson. The characters are in modern dress and the Hamlet is possibly a likeness of Thomas Betterton who played the

part for the last time in 1709. He was then seventy-five. The Hamlet costume, later embellished with the Orders of the Garter and the Elephant, and signifying derangement in its one ungartered stocking, ran with little variation until the time of Kemble.[1] The overturned chair likewise found its way into the tradition of representation, both on stage and in depiction.

(Lewis 1987: 9)

Characters become associated with particular settings and, in a sense, these settings function as stages in the narrative. Lear reaches the stormy heath when he feels he has no family left to turn to and Macbeth is literally trapped within his own castle walls at Dunsinane at the end of the play. More powerfully, however, objects and settings become symbolic of character, become enfolded in their aura. Almost instinctively, we see them as figuring the spiritual and moral condition of those characters – Lear's frustration and rage, for example, Hamlet's morbidity, and Macbeth's isolation and hopelessness.

For readers and audiences, the situation or setting of the characters, has its own familiar pleasures, the pleasures of 'the world of the play', its places, ambiences, encounters and predicaments. The excitement of situation is dense and enticing. It is to do with entering the imaginative domain of a play, which may be fantastic or historical, full of moral challenge, simulated danger, the envelopment of love, or all of these, and more, simultaneously. We enjoy *The Tempest*, partly, for the strangeness of the island with its yellow sands, its sounds and sweet airs, or *King Lear* for its outpourings of storms and madness on the heath or *Othello* for its horrific swell of misguided passion within the castle on Cyprus. In every Shakespearian play, there is a concentration of feeling and emotional colour in the specific situations. *The Merchant of Venice* has its contrasting locations (the commercial Rialto, the courtroom, moonlit Belmont), and its moral visions – Shylock's heroic, but self-destructive resistance to abuse, the power of the appeal for mercy, the fairy-tale truth of the caskets. *Hamlet* has situations of locked-in intensity: subjective alienation too much in the sun of Claudius's court; returning the cavernous gaze of a skull's eye-sockets; Ophelia's private pain, transfixed at the play, or with her herbs in her pitiful performance of madness or in her death by drowning; the forbidden bedroom confrontation of son and mother; the terrible realisation of love buried in a grave; the contemplation of poison in a cup.

Situations such as these, the locations the characters inhabit, are specific to the nature of individual plays and are crucial to what we actually mean by drama. They well up in our minds at the mention of a title or a phrase or a character, and hang there with pictorial clarity and force. We should expect practical work, just as we expect productions in the theatre, to present these situations to us afresh, so that we experience them afresh. As a teacher, I can enthuse about the drama of the Ghost of Hamlet's father checking his son's outbursts against his mother, but a drama exercise should mean that that enthusiasm grows in the imagination of everyone who acts in it.

Mise en scène

In working with situation and setting, the visual is paramount, which is why it is useful to introduce that most visual of concepts from film criticism, mise en scène.

Mise en scène (costume, movement of figures, lighting and setting) is at one level, a structuralist device, permitting analysis of a time-based medium, whose images, like those of theatrical performance, are constantly melting away before our eyes. Mise en scène treats film like photography, freezing the frame and examining structural components as though under a microscope; and just as the microscope can reveal the mechanics of the way a particular organism moves, analysis of the frozen frame can reveal the history, and something of the future, of an action, caught and transfixed, with its origins and its intentions displayed. In Drama, the 'freeze-frame' or tableau, laden with meaning, is a staple teaching device (p. 56). Although not 'dressed, set and lit', the freeze-frame shows the same statuesque characteristic as mise en scène, and from a pedagogical point of view, it allows the unravelling of thoughts and ideas, narratives, perceptions and relationships and offers the disciplinary bonus of renewed focus by consent, working with the energy of a group without the need to check or interrupt that energy with mere authority.

In looking at live performance, too, we need 'snap-shots' or the notion of 'defining moments', in order to analyse the mass of constantly varying images before us. In a similar way, the idea of a set for a play, which can support all the action of a play and yet can itself 'perform' conceptually, acknowledges the need to distil meaning, to remain still long enough for dialogue to be opened, and naive, but necessary questions to be asked: 'What are you saying? What is the theme of the drama? What is this really about?' In composing performance, we can build with the elements of mise en scène and in analysing performance we can separate out those elements in order to infer or deduce. The most fertile aspect of mise en scène, for active work, however, derives from the totality of the concept for it is the imaginative density that the elements can create in conjunction with each other that makes mise en scène so appealing. The mise en scène of a particular section of film is chosen for analysis because of its representativeness and its resonance, the way it encapsulates a particular emotion or mood, a unique 'world'. From mise en scène we take an understanding of the microcosmic and we also take the meticulousness of mise en scène, when structuring the elements of the 'situations' for practical work – as in the exercise *Fixing the mood* (p. 96 below).

TEACHING APPROACHES

Making and playing the characters through the formal qualities of the language is attainable in the theatre and also in practical work with students, so long as the language is a medium for our students, not a barrier. The work suggested in Chapter 2, on language, and elsewhere in this book, does not assume that students are familiar with Shakespearian language, and the speaking of it. Consequently, it does not rely on students' ability to deliver substantial passages of text effectively, though it holds strongly to the principle that it is only through use of the original language that the primacy of speech utterance in the creation of character can be taught.

The shared pleasure of meeting, becoming involved with, and actually being characters in plays, is the bedrock of all active work on character in Shakespeare. In addition, the drama workshop, because it is social, has great potential to enliven and engage students. Even focused, individual work, with students working independently of others, feels heightened and sharpened because it is taking place with and amongst the rest of the class.

In addition to all the activities that follow now, and as suggested in Chapter 3 in the context of work on narrative (p. 56), you can use many of the Group Formation Activities described in 'Introductions' (p. 162) and 'Names' (p. 166), to familiarise students with the characters of a play and to work in more depth with information about those characters. For more detailed Shakespearian character work, two books (written with actors in mind) may nevertheless be very usefully adapted for the educational workshop. The first, *Speaking Shakespeare*, is by Patsy Rodenburg (2002). Her analyses of a range of speeches from Shakespeare illustrate how actors can investigate 'the givens' (semantic, stylistic, informational and locational) of a speech and its different 'imaginative' contexts and dimensions. Students, in pairs, small groups, or as a whole class, might work cooperatively, using her method, towards active class presentations.

The second book, *Secrets of Acting Shakespeare*, by Patrick Tucker (2002), details Tucker's Original Shakespeare Company method of using Cue Scripts (players receive their own lines and cues, but not the rest of the script) for rehearsal. Again, this method could be adapted for educational workshops, using Tucker and Holden's *Shakespeare's Globe Acting Editions* of the plays. The Cue Script approach is not only revealing about Elizabethan theatre practice. As Tucker comments, ' Working at a scroll for just one character is a very different and liberating experience from working at the pages of a book' (Tucker 2002: 2).

As with Chapters 2 and 3, the teaching approaches that follow are arranged in three sections. Any activity may be used as desired, although there is, as before, a broad increase in the demands made on both teacher and students, as we move through the three levels. My suggestions for practical work on character start with focused individual work (in various 'personal encounters with roles') and then move on to techniques which make greater use of the resources and stimulation of the group – 'roles in social settings' and 'roles in action in the narrative'. The suggestions for active work are based on the notion of workshop participants inhabiting and exploring particular roles, using all their own personal skills and abilities (in thought, feeling, imagination, movement, expression) to take up and animate those roles. Students, with their different voices, shapes, styles, gestures and idiosyncracies, become new expressions, in body and presence, of characters. Although temporary and experimental expressions, students are actually 'speaking' or, like Snout playing 'Wall' in *A Midsummer Night's Dream*, 'presenting' these characters. The very diversity of workshop expressions of the same character is, like study of the endless varieties of the same character in performance, evidence of the need to constantly return discussion to the role – the words and lines of the part out of which the character is made.

Accordingly, in all the suggestions for work on 'character' that follow, it is assumed that teacher and students will come out of the practical work and will return to discussion of the text, to the frameworks of roles – out of which characters are made.

Personal encounters with roles

Becoming the character

Simple story-telling can set the scene and focus the class, taking students into the world of the play, as characters within it. The technique is much the same as *Follow my leader speech* (p. 25), but with a greater emphasis on situation and with internalisation of the language, so students are now speaking 'in character' and, briefly, becoming the character.

In this example of the technique, *Caliban's island*, students are immediately framed in role by the voice of the teacher. Here they become Caliban from *The Tempest* (I.ii.331–44):

> 'You are asleep in a dry, comfortable place on a desert island, peacefully curled up at first.' The students look at you quizzically. 'Find a place to curl up . . .' They get the idea and begin to trust the storyteller's voice. 'You become a little restless, as dreams begin to flicker behind your eyes, disturbing your mind. Your all-powerful master is making all your bones and joints ache – you can't get comfortable.' The students imagine this and squirm uncomfortably, as you feed them the information. 'You are being pricked all over your skin, but

you can hardly move because he's pegged you down. As you breathe in, a stabbing side-stitch hits you and now you feel sharp pinches on your arms and legs and your body. You become a tight ball. Gradually the pains go and you lie still. You slowly get to your feet, stretching your limbs. You decide you'll confront your master, Prospero, who's made you his slave.' Now you, the teacher, begin to move around the room, the island, looking at everything as though for the first time. Your Calibans watch you. 'This is your beautiful land, given to you by your own mother, yours by right. You move around it . . .' The students follow suit, moving around the room. 'It's beautiful, but Prospero's taken it from you. Bit by bit, you rehearse the speech you'll give to Prospero: *This island's mine . . .*' The students get the idea and repeat the phrase after you. It's good to repeat the phrase several times in several different ways (quietly, defiantly, angrily, pitifully, etc.), before moving onto the next phrase, holding the idea in your head that this is Caliban's rehearsal, so he has to work to clarify his argument and his expression of it. This repetition by the teacher should be used where it feels right, for deepening understanding of the ramifications of a particular phrase, and certainly not for every phrase. The students now enthusiastically repeat the phrases you give them, copying, and varying, your actions '. . . *by Sycorax my mother*' (you stand remembering her) '. . . *which thou tak'st from me . . .*' (you fix accusingly on the nearest person to you) '. . . *when thou cam'st first . . .*' (you move away and now wag your finger, as you speak, at another person near you) '. . . *Thou strok'st me and made much of me . . .*' (perhaps you caress your own arms and face, and drop into a kneeling position) '. . . *wouldst give me water with berries in it*' (you're back on your feet, drinking, sip by sip, a delicious concoction; you wander away from the person you were addressing) '. . . *and teach me how to name the bigger light*' (your hands indicate the bright sun) '. . . *and how the less, that burn by day and night . . .*' etc., to the end of the speech.

Notice that the students are working individually, but in the social context of a drama workshop. Carried out as above, the work will be focused and personal, even though, at times, participants use each other as 'dummy addressees'. There should be no reaction or interaction, as everyone's point of concentration is firmly their own personal encounter with the (same) character – though the setting is actually 'dramatised' by the teacher.

Some of this sort of work can be done in a purely imaginative way. The class, as 'Juliets', can sit with eyes closed listening to the workshop leader, moving among them, describing her vision of terror about waking in the tomb of the Capulets; as Macbeth, the class can imagine the despair of 'Tomorrow and tomorrow . . .'

Revealing characters

This activity is a development of *Becoming the character*, but now the students read the text themselves and work on it, using a particular, revelatory style. Some characters, such as Iago or Edmund have been given 'disclosure' or 'confessional' speeches, which are innately dramatic, by the playwright, and others (Lady Macbeth sleep-walking; Richard III dreaming before the Battle of Bosworth and Hamlet in his soliloquys) have speeches that enact disclosure as part of the drama, although the language of any character can be treated as disclosure and that character can be imaginatively placed in an appropriate setting. The speech chosen can then be dramatised as the character planning, or working through an issue by 'thinking aloud' or preparing a defence speech for a court appearance or writing a letter or diary entry, etc. To prepare, first use one of the 'Active reading' techniques (pp. 33–43) to ensure that everyone is comfortable with the lines and then ask the students to rehearse their own readings, either the whole class simultaneously (preparation for which might be *Walking the grid*, p. 152) or in pairs, taking it in turns to perform, while the other member of the pair is their audience, a silent 'auditor', who does not engage with them, but just sits on a chair watching the performance as though at a play. For example, we could take Angelo's soliloquy at the start of II.iv in *Measure for Measure* and ask for it to be given as though he is trying, with some difficulty and hesitation, to confess his feelings to a friend, or describe some personal symptoms to his doctor. The speech begins:

> When I would pray and think, I think and pray
> To several subjects. Heaven hath my empty words
> Whilst my invention, hearing not my tongue,
> Anchors on Isabel: Heaven in my mouth,
> As if I did but only chew his name;
> And in my heart the strong and swelling evil
> Of my conception . . .

The thought of the speech is not easy to disentangle, mainly because it is equivocal, but discussion of the thought, the meaning of the language of the speech and Angelo's state of mind and conscience, should all be more fluent and focused after first dramatising it through *Revealing characters*.

Emblematic objects

This activity is a variation of *Language across the circle* (p. 28 above) and may be used where a particular object seems emblematic of a character. Some imagination may be required: blunt dinner knives, perhaps, for Macbeth's daggers and a (preferably) life-size doll for the baby Perdita in

The Winter's Tale. The object is passed round the circle or taken across to give to another person, with a line from the text accompanying the action: Macbeth's 'I go, and it is done: the bell invites me' or Lady Macbeth's 'Why did you bring these daggers from the place?' or 'This brat is none of mine' (Leontes's line, perhaps alternated with Antigonus's tender 'Blossom, speed thee well!'). For a more extended *Hamlet* micro-drama, using the line 'Alas, poor Yorick! I knew him, Horatio' and the skull of Yorick, see p. 30.

Mimed character routines

In the case of comic characters, mime routines can be used, with, perhaps, a single (learnt) line as conclusion. A class of Malvolio's can be 'talked' through a mimed routine of preening and vanity, leading up to the donning of his yellow stockings and tight cross-garters. The whole class can be asked to advance down the room together, tottering and smiling: a 'freeze' command can be used to halt them all in their tracks, with different participants called on to then deliver their line, whether 'Sad, lady? I could be sad. This does make some obstruction in the blood, this cross-gartering, but what of that?' or 'Not black in my mind, though yellow in my legs' or 'Be not afraid of greatness: some are born great, some achieve greatness and some have greatness thrust upon them', etc. Other *Twelfth Night* mimed routines could be devised, leading up to concluding lines chosen from the text, for Viola/Cesario changing into boys' clothes and swaggering into Olivia's court; Toby Belch waking up drunk, putting his boots on and going to explain himself to his niece; or Andrew Aguecheek practising, in some terror, his sword-handling before meeting Cesario. Again, all this work is done individually, but in the social environment of the drama workshop. The emphasis is on taking up a role and becoming the character, entirely in one's own way, through personal encounter.

Roles in social settings

These activities harness the social energy of the play and of the class itself. The exercises involve two or more characters and once again all participants will be involved all the time, so exercises will be organised as simultaneous encounters and engagements. In paired work, the whole class works with just two characters at a time (i.e. in pairs, half the class play Othello and half play Iago). Gender, age and class differences (between lovers; parents and children; masters and servants) underlie and energise particular sections of dialogue, and such sections are especially suitable for practical work. Group work can vary from small groups focusing on particular episodes, to 'whole play' improvisations in which every student is briefed to play a different role. Sometimes a few lines are given to characters to use in the exercises and many language activities, such as *One word reductions* (p. 46), are also very appropriate for work on character.

Situating characters

For first encounters with a new play, situational work in role can have great impact. Students can feel they have arrived in the play before the cast itself, as when a class first encounters *The Tempest* through the shipwreck of its own boat, or when it finds itself drafted into the King's army and camped before Harfleur with the King, in *Henry V*, or set to guard the battlements and watch out for the Ghost, in *Hamlet*.

The tradition of Drama in Education as developed by Dorothy Heathcote, Gavin Bolton, Jonothan Neelands and others, lies behind such work 'in role'. Using their approach, of a flexible dramatic structure for the creative and moral exploration of an issue by a group of children in role, with their teacher in role, may be adapted for work on Shakespeare by those familiar with the methodologies of Drama in Education. Alternatively, using work in role as an active approach to teaching texts can be a much simpler matter, if it takes place within the narrower limits of the text. Take, for example, the teacher going into role as Lady Macbeth and the children as servants. This could lead to an open-ended dilemma (the servants read Macbeth's letter to his wife, before she receives it, or they hear Macbeth briefing the murderers to kill Banquo and Fleance or they see Lady Macbeth take the daggers back to Duncan's body: what should they do?). Such dramas can be rich, but they are, inevitably, tangential and it's uncertain where they might end, while work in role more focused on the text might involve preparing the castle for Macbeth's arrival ('who are the cooks, who's getting the tables out?' – while all this is going on, Lady Macbeth tells the servants about the battle with Macdonwald, Sweno and Cawdor) and practising greeting him with his various titles – much less dramatic, but still effective ways of situating the main characters and taking children's imaginations into the world of the play.

A different approach to *Situating characters* is described by Peter Thomas in 'Shakespeare: Page to Stage: An A Level Approach to *Antony and Cleopatra*'. He argues that 'it is a context of action, rather than of scene which is most needed, especially for those who have little experience of the theatre, let alone of Shakespeare'. Thomas asked pairs to create a context for Philo's opening line to Demetrius. 'The only guidance given was that the context should give answers to such questions as: "*Who* is the speaker?", "*Why* does he say this?", "*How* does he say this?", "*Where* does he say this?" and "*Who* is listening to him?".' After presentations and discussions, students knew 'they were still lacking a proper social and dramatic context for the line. So, once again, they went off in pairs to plan *the minute before Philo's speech begins* . . .' Thomas says that the best version began with off-stage drinking sound-effects, hand-clapping to accompany someone drinking a draught, and laughter: 'In from the rear of the stage area staggered a hair-drenched Philo wiping wine out of his eyes and throwing his glass in disgust into the corner. "Nay but this dotage of our general's o'erflows the measure" bristled now with the humiliation of the butt of the joke, the anger of the Roman functionary ridiculed in front of Egyptians, and the contempt of the man who sees drink as a source of unnobling weakness. We had found our context!' (Thomas 1987: 9).

Fixing the mood

This is similar to *Becoming the character* (p. 91), but now theatricality is fore-grounded. 'Mise en scène' (p. 89) is the starting-point. *Frames* are created around characters or are set for them to enter. A feeling of period and location precedes performance of the text and then accompanies it. Examples of such fixing of mood or 'naturalistic framing' as a theatrical technique were plentiful in David Thacker's 1993 *Merchant* for the RSC – from Launcelot Gobbo's ignorantly toying with a computer keyboard in the modern city office world of Thacker's Venice, to the beautifully composed picture of David Calder's Shylock in his leather wing-backed chair, listening to chamber music on his hi-fi, a framed photograph of his dead wife on the polished table beside him. In this sympathetic con-textual detail, reminiscent in its emotional pull of accounts of Henry Irving's 1879 Shylock silhouetted on a bridge on his way home, unaware of Jessica's treachery, a whole perspective on the character was suggested – but for this production only. It is plain that in the theatre 'character' is transitory and unstable[2]. *Fixing the mood* encourages students to recognise this, by composing settings for characters and playing the text through the mood created.

An example of the activity is to frame Shylock at his desk, in *The Merchant of Venice*. Antonio's approach to Shylock to borrow money, in I.iii, can be preceded, in a paired exercise, by the 'Shylocks' using a handful of coins to establish mood. These coins are meticulously counted and arranged while the Antonios watch from a distance. At a signal, the Antonios approach. The Shylocks finally look up and speak: 'Three thousand ducats; well'. The scene runs on, the Shylocks maintaining, however irregularly, their counting routines. The pace of this exercise makes it easy for students to both act and read.

Another example rehearses the start of the Gravediggers' scene in *Hamlet* V.i. The scene-setting is done as 'arriving and preparing for work', using props such as coats, bags, newspapers, packed lunches, etc. If you have canes or poles available which can be used as shovels and picks, so much the better. This activity may be done with the class in pairs, starting with all the First Gravediggers arriving at their gravesides (side-coached by the teacher) to prepare for work and await the arrival of the Second Gravediggers – who eventually appear and, all in silence, get ready for the day's labour too. Encourage personal invention in the use of time and space: the Gravediggers are in their own worlds until they actually engage with each other to start thinking about work. The opening two lines of the scene may now be built in to the improvisation.

A good way of teaching the lines, which will need a little glossing, is to have the First Gravediggers on one side of the room and the Second on the other, facing them. Stepping off as First Gravedigger, you say, 'Is she to be buried . . . ' and then halt, indicating to the line behind you that they should follow, repeating the words. Then you set off again, saying '. . . in Christian burial . . .' (halt again; they follow again, repeating the new phrase) '. . . that wilfully seeks . . .' (halt etc. as before) '. . . her own salvation?' Now, leaving the First Gravediggers standing in their line (by now near the middle of the room), go over to the Second Gravediggers and teach them their line in the same way – which also falls neatly into four parts, but, as though to emphasise the Second Gravedigger's superior knowledge, is a little longer: 'I tell thee she is . . .' '. . . and therefore make her grave straight . . .' '. . . the crowner hath sat on her . . .' '. . . and finds it Christian burial.' Now the two lines are facing each other down the centre of the room. Ask them to look at their pair, long and hard, the First taking in the words of the Second, and the Second looking to see if their words have been understood and then, in their own time, to part and return to their side-wall. This can be repeated a few times, until word-perfect. Finally, pairs are given time to rehearse their own versions of the scene, with actions and words combined however they choose, before some, or all, are shown and discussed.

Students can be asked, in pairs or threes, to discuss what simple hand props or items of costume of their own they might bring in to the next class, to fix the mood of a particular scene. Allowing such preparation to a class means *Fixing the mood* can become an opportunity for extending the drama workshop's usual 'Poor Theatre' approach (reliant on the physical resources of the participants alone). It will also bring home the point that there are numerous ways of imagining how the text can be performed.

Status work

Chapter 1 in Keith Johnstone's indispensable *Impro* (1979), is devoted to status work and is full of insights, both about theatre and about human behaviour. Status play is something that we all recognise and we are all constantly involved in, during our everyday lives.

Johnstone set the first of his status exercises when he was finding it hard to get his actors to talk realistically, as though in 'ordinary' conversation:

> 'Try to get your status just a little above or below your partner's,' I said, and I insisted that the gap should be minimal. The actors seemed to know exactly what I meant and the work was transformed.

The scenes became 'authentic', and actors seemed marvellously observant. Suddenly we understood that every inflection and movement implies a status, and that no action is due to chance, or really 'motiveless'. It was hysterically funny, but at the same time very alarming. All our secret manoeuvrings were exposed.

(Johnstone 1979: 33)

Students introduced to the idea of pitching their status just above or below their partner's, show the same instinctive understanding that Johnstone's actors did. Without further instruction, pairs act the same scene over as requested, with both playing high status; one playing high and one low; both low; status changing over during the scene, etc. They understand that an inferior social role, such as that of a servant, may still be played high, and that a King's role may be played low. They can point out the preferred 'status plays' of different characters (and of themselves in their own lives) and recognise the 'status experts' in Shakespeare, who are able, like Portia in *The Merchant*, to adapt their status according to the situation. The analysis of status transactions in a given scene, unsurprisingly, has much in common with analyses of the 'social gaming' and 'language gaming' in that scene, for participants in both these forms of gaming are also acutely aware of status. The beauty of status work for the drama workshop is the ease with which students can use it to test out the possibilities offered by the drama and the language of the drama.

Johnstone's *Master–servant* scenes are excellent preparation for workshops on Shakespeare's plays, most of which include master–servant relationships in some form, and they are especially useful for work on those plays with Classical New Comedy roots such as *The Comedy of Errors* or *The Taming of the Shrew*, in which master–servant comedy is prominent.

The variation *Hierarchy* is conveniently played in groups of four, in which No. 1 is the master, No. 2 is the first servant, No. 3 the second and No. 4 the lowest. No.1 can talk to anyone and request any task to be done, by anyone below them, but normally they communicate only with No. 2. 'Orders and blame are passed one way along the hierarchy, excuses and problems are passed the other way. So far as possible, each person is to interact with the next one to him in rank' (Johnstone 1979: 67).

Another excellent *Master–servant* game, Johnstone calls *Maximum status gaps* (pp. 70–1). The 'master' has the highest possible status and the servants the lowest possible. Whenever the master is irritated by a servant in any way, the master snaps their fingers, which means that servant must commit suicide. The game may be prolonged by giving each servant three lives. Taking up Johnstone's reference to Queen Victoria's reputed practice of sitting whenever she felt like it, and there *had* to be a chair to receive her, I encourage the master to behave in a similar way. The stakes can be raised by the master irritably calling out, 'stop following me around with that chair' and snapping their fingers to emphasise the point. Awareness of 'Johnstone's law', which teaches that 'a master–servant scene is one in which both parties act as if all the space belonged to the master' (Johnstone 1979: 63) will sharpen the scenes greatly.

With *Maximum status gaps* for preparation, a whole-class improvisation, *Petruchio brings home his bride*, on Petruchio's bringing home of his bride Katherina in Act IV of *The Taming of the Shrew*[3] can be entertaining and rewarding. You cast Grumio, Katherina and Petruchio (Petruchio's the only one to have the text, however, which he uses at will, interpolating at will too), with everyone else as servants. Katherina must play low status and is given two lines, which she may repeat whenever she wishes, but with hesitation and great caution, 'Patience I pray you' and 'I pray you, husband, be not so disquiet'. Grumio plays below Petruchio, but not greatly below, and the servants must play the lowest status possible. Having demonstrated *Petruchio brings home his bride* playing Petruchio yourself, the roles may be re-cast and the scene played again, perhaps with some variations, e.g. the servants don't understand or speak Petruchio's language very well, or they all have painful ailments which make it difficult for them to move quickly – though they are still bound to play the lowest possible status.

Images

We can develop the approaches used in the section on structural approaches to teaching narrative, where the emphasis was on story (see pp. 56–61 above), as part of practical work on character. In addition to name-cards on elastic necklaces or labels, more detailed information about their characters can be given to students, together with a few of their character's lines. First, all rehearsing simultaneously, you can ask every-one to pose as a statue of their character: then, in pairs they can ask questions of each other's work in turn, making suggestions and, perhaps, speaking a personal line or phrase allocated to them. You can then ask for a 'cast photograph', followed, perhaps, by 'thought-tracking' (when you signal, a particular character's thoughts become audible; they 'muse' aloud and the group eavesdrops on their private thoughts). Here are some examples of 'character cards' prepared for work on *Measure for Measure*:

Vincentio, Duke of Vienna

You have allowed Vienna's strict morality laws to be ignored and it is now difficult for you to do much yourself to change things. You decide to announce you are going to Poland and that Angelo will have full powers as your deputy, during your absence. In fact, you disguise yourself as a friar and you secretly observe Angelo's behaviour as ruler.

Sith 'twas my fault to give the people scope,
'Twould be my tyranny to strike and gall them.

*

Like doth quit like, and measure still for measure . . .

Angelo, the Duke's Deputy

When the Duke leaves Vienna, he puts you in charge. You are known as a very moral, severe person and as soon as you take over responsibility for the law, you set about cleaning up the city. You have a guilty secret in your own life, however: you promised to marry Mariana and then you abandoned her.

When Isabella, who's about to become a nun, comes to plead with you for her brother Claudio, who has fathered a child outside marriage, you abuse your power by demanding she sleep with you in order to save her brother's life.

'Tis one thing to be tempted, Escalus/ Another thing to fall.

*

I have begun,
And give my sensual race the rein.

Isabella, Sister to Claudio

You enter a convent as a novitiate. Your brother Claudio is condemned to die for fathering Juliet's child before marriage and you plead with Angelo for your brother's life. Angelo offers you a bargain which is abhorrent to you: to save your brother, you must sleep with Angelo, the outwardly moral judge.

Then Isabel live chaste, and brother die:
More than our brother is our chastity.

*

Th'impression of keen whips I'd wear as rubies
And strip myself to death as to a bed . . .

Lucio, a Fantastic

You are a rather cynical 'man about town' and you have no sympathy with the attempts of the deputy Angelo, to clean up Vienna in the Duke's absence. You help Isabella in her attempts to save the life of her brother, Claudio. You pretend to know the Duke well, but you are quite prepared to slander him in order to impress people.

Hail virgin, if you be – as those cheek-roses
Proclaim you are no less –

*

Marrying a punk, my lord, is pressing to death, whipping, and hanging!

Mistress Overdone, a Bawd

You work with Pompey (a pimp, who claims you've had nine husbands). You are arrested and taken off to prison, when Angelo, the Duke's severe Deputy, begins his campaign to clean up Vienna.

What with the war, what with the sweat, what with the gallows, and
    what with poverty,
I am custom-shrunk.

*

What shall become of me?

Collective events in role, discussing and deciding where we all fit in and what we do, may be improvised without preparation. The cast of *Hamlet* devises, and holds, a procession; the characters in *A Midsummer Night's Dream* meet first to plan, and then to attend a party; those in *Henry V* must organise themselves into a fighting unit and then march off to war together, and so on

Any play may also be represented, out of its time-frame, as an assembly in which the characters must speak for themselves – as, for example, a *Courtroom* or an *Election meeting* with Judge or Chair keeping order and each character speaking their lines imagining that particular context, adversarially for the court, persuasively for the election meeting. You can ask characters to answer the question 'what did you do in the play?' using only their given lines, but conveying a 'defence' of their role in the play through accompanying gestures. The effect of all this is to naturalise the language of dramatic characters, as they speak. If so desired, more resourcing can be given in advance. Students can be cast the day before and then asked to bring a suitable article of clothing or object to the next workshop, or they are given a few lines or a short speech to learn. *Trials, tribunals and enquiries* (pp. 76–7 above) develops these ideas further.

Meeting and greeting

Much active work on Shakespeare combines two principles: providing students with lines of text through which to communicate, and setting them in motion, which is liberating and stimulating. For the latter, a good preparatory exercise is *Sword and shield* (p. 177). Alternatively, use *Walking the grid* (p. 152): if you wish, free students from the imaginary fixed points on the walls in this exercise, by asking them to simply move at will, turning and avoiding people as they go. Now character work can be introduced, using any number of characters from the play, depending on what you wish to explore. For *Measure for Measure*, for example, you might work with just the roles of Angelo and Isabella, giving seven or eight lines to students and asking them to choose one to learn and use, or you might take just the five characters listed above, or the whole cast.

'Meetings' may be silent ('how does your character walk, smile, greet?') or characters may be asked to meet and greet each other with the tags of language already learnt, e.g. 'What shall become of me?' (Mistress Overdone); ' 'twas my fault to give the people scope' (Vincentio). You may vary your instructions to the class: 'choose whether to meet as an old friend or an old enemy; quickly meet and greet as many as you can, still using your language tag to communicate; choose whether to greet as though telling a secret, or as though you want everyone around to share your pleasure; choose to make your greeting 'big' or 'small', or choose to play high status or low status (see pp. 97–9 above) to those you meet', etc. To get students to experience different characters, have them swap their character briefs (elastic necklaces work best here) or place a pile of character cards in the middle of the room, so students can change roles to explore at will. They should do this 'blind'; however – no static sorting through to find a particular role! The work must remain fluid and improvisatory.

Characters co-operating

For more sustained work, characters need to be developed, or 'resourced' more fully. Just from basic character card information, individuals can be drawn into development: how does your character make a cup of tea, eat an ice-cream or an apple, take their dog for a walk, read a train timetable, sit down on a chair? Or, take the class back a stage, asking them what part of their body might most suitably lead their character's movement – eye, stomach, finger, nose, knees, big toe? Ask the class to practise this body-part leading by 'tipping' into their next movement: you lean into the direction in which your body-part is leading you until you can balance no longer and must 'tip' into moving on. Then you pause, change direction and tip again. How, then, without tipping any longer but retaining the sharpness it gives, would they walk down the street, meet others or buy a newspaper?

Alternatively, what kind of animal might their character be? You could spend some time coaching everyone, having selected their animal, in simultaneous individual work, starting with everyone waking up in their lair or hole, then going out to search for food etc. All this can then be refined down into particular gestures, mannerisms, ways of moving or looking, so human versions of the animals emerge which are then used in making, or 'mediating', characters from the play.

This mediation of characters may be explored in numerous ways. As well as the ones mentioned so far, teachers can suggest students play characters through well-known personalities, through trades or occupational types or by using a 'hat-box', from which they select, or are given, a particular cap, hat or piece of head-gear in which to play their character. For comedy, especially for plays such as *The Taming of the Shrew* and *The Comedy of Errors*, which clearly draw on Roman New Comedy, mediation through the types of Commedia dell'Arte is very rewarding. Even if you have no experience of using Commedia and no opportunity to try out its techniques for yourself in a professional workshop (the ideal), you can still obtain descriptions of the main roles of Commedia and use them, through simple movement or mime work (see pp. 194 and 196–7), as character types in workshops.

Once some individualisation has been achieved, characters can be asked to co-operate. Accepting and working with an improvisational offer adds to development, replacing the confrontational dead-end of blocking or resisting what is offered, and the same is true of set exercises. If your students are unfamiliar with improvisation, play *Offer/block/accept* (p. 199) for a little while, in groups of four. Other preparatory co-operative exercises are *Paired* and *Group mime exercises* (p. 197) and some of these exercises may also be used directly in work on texts. For example, pairs can manoeuvre an invisible ladder or plank of wood, while speaking their dialogue, or, using lines they have been given to learn (as in *Images*, p. 99 above) the whole cast can, in character (!), set out furniture in the room for a visit from an important person and their entourage or prepare dinner together.

An example of a paired exercise, from *King Lear*, is *Poor Tom shall lead me*, Gloucester's journey to the top of Dover Cliff, with one pair member, Edgar, who is disguised as Poor Tom, leading the other, his father, the blinded Earl of Gloucester, who does not know that his helper is his own son. In the exercise, Gloucester is blindfolded or keeps his eyes closed. This is an entirely silent activity except for the voice of the workshop leader, who uses lines from IV.i and IV.v to describe the journey to the point of despair at the cliff-top, at which point Gloucester kneels, and hears the speech 'Come on, sir, here's the place . . . topple down headlong' (IV.vi.11–24). At these words, Gloucester (forewarned at the start of the exercise), topples forwards, as in the play, thinking he is falling to his death. To prepare for this, you can use the trust exercise, *Trust leading* (p. 169), in which *A* leads or guides *B* (who has a blindfold or has eyes closed) around the room, simultaneously with other pairs, finally leading to 'parking' and 'exchanging' the blindfolded ones in a co-operative group exercise. Students can prepare for Gloucester's final 'gossamer' fall in advance, using a safe, trusting process of *A* gently taking blindfolded B's weight and helping *B* to 'fall' in slow motion to the floor. Check, first, that pairs have the necessary physical abilities to do this.

The co-operative nature of this exercise, and the empathy with the characters that it generates, should allow a class to take on yet more demanding moments in the play, such as the blinding of Gloucester itself or the final entry of Lear with Cordelia in his arms.

Discussions, arguments and confrontations may be handled through this idea of dramatic co-operation between characters. Using *The action and reaction fight* (p. 195), students, playing a character each, can present an exchange, taking it in turns to present an appropriate slow-motion action to accompany each line. Lines may be read or, if learnt, groups can form *Composite characters* (p. 111) and speeches may be distributed (see p. 44). The 'fight' might be boxing, fencing, knife-fighting or wrestling – tag-wrestling for small group work, perhaps, as in Angela Dale's vivid account of working on Macbeth and Lady Macbeth with '3G' (1989: 13); or you can use sports and games, such as tennis or chess. In *The Tempest*, Shakespeare presents the loving banter of Ferdinand and Miranda, through the device of their being 'discovered' to the court playing chess. Some contemporary dramas have been conceived entirely in such ways. Claire Luckham's *Trafford Tanzi*, first produced in 1978, used wrestling to explore gender relations, and Albert Hunt staged the Cuban Missile Crisis as though it were a Western. It became *John Ford's Cuban Missile Crisis*:

> So we came to present the Cuban Missile Crisis as if it were a movie being directed by John Ford – with Henry Fonda as Jack Kennedy, Lee Marvin as Nicki Krushchev, and Groucho Marx (out of place in a John Ford movie, but right for the part) as President Batista.
>
> (Hunt 1976: 108)

Another approach to *Characters co-operating* is to borrow Stanislavsky's concept of 'objectives', what a character wants to achieve or obtain in a particular exchange. In 'W.H. Smith Interact: A National Theatre *Twelfth Night* Workshop', Rex Gibson describes Brigid Panet demonstrating this:

> She has marked out a series of circles on the stage. Standing in one of them she waves a cloth at Sherrie – who wants it. 'Give me the cloth please' implores Sherrie who must somehow seize it without entering the circle. Brigid taunts her. The students are obviously eager to join in. They suggest two characters from *Twelfth Night*. Soon the whole stage is filled with circling, snatching, wheedling, pleading Orsinos and Violas: 'I want you to love me', with a cloth symbolizing that love. Brigid encourages them increasingly to include lines from the play – 'Pity me'; 'That's a degree to love.'
>
> Brigid plays variations on the power game using assorted Malvolios and Toby Belches. 'Shakespeare always makes characters' objectives clear – and they go all out to get what they want.'
>
> (Gibson 1989b: 10)

Mimed character routines: in groups

Some plays have comic routines which it's vital, on stage, to show as funny. Group work on *Mimed character routines* will often bring out the comedy of these routines very effectively, sometimes more effectively than in the theatre – Malvolio reading the letter he thinks is from Olivia, while Aguecheek, Belch and Fabian peer out from the box-tree in *Twelfth Night*; Benedick and Beatrice hiding while they listen to conversations which appear to indicate that each has an admirer in the other in *Much Ado*; the scene in *The Tempest* in which Stephano finds Trinculo sheltering under Caliban's gaberdine.

Comic business

Well-conceived comic business, best when integrated into the narrative and characterisation, is always welcome in productions, especially if there are textual prompts indicating suitable moments for its introduction – when Petruchio arrives home with his bride, for example (see *Status work* above, p. 97), Shakespeare includes phrases about the servants having difficulty pulling off their master's boots and then spilling water (cue comic routines). As well as the stage direction 'strikes him', there are questions ('Where's my spaniel Troilus?' and 'Where are my slippers?'), which are unanswered. I remember one production in which, when Petruchio asked about his spaniel, all the servants went immediately into 'a dog-searching routine', whistling, looking under chairs, snapping their fingers and calling out 'come on, boy, come on Troilus!' This only lasted a few seconds – they all very amusingly dropped it, as one, on Petruchio's next word. Another production of *The Taming of the Shrew*, used a number of slap-stick favourites, including one involving Petruchio's half-sitting on a three-legged stool, legs stretched out and elbow on the table. When Kate swept the stool from beneath him, instead of falling flat on the floor, he remained undisturbed in his original position, still stretched out, elbow on the table. There are many such familiar pieces of comic business, some of which find their way into stage tradition, often for quite long periods of time, and there are many more which may be freshly invented.

For students, either being taught a particular comic routine, which they must then adapt and fit into their playing of a scene, or (following some introductory practical work) being asked to devise their own comic business, can be an excellent exercise. It soon becomes apparent that crude 'add-ins' are not very revealing, or convincing: the business needs to be crafted into the text and the action and it needs to be in character.

Contemporary contexts

This is a more developed and extended version of *Style shifts* (p. 42). Students work in pairs or small groups, over a period of time, on a scene or scenes, with the brief to choose text which seems especially interesting or pertinent today, and to find a contemporary context for their text and ideas. They must use the original text, though the odd interpolation, especially in comedy, is not ruled out. They may also edit, reorganise or redistribute the language. Depending on how much time you have, and how elaborate you want the exercise to be, you can permit light furniture, hand-props and some costuming, but there should be no scenery, lighting, music or sound effects, other than those which can be integrated into the performance by the actors (e.g. effects from portable instruments). I used to use this exercise as a practical assessment with First Year undergraduates, and it often produced inventive and revealing work. Lines were learnt (though you could use a scaled-down, 'rehearsal' version without the learning of lines), and we presented the scenes 'in the round', with minimum setting-up time. Students were asked to produce a brief note on their 'update', which was distributed just before they played their scene. The early work, selecting text from one of the set plays and hammering out how it would actually work in a contemporary updating, was monitored by staff who first met groups regularly for discussions, and then commented on rehearsals. Prior to our showing in the round, we would carry out a 'cue to cue' rehearsal, so the actual performance moved with little interruption from piece to piece.

Roles in action in the narrative

This section is closely related to the section on dynamic approaches to teaching narrative (pp. 61–73) in the previous chapter, but the emphasis now is on the perspective of individual characters, and on their experience as it unfolds through the action.

When Aristotle argued, in Section 6 of the *Poetics*, that characters are included in plays for the sake of the action, he was underlining the dramatic primacy of plot or narrative. We are certainly left, after reading or seeing a play, with an impression of fictional people, what they were like and how they spoke, but it is what they did that determines how we conceptualise their chararacters. In this final section, we are working with the idea of action producing character and it will not be surprising if the characters now seem to be three-dimensional and richer. In the theatre, in contrast to literary criticism, we may imagine characters' motivation and their lives before and outside the play and productions may even direct us to think in this way (audiences are sometimes supplied with suppositional information about the reasons for Iago's hatred of Othello, for instance), but in the activities that follow, the focus is on what we experience of the characters in the action of the play.

A dominant motif in this section, especially in the first four activities, is rhetoric – language used formally to argue and persuade. Identifying the rhetorical impulse of a particular scene will often lead directly to ideas on how to work on it with students, as many of the examples demonstrate.

Group interview

Actors, including students in workshops, playing a given classic role, speaking its words, are literally inserted into, often conflicting, discourses. The role of Lear, for example, can be fragmented into different roles and strands of discourse deriving from paternalism, regality, friendship, humanism, religion etc. Students can themselves research and resource these strands and roles and Charles Marowitz's brilliant *Group interview* exercise (Marowitz and Trussler 1967: 170–1) can then be easily adapted to collective dramatisation of Lear's 'character'. Here is an outline of *Group interview*:

> *A*, a social outcast who's been in jail and is now being interviewed for a job by an Interviewer who knows *A*'s background but will consider *A* for employment, is backed by a semi-circle of his own 'Personality Adjuncts' (hostility, need for work, conformity, etc). These figures, each played by one actor, cannot initiate, but they simultaneously 'gloss', quietly making their own comments out loud on every comment or reply *A* makes, as it is made.

In *Lear's group interview*, class-room discussion can be used to identify the elements of character to be dramatised and then paired discussion of the actual passage selected for the exercise, can be used to prepare the 'Personality Adjuncts' for their parts. It may help to cast each pair as one of these adjuncts, or you may want to keep one actor for each adjunct. Now the interview is played out. Almost any of Lear's substantial speeches, or a whole section of dialogue, may be used. The Interviewer faces Lear, and gives him his cue-line, while the 'Personality Adjuncts' stand in a semi-circle behind. Using the dialogue beginning 'Peace, Kent, come not between the dragon and his wrath' (I.i.121), for example, Kent is Interviewer and begins with the cue-line 'Good my liege – '. Lear reads his lines slowly, with pauses made as though to explain his meaning to Kent, but it is important that he doesn't pause for comment or reaction from the adjuncts. They must 'gloss' as he speaks. The 'interview' ends at line 180:

> Fare thee well, king, sith thus thou wilt appear,
> Freedom lives hence, and banishment is here.

Victimisation

Many Shakespearian characters, especially female characters (Juliet, Ophelia, Desdemona, Katharina) face collective pressures. In choral

Victimisation exercises, group members each receive an oppressive line or phrase from the text and are briefly familiarised with it, using techniques from *Choral distribution* (p. 44) in keeping with the mood of *Victimisation*, i.e. using whispering and subdued, introverted repetition. Next the group encircles the person who has volunteered to be the victim, who must turn rapidly from speaker to speaker making an agreed kind of response, e.g. she may have some fragments of her own language with which to ward off the attacks, or she may repeat (defeated or defiant) the phrases hurled at her, or she may be asked to improvise her replies. Physical contact, such as jostling, may be added, provided the group is working in a focused and controlled way, but this whole exercise needs careful handling. The experience can be upsetting and it's important to make the first volunteer aware of that. The volunteer needs to be mature enough to understand what volunteering to be victim is likely to entail. Also, watch out for any signs of 'victimisers' becoming distressed by their role.

A good warm-up for *Victimisation*, is the circle game *Why?* (p. 187) in which the victim must turn to each accuser and reply immediately, to such questions as 'Why have you got dirty shoes?' . . . 'Why didn't you do the washing up?'

Persuasion

For speeches where persuasion is the leading motif, especially where the persuader is dominant and the listener has little to say in response, a milder version of *Victimisation* may be played. In *Julius Caesar* I.ii, Cassius has two long speeches ('I know that virtue to be in you, Brutus' and 'Why, man, he doth bestride the narrow world') in which he relentlessly attacks Caesar's reputation, in order to persuade Brutus to turn against Caesar. One person, blindfolded, plays Brutus and everyone else, surrounding him, Cassius. Using a 'tag' system, so students read a few lines and then fall back with someone else taking over reading, Cassius delivers his lines. The objective of Cassius is to persuade Brutus, so at times Cassius should physically 'act' on Brutus (leading him, taking his arm, holding him by both shoulders, etc.). Encourage movement around the space and all kinds of persuasive tone too, from loud and brow-beating to hushed and wheedling – the speeches are *tours-de-force* in the art of rhetoric.

As an example of *Persuasion*, but this time working in pairs, consider another sequence from *Julius Caesar* (II.i.237–302: 'Nor for yours neither . . .' to '. . . And not my husband's secrets?'). Here Portia is trying to persuade Brutus to tell her what is troubling him. Again the assault is prolonged and intense. Pairs can take it in turns to read, as Portia (Brutus should not have a text and all his speeches should be left out). Portia's objective is to get Brutus to stand still and look at her, but every time he feels the pressure mounting, he must move away. Portia must stalk him, imploring him to be open with her. A warm-up might be trying to put a halter on a horse's neck or catch a skittish cat.

Alternatively, start with Portia angrily trying to corner Brutus, as she speaks her lines, 'hands on' him – she is determined to make him listen. When he can't take any more, he breaks away, only to be caught again. A variation is for Brutus to have to answer 'yes' or 'no', every time she insists, and she insists by repeating herself. So, she might begin like this:

Portia:	You've ungently, Brutus,
	Stole from my bed: *she looks for an answer, but he avoids her look*
	. . . ungently from my bed . . . *still no response* . . . ungently from my bed . . .
Brutus:	*Yes!*
Portia:	. . . and yesternight at supper
	You suddenly arose and walk'd about, *she pauses* . . .
Brutus:	*Yes!*

As a contrasting approach, you could instruct Portia to pamper and molly-coddle Brutus while she speaks, doing everything to soothe and comfort him, to make him take her into his confidence.

Pairs may take it in turns to play Portia, experimenting with a variety of persuasive tones. Side-coach use of the acting-space and also pauses during which the characters feel their thoughts. If you wish, give different pairs different sets of instructions for playing the scene, without anyone knowing how other pairs have been briefed, and then hold a class showing.

Other plays suitable for *Persuasion* exercises include *Coriolanus* (Volumnia trying to persuade Coriolanus not to invade Rome) and *Othello* (Iago trying to persuade Othello of Desdemona's infidelity).

Discontinuity

Another of Charles Marowitz's 'Theatre of Cruelty' exercises, which adapts in an interesting way to *Hamlet*, is *Discontinuity* (Marowitz and Trussler 1967: 168–9). In *Discontinuity*, a writer or student is set up in a bed-sit and then must face escalating demands. Parents wish the victim to get 'a proper job', the victim's partner wants to get married, the landlady wants the rent, friends want the victim to go out for a drink, the gasman wants payment, the H.P. company wants the next instalment on the television, etc. At first, each 'demander' (arranged in a circle around the victim) enters the bed-sit and makes one comment 'on the move', one after another. Next, mini-scenes with each demander are improvised. Then scenes follow hard upon each other, the workshop leader coaching demanders to stay briefly and then exit as soon as another person arrives. Then two or three demanders enter and play their scenes simultaneously. Finally, and inevitably, the pressure is too much for the victim.

I call the *Hamlet* version of this *Discontinuity* exercise, *Hamlet demands*. First, set up Hamlet (rehearsing one of his soliloquies) in isolation. Using the characters and lines extracted from the text, given below, play a version of *Discontinuity*, as described above. Gertrude and Claudius have more lines from which to choose, but it is just as effective if characters repeat the same lines a number of times. Hamlet may only be allowed to reply using bits of the speech he is reading and rehearsing, or by repeating bits of the demands addressed to him.

Gertrude: Do not for ever with thy vailed lids
          Seek for thy noble father in the dust.

Gertrude: Thou know'st 'tis common – all that lives must die,
          Passing through nature to eternity

Gertrude: If it be,
          Why seems it so particular with thee?

Gertrude: Let not thy mother lose her prayers, Hamlet.
          I prithee stay with us, go not to Wittenberg.

Gertrude: Come hither, my good Hamlet, sit by me.

Gertrude: Hamlet, thou hast thy father much offended.

Gertrude: Why, how now, Hamlet?

Gertrude: Have you forgot me?

Gertrude: What wilt thou do? Thou wilt not murder me?

Gertrude: O me, what hast thou done?

Gertrude: Alas, how is't with you? Whereon do you look?

Gertrude: What shall I do?

*

Claudius: But you must know your father lost a father:
          That father lost, lost his

Claudius: For your intent,
          In going back to school in Wittenberg,
          It is most retrograde to our desire.

Claudius: . . .'tis unmanly grief,
          It shows a will most incorrect to heaven.

Claudius: How fares our cousin Hamlet?

Claudius: Have you heard the argument? Is there no offence in'it?

Claudius: What do you call the play?

Claudius: Now Hamlet, where's Polonius?

Claudius: What dost thou mean by this?

Claudius: Where is Polonius?

*

Ghost: List, Hamlet, O list!
          If thou didst ever thy dear father love –
          Revenge his foul and most unnatural murder.

Ghost:	Let not the royal bed of Denmark be
	A couch for luxury and damned incest.
Ghost:	Adieu, adieu, Hamlet. Remember me.
Ghost:	Do not forget

*

Polonius:	How does my good lord Hamlet?
Polonius:	Do you know me, my lord?
Polonius:	What do you read?
Polonius:	What is the matter my lord?
Polonius:	Will you walk out of the air, my lord?
Polonius:	My lord, I have news to tell you.
Polonius:	The actors are come hither, my lord.
Polonius:	My lord, the Queen would speak with you

*

Guildenstern:	What should we say, my lord?
Guildenstern:	Good my lord, vouchsafe me a word with you.
Guildenstern:	The Queen your mother, in most great affliction of spirit, hath sent me to you.

*

Rosencrantz:	Good my lord, what is your cause of distemper?
Rosencrantz:	What have you done, my lord, with the dead body?
Rosencrantz:	Take you me for a sponge, my lord?

*

Ophelia:	Good my lord
	How does your honour for this many a day?
Ophelia:	What means your lordship?
Ophelia:	Could beauty, my lord, have better commerce than with honesty?
Ophelia:	What means this my lord?
Ophelia:	You are keen, my lord, you are keen

Composite characters

This activity, reminiscent of the work of such ensemble companies as Volcano, Théâtre de Complicité and Cheek by Jowl, is really choral speech physicalised and treated expressionistically. A group of students presents a character collectively by first distributing the text and then finding an appropriate collective physical mode of expression. A drum or other instrument may be given as an optional extra. Everyone in the group must speak part of the speech. For example, Touchstone's nomination of the seven 'degrees of the lie' (*As You Like It* V.iv.70–108), invites enactment in its escalation from the Retort Courteous to the Quip Modest, the

Reply Churlish, the Reproof Valiant, the Countercheck Quarrelsome and, finally, the Lie Direct. Conditions may be imposed on the group's delivery in order to sharpen the enactment (and, in this case, its humour), e.g. each 'degree' must be illustrated with movement involving the whole group. If you have several groups, they can be asked to encounter each other, while sticking to their own delivery.

Another example, from *Julius Caesar*, is to divide the class into three *Composite characters*, Brutus, Cassius and Antony, and ask for three *Funeral orations* to be rehearsed and delivered over Caesar's body to the plebeians. Brutus and Antony's speeches are based on their actual orations in III.ii and Cassius's on 'Why, man, he doth bestride the narrow world . . .' in I.ii. Students listen, and respond, as the crowd now, when one of the other 'composite characters' is speaking.

Composite characters can also take part in passages of dialogue or exchanges between two characters, each member learning a particular phrase or line (see *Characters co-operating*, p. 102).

Useful warm-ups for *Composite characters* include *Simon says* (p. 181) and *N.S.E.W.* in which groups are asked to find a collective action for each of the four cardinal points of the compass, as they move across the room towards each point in turn. At the same time, they develop a way of speaking the accompanying words 'north, south, east and west'.

A simple, but effective 'composite character' can be made using speech fragments and a characteristic of the character in question. Dickens and Shakespeare share the ability to conjure characters from a habit, catch-phrase or trick of speech. To create Corporal Nym in *Henry V*, for example, Shakespeare uses language mannerisms, his portentous 'I can-not tell' and his knowing 'that's the humour of it', with humour and delicacy, drawing a warmth of response from the reader or audience. Nym's language, broken into phrases and distributed round the class, evokes a whole attitude and personality. An appropriate activity within which to set Nym's language, is marching, for, along with Pistol and Bardolph, he is a camp-follower, part of the lowest layer of Henry's (emblematically) 'layered' army, with its yeoman group of Bates, Court and Williams, the Welsh, Scottish, English and Irish captains and the aristocratic and royal com-manders. On one occasion, trying to capture some of the delight an audi-ence may feel on encountering this bizarre, new character in the play, and with half an eye on the Falstaff recruitment scenes from *Henry IV*, I went into role as Drill Sergeant, framing the class of 'Nyms' as poor English rabble, drilling them for five minutes and then marching them away from their ale-houses, 'Doll Tearsheets' and 'Nell Quicklys', off to France. As they marched they called out their lines, as though to boost their own courage: 'For my part I care not', 'I dare not fight, but I will wink and hold out mine iron', 'Faith, I will live so long as I may, that's the certain of it', 'I cannot tell: things must be as they may . . .' etc. The pathos of Nym, the common soldier who must fight his country's wars, came sharply to life in his language, spoken by the different voices of a company tramping off to war.

Once students are familiar with physicalising speech, they can be given different sections of a speech or series of speeches to rehearse and present in small groups. This technique can point up the way that characters come into dramatic existence through the deployment of different kinds of discourse. Lady Macbeth's language in I.v–vii is a striking example. The subject of her speech certainly changes, as the head-lines or topics listed below make clear, but her discourse is also made up of distinctively different strands:

I.v.16–31:	Problems with Macbeth's Nature
I.v.41–55:	Evil Prayer
I.v. 64–71:	Advice
I.v.14–20 and 25–28:	Courtly Greeting
I.vii.35–45:	Questions
I.vii.47–61:	Recrimination and Determination
I.vii.61–72:	Murder Plan

Journeys

The progress of the central character through a tragedy, its plot, was famously described in Section 13 of Aristotle's *Poetics* as dealing with a change in fortune, from happiness to misery, brought about by some personal error of judgement on the part of the protagonist. If we break down this progress into elements of the story, we can begin to understand its structure, and if we give students the opportunity to experience the elements, as they unravel, then they will internalise that structure and the drama of the story. The technique of *Journeys* will help to teach such structural elements effectively and it's especially good for sorting out exactly how action unfolds character in, for example, the *Temptation and corruption* of Othello by Iago or in Hamlet's *Moments of delay*, Macbeth's *Journey to damnation*, or, the example illustrated below, *Lear's journey to storm and madness*. (We might, of course, take the journeys of other characters, Edgar, Cordelia or Albany, for example, to bring out particular themes and structural subtleties in the play.)

In *Lear's journey to storm and madness*, King Lear's 'personal journey' from regal control to 'storm and madness' is divided into eleven scenes. The first nine scenes are played in pairs or fours and the last two scenes are played in threes. In these small groups, the class works through the scenes in order, so every student acts in every scene. The objective of this exercise is to give students the imaginative experience of King Lear's journey of suffering, his 'Via Dolorosa', and through this, to fix both the stages and structure of the narrative and our sense of the 'development' of the King's character.

Students use the lines indicated for the first scene, to prepare an 'explanation' of Cordelia's thoughts and behaviour. Cordelia can then give this explanation to her fellow pair-member, Lear, either in modern speech and in her own words, or using fragments from the text. When students have completed their preparations, the scene is played, with Lear starting it off by saying: 'Explain yourself!' to Cordelia. She, in role, then speaks her explanation. As rejoinder, at the conclusion of the scene, Lear chooses, and reads, one or more of his lines, given below. After discussion and, perhaps, a certain amount of presentation, the class then turns to Scene 2 and the process is repeated, through all the scenes. Remember that each new scene is set in motion, after preparation, by Lear's command 'Explain yourelf' or 'Explain yourselves', and ends, after the improvised explanations, with one or more of Lear's lines.

As a 'summary' activity for presentation, focusing on the experience of Lear's mounting frustration and anger, you could ask each acting group to cut down their words of explanation to a few key words or phrases, accompanied by gestures (rather like *One word reductions*, p. 46 above), so that the essence of the scene is clarified. Here are the scenes, together with Lear's choice of rejoinders:

Scene 1: Cordelia Rejected   *Actors: Lear and Cordelia*

Lear rejects his favorite daughter, because she will not say how much she loves him.
Based on I.i.96–105: 'Good my lord . . . father all.'

> *Lear*: Here I disclaim all my paternal care.

*

> Thou, my sometime daughter.

*

> I loved her most.

Scene 2: Kent Banished   *Actors: Lear and Kent*

The loyal Earl of Kent is banished by Lear for criticising him about his rejection of Cordelia. Based on I.i.120–167: 'Good my liege . . . dost evil.'

> *Lear:* Turn thy hated back upon our kingdom.

Scene 3: Cordelia's Husband   *Actors: Lear, Cordelia (silent), King of France, Duke of Burgundy*

Cordelia's suitors, the King of France and Duke of Burgundy, learn that Cordelia has been disinherited, has no dowry. Lear continues to upbraid Cordelia.
Based on I.i.188–261: 'Here's France . . . where to find.'

Lear: Her price is fallen.

*

Better thou hadst not been born than not t'have loved me
better.

*

We have no such daughter, nor shall ever see that face of
hers again.

Scene 4: Fool   *Actors: Lear and Fool*

The Fool, in a song, tells Lear that he is foolish – he's given away all
his 'titles' and claims to greatness.
Based on I.4.138–45: 'That lord . . . out there.'

Lear: Dost thou call me fool, boy?

Scene 5: Gonerill's Complaint   *Actors: Lear and Gonerill*

Gonerill complains about the unruly behaviour of Lear's Fool and his
knights.
Based on I.iv.196–209: 'Not only, sir . . . proceeding.'

Lear: Are you our daughter ?

*

Does any here know me?

Scene 6: Gonerill's Ultimatum   *Actors: Lear and Gonerill*

Based on I.iv.233–48: 'This admiration . . . themselves and you.'

Lear: Saddle my horses!

*

Degenerate bastard, I'll not trouble thee.

*

Into her womb convey sterility,
Dry up in her the organs of increase.

*

Yet have I left a daughter . . .
She'll flay thy wolvish visage.

*

A father's curse pierce every sense about thee!

*

O let me not be mad, not mad, sweet heaven!

Scene 7: Stocks   *Actors: Lear and Kent (in the stocks)*

Arriving at Gloucester's castle, Lear discovers his servant (Kent in disguise) has been put in the stocks by Cornwall (because Kent quarrelled with Oswald, Cornwall's servant, who had earlier insulted Lear).
Based on II.iv.1–20: ''Tis strange . . . I swear no!'

> *Lear:*   How came my man i'the stocks?
>
> *
>
> They durst not do't; they could not, would not do't.
>
> *
>
> O how this mother swells up toward my heart!
>
> *
>
> *Hysterica passio*, down, thou climbing sorrow!

Scene 8: Cornwall and Regan Stay Inside   *Actors: Lear and Cornwall*

Cornwall and Regan refuse to come out of Gloucester's castle to meet Lear.
Based on II.iv.84: 'Deny to speak with me?'
(In this scene, Cornwall and Regan remain with their backs turned on Lear, refusing to speak to him.)

> *Lear:*   Deny to speak with me?
>
> *
>
> Bid them come forth and hear me.
>
> *
>
> O me, my heart, my rising heart !

Scene 9: Cornwall and Regan Come Out   *Actors: Lear, Cornwall, Regan, Gonerill*

Cornwall and Regan disrespectfully saunter out to meet Lear. Then Gonerill arrives too; Lear is angry that Regan greets Gonerill.
Based on II.iv.121: 'Good morrow to you both' and II.iv.185: 'Who comes here?'

> *Lear:*   Beloved Regan, thy sister's naught.
>
> *
>
> Strike her young bones, you taking airs, with lameness!
> *(said of Gonerill)*
>
> *

You nimble lightnings, dart your blinding flames
Into her scornful eyes.   *(said of Gonerill)*

*

Infect her beauty, you fen-sucked fogs. *(said of Gonerill)*

*

O Regan, will you take her by the hand?

*

Art not ashamed to look upon this beard?

Scene 10: Regan's Offer   *Actors: Lear, Gonerill, Regan*

Regan asks Lear to cut his train of knights in half and go back to stay
with Gonerill.
Based on II.iv.196–20: 'pray you, father . . .'

Lear: Return with her? *(spoken to Regan about Gonerill)*

*

I prithee daughter do not make me mad. *(to Gonerill)*

*

But yet thou art my flesh, my blood, my daughter.
Or rather a disease, that's in my flesh, *(to Gonerill)*

*

Thou art a boil, a plague-sore. *(to Gonerill)*

Scene 11: Sisters United   *Actors: Lear, Gonerill, Regan*

Regan and Gonerill join together to humiliate Lear: they cut down
his suggested 'allowance' of knights to none. The King goes out into
the storm, in a rage.
Based on II.iv.225–58: 'I can be patient . . . What need one?'

Lear: You unnatural hags, I will have revenges on you both.

*

I will do such things – what they are yet I know not.

*

You think I'll weep. No, I'll not weep.

*

O Fool, I shall go mad!

EXIT KING LEAR: STORM AND TEMPEST

Hot-seating

Hot-seating, like trials, interviews, investigations, imitation game-shows, is a familiar technique which puts a student in role as a particular character to deal with questions from the rest of the class, on their behaviour, attitudes, motivation, feelings, etc. Here is a brief[4] for Jessica, from *The Merchant of Venice*:

> JESSICA: the facts
>
> She is Jewish. Her father is Shylock; her mother (deceased) was Leah. She is not happy at home, describing it as 'hell' and tedious, and, although she admits it is a 'heinous sin', she says she is ashamed to be her father's child. She falls in love with Lorenzo, a Christian, and devises a plan to elope with him and become a Christian. This she communicates to Lorenzo by letter. When her father goes out to dine with Bassanio, leaving her with the house keys, she disguises herself as a boy, steals her father's money and jewellery and runs off with Lorenzo. They take a gondola to the mainland. Eventually they arrive at Belmont but only after spending four score of the ducats in Genoa and exchanging the ring Leah gave Shylock when he was a bachelor, for a monkey. When Portia and Nerissa leave for Venice, Jessica and Lorenzo are left in charge at Belmont. Under the terms of the settlement of the legal action between Shylock and Antonio, Jessica and Lorenzo stand to inherit all Shylock's wealth when he dies.

Such briefs do not always have to be prepared by the teacher. Students, singly or in groups, can be asked to prepare first drafts, or Study Guides can be used – though beware of interpretative information. It is important that the briefs stay factual.

*

All the approaches I have been discussing depend on the teacher's drawing out particular features of roles, from the narrative, language and stage-directions of the chosen text. These features are then presented to students within active exercises, in ways which allow them, using their own living feelings and personalities, to create the characters of the drama. So it is that we hope to go beyond those stumbling play-readings and teacher commentaries, that may be effective for some in the class, the 'good readers' especially perhaps, but which leave many others passive and subject to boredom or distraction. Our aim, in using practical ways of teaching character in Shakepeare, is to people the class-room with the characters of the plays, ensuring that every student is 'on stage', immersed in the 'fields of power' that are the roles of the drama, the whole class making and experiencing the characters for themselves.

Section II

General workshop activities and the Shakespeare workshop

Chapter 5

Practical work and drama workshops

Activities in conventional teaching sessions

This chapter is mostly about planning and running drama workshops, with particular attention to workshops on Shakespearian texts, but for many teachers, practical work will occur in a much less formal way, perhaps as a single exercise or activity introduced at an appropriate moment. Whether you are quite new to practical work or whether you use it extensively, you may want to use one or two simple, active techniques as part of a more conventional teaching session. These techniques may not require any particular preparation. For instance, you might be working on a speech with a class and want to start with some kind of reading of it, to refresh everyone's memory. If the class knows the speech fairly well, you could ask them to read the first phrase silently, and then speak it aloud to themselves, but under their breath, from memory, while miming the action of writing a letter – and so on, through the whole speech, following strictly the rule of 'read a phrase silently and repeat it from memory, as you mime writing it'. If the speech is new to them, you might decide to read it aloud yourself, slowly, with the class listening (not following in their own texts) and whispering the words after you, as closely as they can, as though making a promise. This can be done, so that they are almost speaking along with you; the simple dramatic context of 'making a promise' (as with the dramatic context of the first example of 'writing a letter') helps greatly in achieving the concentration needed to do this. At the end of the reading, you might ask them to now look at their texts and check back to see which particular phrases they remember speaking. Saying which phrases they recall most vividly, can be a way in to discussing what is happening in the speech, and how it works.

For those who give lectures, large groups can be subdivided into pairs or threes, or, if the seating is flexible, into larger groups. Many forms of discussion, from brain-storming to buzz groups can then be organised at appropriate points in the lecture, as well as creative activities. Once, when teaching a whole year group about verse forms, for example, I set a 'Sonnet Race'. Everyone worked with a partner. I gave them the rhyming words of a sonnet (dead/ bell/ fled/ dwell/ not/ so/ forgot/ woe/ verse/ clay/ rehearse/ decay/ moan/ gone) and the first pair to finish their own sonnet, using those line endings, and writing lines strictly alternately, stood up, followed by the next two pairs to finish. After that, everyone was given another minute or two to get as far as they could (but with no more standing up for finishers), before pairs were invited to read out their efforts. As we turned to the original, there was a high level of interest, a general eagerness to discover Shakespeare's art. It is this shared focus and involvement that makes practical work so valuable, not only as preparation for learning, but for learning itself.

Some of the activities discussed in the chapters that follow, especially language activities, may be adapted for 'sedentary' use, as part of conventional lessons, lectures or seminars. Good examples would be *One word reductions* (p. 46) or *Brief intense exchanges* (p. 47), both of which are done in pairs, or *Hot-seating* (p. 118), in which one or more people come out in front of the class to answer questions in role. More adventurously, TV formats, from *This Is Your Life* to *Blind Date* or *Oprah Winfrey* may be used, and these, if kept brief and focused, can be effective. Students will enjoy using the text to prepare briefing cards for themselves, and it usually pays to hand the compère's role over too.

To work practically in conventional teaching sessions, as in the examples above, it is unnecessary to carry out any kind of group formation. However, once you are using practical work in a more sustained way, have moved into holding a 'drama workshop' in other words, group formation and preparatory activities are essential. But before doing any planning of the drama workshop, the first priority is that of safety.

Safety: physical and emotional

Every educational institution needs to have its own Health and Safety Policy and many institutions, especially schools, are also bound by particular nationwide requirements. Because Drama involves physical activity, sometimes in arenas where this does not normally take place (such as the classroom where English is being taught), teachers always need to check and follow all such material carefully.

Views about the safety of particular activities can vary from institution to institution. Such views often relate to local experiences and knowledge and, of course, age range. Some schools, for example, do not allow any kind of chasing games, or activities that involve jostling or forming chains of students. Whatever school or college policies are in force, it is essential that we follow them diligently. It is up to us, as individual teachers, as I emphasized in the Introduction (pp. xii–xiii) to take responsibility for the physical and emotional safety of our students, while they are in our care: '*In choosing, planning and carrying out any activity, can we always demonstrate (if necessary with the aid of our syllabus and teaching notes) that we have exercised appropriate care and due regard for the safety of all involved, including ourselves? This is the question we must always be able to answer about any practical work we undertake with students. If necessary, exercises should be adapted, or others, with the same learning objectives but which present less risk to the group in question, should be substituted.'* If, for example, you have planned an active session in a drama workshop, expecting that your students will be suitably dressed and in suitable foot-wear, only to find that the students' shoes and clothing are unsuitable for active work or that you have to make do with a cleared class-room, you may need to change, substitute or abandon some activities altogether. Part of every teacher's skill is identifying what is safe and appropriate for a particular group in a particular set of circumstances. But how might we go about the making of such safety decisions more systematically? I am grateful to Malcolm Griffin for the following account of how you might carry out 'risk assessment' in your own teaching situation:

> Modern safety policies are constructed around the concept of 'risk assessment' – a concept which pervades health, safety and welfare legislation. *The Management of Health and Safety at Work Regulations 1999: Approved Code of Practice and Guidance* (ISBN 0717624889) provides useful information about topics including Risk Assessment and Principles of Prevention. *Five Steps to Risk Assessment* (ISBN 0717615650) provides guidance on the risk assessment process. Material related directly to education may be found in *Everyday Safety for Secondary Schools* (Griffin 2001).
>
> First, you need to be clear about the activities you plan to do and why you plan to do them. Once you have a clear picture of what is planned, set in its fullest context (physical environment, people, equipment, group size, culture, etc.) you can then identify what could cause harm or loss. Such harm or loss needs to be reasonably predictable; there is no need to consider the impact of a possible earthquake when planning a drama session!
>
> Having done this, consider how high or low the risk is. If it is extremely likely that something will happen and that it will cause serious harm or loss, it is 'high risk'. On the other hand, 'low risk' activities are those where it is unlikely that a particular incident would occur and, even if it did, the level of harm or loss would itself be minor. There are obviously gradations and variations between these factors. The next stage is to make a decision about how to proceed. Is it so highly risky that it's best not to do it? Can ways be found of making harmful incidents less likely to occur? Similarly, can potentially harmful outcomes be made less severe? In drama activities, once

physical considerations have been addressed, much depends upon the competence of those involved (teacher and taught). Competence involves a whole range of considerations, including, for instance, maturity, qualification, experience, attitude, training, physical ability. If you are a 'more competent' teacher (not just in your own view) then, by definition, you should be able to handle activities better than the less competent. If you are 'less competent' (this does not mean you are bad at your job, but, perhaps, just less experienced), then you will need to take great care. Similarly, if you have a group students of low (or unknown) competence, then they will need a high level of supervision and carefully chosen activities. I would sum it up thus: 'Taking into account what we know about the people we are dealing with, and the hazards that they face, have we done all that is reasonable to reduce and control risks?'

The points given above would make the basis of a useful checklist to have at hand when planning work. It is a good idea to check such a list with your school or college health and safety co-ordinator, but it might well include the following points:

- Activities to be included in the session
- Description of the context – both the 'physical context' and the 'people context'
- Identification of significant hazards
- Assessment of the levels of risks involved
- Measures that will be put in place, which might include:

    o Proceeding as normal
    o Removing physical hazards
    o Adapting activities to take into account the limiting effects of physical hazards
    o Adapting activities to take into account what you know about the group
    o Providing higher levels of supervision
    o Sub-dividing groups
    o Providing training and returning to the activity at a later date
    o Abandoning the activity

No doubt you will think of all sorts of other measures but it is always important to note the main points of your risk assessment in your lesson notes and review what happened so that you gain in competence.

Any physical work will have safety issues, though a proper sense of safety is a continuosly evolving thing. It is not just that we are in a more litigious age. It is more that awareness of the dangers of different behaviour is constantly changing. (Extreme examples might include any of the hundreds of varied activities, until quite recently accepted as harmless, such as smoking or breathing in fume-laden air or sun-bathing.) So it is with active work, sometimes even of the simplest kind. Not long ago it was a general rule for Drama teachers that, in 'warming up' classes, then calming them down again, ready to focus on the topic, strenuous physical activity was desirable. There would inevitably be a lot of running around, probably physical contact too, especially with difficult or boisterous classes. When I worked in Further Education, General Studies formed part of my teaching. I was often given last period of the afternoon with 'Day Release' students, all male aged sixteen to twenty or so. They had spent the day sitting in class or working on practical skills to do with their vocational qualifications and future careers, and by four o'clock they were ready for some energetic activity. I remember using games, as openers, which recognised this. *Bull in the ring* was one favourite. The class formed a circle with linked arms and one person at a time volunteered to enter it. Next they were invited to escape. Another was *Deadly swamp*, also played in a circle with linked arms, but this time with a heap of coats (the deadly swamp) in the middle: anyone touching any part of the swamp was 'sunk', out of the game. Another traditional game they loved, was *Fox and geese* (p. 178). A fourth example was *Sinking raft*. The class was invited to form a tight group in the centre of the room. I would chalk a circle around them, stand back, and say: 'you're on a raft in the middle of the ocean; it's sinking and only the last person left on it will survive.' Normally when I introduced this game to any class, there would be a brief pause, followed by an eruption of pushing and shoving, though a class of *Gymnasium* students in Germany with whom I once played this game, gave a beautiful demonstration of how the unexpected can always happen in active work – and, incidentally, how aggressive human behaviour does not have to be the norm, even in play. They absorbed the instructions, talked briefly for a minute or so and then said they would rather all sink together than push the weakest into the sea.

Nowadays, of these four games, I would only use *Fox and geese* and, perhaps, *Deadly swamp*, but only then with considerable caution. Any running around presents some level of risk (note how running around the edge of swimming-pools was banned long ago), particularly running in unsuitable spaces, with unsuitable foot-wear or on slippery floors. Yet tag games are useful and can be set up so that they are not dangerous. One can insist on fast walking only, rubber-soled shoes or bare feet only (though working in bare feet is frequently considered to be unacceptable on health grounds now) and a delimited space, perhaps chalked on the floor, well away from any furniture or hazards. Other traditional drama activities simply should not be done anymore: such as *Chair relay*, in which teams, standing on chairs, advanced to the winning line, stepping-stone fashion, passing the last chair up the line to be used as the next stepping-stone – which involved two on a chair at any given moment and much clinging together, with the danger of falling off . . . or, *Trust charge*, in which a blindfolded runner ran full tilt into a 'safety-net' made up of the rest of the class, who caught, and held the runner. Apart from the experience of the enthusiastic teacher who wanted to demonstrate how safe this trust exercise is to his rowdy group, and was allowed, by them, to charge into a wall, there is my own memory of a powerful undergraduate who was completely disorientated by the blindfold and set off like a Rugby forward on the burst – at right-angles to the safety-net. Fortunately some of us were standing to the side, in his path. Other, once taken-for-granted physical activities, especially those involving lifting, balancing or heavy contact (such group exercises as building *Human pyramids* or *Log rolling*, which involved all lying next to each other like pencils in a case and then taking turns to roll from the back to the front over each other, as a way of progressing down the room) must also pass into history, unless, say, part of professionally-taught movement classes, at more advanced levels.

The general rule for all physical work is that one should first identify the hazards involved (bearing in mind that different groups, working conditions and spaces may mean radical differences in the associated levels of risk) and then plan to prevent harm, or reduce its likelihood and severity so far as is reasonably possible. Dance and movement teachers are trained to anticipate such differences in levels of risk, whether in individual students or in working conditions (whether floors are sprung or rigid, for exampe). They will check their classes carefully before starting work: even easy bending and stretching exercises, sequenced properly to allow people to warm up, may be hazardous for someone with back problems. Clive Barker tells (in Johnston 1998: 62) how, in a long career teaching a great deal of physical work, he had two serious accidents: both were snapped Achilles tendons and both occurred during the apparently innocuous activity of hopping. Although reassured by the surgeons that this can happen to anyone at any time, Barker feared that, perhaps, he might not have warmed up the groups sufficiently. The warm-up *Walking on the spot* (p. 193), incidentally, is a good preliminary for any exercise involving sudden foot movements, such as hopping or dodging about. It is not that one should become lost in a web of complexity about what is safe and what is not – more that one needs to develop a habit of mind that makes no assumptions about safety (just as the same mental drills should be applied to the quiet lane that hardly has any traffic, as to the street that is always busy).

Furthermore, physical safety is not just about possible accidents or injury. Today, almost any form of physical contact, without which most people would say Drama is impossible, may be contentious. Perhaps because professional actor training requires people to dispense with their inhibitions during rehearsal and performance, it has also been a tradition of Drama classes, that a degree of physical contact is inevitable, and desirable, in practical work. Yet social attitudes to touch have shifted greatly in the last ten or twenty years. Uninvited touching is unacceptable and something that might once have been justified as 'harmless' or 'friendly', might now be viewed, by some people – and by the courts, as molestation or assault. It is difficult to be prescriptive about touch in practical work, and the existing practice and expectations of classes will vary widely, but, as with physical safety, one needs to think in ways that avoid assumptions. *Finger-tip massage*, for instance, in which pairs in turn loosen up each other's neck, shoulder and back muscles, or *Face exploration*, an old sensitivity-training exercise involving pairs taking it in turns to close their eyes and run their fingers gently over their partner's features, may not now be acceptable to everyone. My own feeling is that such exercises should not be used initially with groups, but that as trust in the seriousness and appropriateness of practical work grows, so greater levels of physical contact may become more relevant – and acceptable. With very reserved groups, one might begin by making use of only the first level of socially acceptable physical contact, shaking hands. Even taking hands to make a circle (with the word of invitation being to 'take' or 'join', rather than 'hold' hands!) may cause embarrassment for children of a certain age, leading one to avoiding starting a workshop with such a request.

Safety awareness is vital, too, in imaginative work, which may disturb areas of the mind and the emotions, and reveal them to others, in ways that have not been anticipated and which may be distressing. This can happen, of course, in serious work of any kind. In an apparently academic classroom discussion, personal memory may be touched very painfully for a particular individual, causing an unexpected and unwelcome breaking out of feeling. In practical work, when 'acting out' and imaginative intensity are part of the procedure, such feeling may be nearer the surface, though there may also be a heightened sense of group responsibility and readier ways of giving immediate support. If educational work is serious, and sensitive to differences of all kinds within groups, it should have the resources to withstand the potentially negative effects of such rare incidents – and, quite probably, to turn them into positive experiences. This is not to say that it is easy to address all the issues that may arise in imaginative work on Shakespeare. When I was working on *Pericles*, in a London primary school, with the Cambridge Shakespeare in Schools project, we debated the question of how to deal with the incest involving Antiochus and his daughter, knowing that, in the large group with which we were working, there might be abused children. Our conclusion, essentially that we would trust the text, reflected our belief in the mythologising and story-telling qualities of literature, its ability, perhaps, to create a relatively safe space for children's mental 'processing' of their own fears and their own experience, however shocking. All the children followed, wherever the story went. We could only hope (as with the fictionalisation of other traumatic events that some would actually have experienced, such as the loss of a parent), that there might be a certain comfort, for any child personally affected, in knowing that their peer group was sharing an experience with them, imaginatively, which that child also knew in their own life as reality. We were agreed that ignoring or removing crucial elments of the play, was unnecessary. It is not possible to sanitise and censor literature, and maintain its complexity and totality, the very things which, in turn, may permit the kind of valuable catharsis described above.

Finally, students' footwear and clothes, and the working space itself, should be appropriate for the activities you plan to carry out. 'Dress', including footwear, watches and jewellery, may present hazards to students themselves and to others. Always watch out, too, for particular hazards of the working space you are in (surfaces, obstructions, 'non-safety' glazing, temporary structures, as well as students' own books and bags, etc.) and for hazards associated with any equipment or props you are using. There should also be sufficient privacy so that work is not inhibited by, for instance, passers-by peering in to see what is going on.

Different needs and abilities

Everyone in a workshop, of course, does not share the same character-istics and abilities. Memories come back to me of times when I was taken by surprise, having failed to anticipate what differences there might be in a class and how they might impact on the work and on the needs of individuals. If you do not know a group well, all kinds of things may happen. You may prepare simple 'speech tags' for children to read out, only to find that the language is too difficult or that a lively student chosen to read something aloud, is dyslexic and cannot sight-read. On one occasion, I'd planned a very active workshop for my opening meeting with a class of First Year undergraduates (including exercises like *Spot challenges* (p. 160), which has commands such as 'In groups of three, only three feet, belonging to different people, can touch the floor . . .' or 'Put your left hand behind your back; now try and touch other people's left hands with your right, but don't let your own left hand be touched'). One student was in a wheel-chair. My first instinct, which I did not follow, was to alter my workshop plan, or make lots of revisions, though the important thing was, of course, not to make any special announcements, but to carry on as planned and, at the same time, discreetly check that that student, as every other, was comfortable. As I gave my opening instruction, for *Names across the circle* (p. 166), I glanced at him: his hands were gripping the chair wheels and he was leaning forward, raring to go.

He did the whole workshop with relish. Once or twice I'd say to him quietly 'OK for this one?' and, for safety, I slightly modified the odd exercise, but, as you might expect, that was all that was necessary.

On another occasion, again with a group new to me working together for the first time, I'd decided to use *Lost hands* as a warm-up for work on 'Lost Twins' in *Twelfth Night*. In *Lost hands*, rings and bracelets were removed, a circle was formed, eyes were closed and participants gingerly set off on tangents until they encountered another pair of hands, which, eyes still tightly shut, they explored, noting, by touch alone, all their special characteristics. Then they all separated and moved around the room, seeking, by touch only, to find their partner's hands again. The effect was of ants meeting antennae, before, eventually, locating their lost twin. As soon as we started the game, I noticed that one student's left hand was missing several fingers, while his other fingers were much shortened. Once again, the student enthusiastically participated in the game, perhaps welcomed it – just as once, when I was doing the relaxing trust exercise *Fall-guy* (p. 170) with a class of mature students, one woman who was self-conscious about her weight, welcomed the opportunity to join in. Initially she had said she would not, but when everyone had taken their turn standing to attention in the middle, eyes shut, trusting to the group to hold them up as they were rocked this way and that around the circle of hands, she suddenly said, in response to a friend's 'go on, we'll look after you', that she wanted to try the experience. At first she was only rocked around a few inches, then a little more as she came to trust the group to bear her up; afterwards, glowing with pride that she had done the exercise, she told us that, normally, even standing still with her eyes closed was frightening for her, making her feel she was going to fall. Moving slightly off-balance, through trusting the group, clearly gave her far more than a certain physical satisfaction.

Every teacher's awareness of special needs increases with training, but much can be learned, following a student-centred approach, from observing individuals and from simply asking people what they require. A deaf student's experience of my Shakespeare workshops was transformed, for instance, when he told me he'd appreciate a copy of my workshop plan, and the sections of text involved, in advance or at the start of the class – something I should have thought of, it's true. These things only took a little effort to provide, but made a great difference to the student's ability to participate fully and, therefore, to his learning. Active methods of teaching do, perhaps, give rise to a broader range of pedagogical questions and concerns about special needs and abilities, than do more traditional approaches, but their philosophical foundations in student-centred and progressive thinking, may also mean that the 'active class-room' is a particularly receptive and responsive environment. By valuing and harnessing positive social connections and foregrounding participatory procedures, it has available, I would argue, a broader, richer and more versatile means of supporting students, whatever their needs and abilities, than is normally found in traditional class-rooms.

Workshop practices

In writing this chapter, I have felt that certain points should be made although they might seem obvious, or even, because they are obvious. Safety drills, for example, sometimes seem obvious, and for that reason they are sometimes ignored. In writing the next section, I have reminded myself that problems in workshops often have familiar and simple solutions to them that one habitually overlooks – things like not trying to do too much, leaving enough time for any final presentations required and keeping instructions brief and to the point. When I wondered about leaving a particular point out, because it might seem too obvious to retain, I then thought of how often I'd overlooked it in my own practice – and kept it in!

Workshop discipline

When I was a student teacher, I visited Stratford-upon-Avon High School to observe a series of Dance/Drama lessons. I remember going along the corridor to the Studio and finding a line of children standing quietly outside. When the teacher let the children into the space, they immediately went to one end of the room, put their books and bags against the wall and changed into soft shoes, before going to sit in a circle in the middle of the room – all still in silence. There was a tremendous sense of expectation and when the work began it was easy to see why: they were devising their own dance/dramas to Copland's *Rodeo* and they were all itching to get back to their work, which was, I recall, extremely exciting to watch. Their teacher explained to me that he always insisted on the same routine for the start of classes, just as, at their conclusion, he always spent five minutes 'winding down' so the children went calmly into the Maths or French lesson to follow. Many workshop leaders adopt such disciplined approaches. Some voice and movement teachers will not allow anyone to join a class late – on safety grounds. If you have not been through the appropriate warm-ups, then you cannot safely suddenly start doing demanding work. In any workshop, I will only call late-comers into activities already underway, at an appropriate moment, but I do not make people sit out just 'to teach them to come on time'. The important thing, as with all discipline, is that the need for it is clearly understood – and agreed. That's why workshop discipline that obviously contributes to the seriousness and quality of work, is invariably accepted by students. Even for rebels, the temptation to fight against it is far less than the temptation to attack the authority of the teacher who seems to be primarily working to their own agenda.

Discipline will obviously be partly determined by one's usual class-room practice. What is your customary 'stop signal', for example? In practical work it is useful, and sometimes important for safety reasons, to train your class to stop what they are doing immediately, on a given signal – when you clap your hands twice, perhaps, but, contrary to the expectations of some unfamiliar with practical work, discipline is built into practical work at every stage. Just as no sport can be played without the adherence of participants to agreed rules, so no practical drama, whether it be game, exercise, rehearsal or presentation, can take place without the same adherence to rules and conventions. Public perfor-mance itself, of course, requires the utmost discipline and team-work, and this is constantly reinforced in workshops through even the simplest presentations. Following the same procedures, day in, day out – how we listen to each other, how we watch each other's work, how we give instructions and how we expect the class to respond – all these things are as essential in workshops as they are in other kinds of classroom activity.

Texts and note-books

For many activities, students need to be unencumbered by their texts and note-books, but it's important to avoid that disruptive, chaotic searching in bags and piles of books that normally accompanies the request to 'now get your copy of the play' or 'please note this down . . .'. At the start of a workshop, ask students to place their texts, note-books and pencils or pens somewhere accessible (under their chairs around the edge of the room is my preferred place). It's easy to forget, in all the activity of a practical session, to give students the time and opportunity to look back at the text itself or to note down ideas, thoughts and brief accounts of potentially useful material from the workshop.

Giving instructions

Instructions should be simple and brief. They should not hinder the impending activity with long-windedness or complexity. One needs to make a conscious effort, every time one is giving instructions, to follow this 'simple and brief' rule. Sometimes, especially with more intricate exercises, perhaps tailor-made for a workshop, it pays to write instruc-tions out in advance, or at least to list the main point about each in turn. It is also sensible to give instructions in stages, e.g. 'your partner is the person nearest to you – stand facing each other' (the class does this); 'one of you is A and will stand still, at first; decide who this is' (they do); 'the other is B and now B moves fifteen or twenty feet away, in any direction' (they do so). This is a better way to set up an exercise, more controlled and focused, than to say, all in one go: 'get into pairs with someone near you, decide who is *A* and who is *B* and then, if you're *B*, move away fifteen or twenty feet in any direction'.

Demonstrations and dummy runs are very helpful devices. Demonstrations allow one to dispense altogether with a lot of complicated speech, and dummy runs, which involve the whole class, are particularly useful when one wants to take a group through the stages of an activity. Similarly, if one is giving an exercise which involves, say, working through a piece of text and extracting a series of points or features, it's good to get everyone to show their first stage. Not only can one check that everyone has the right idea, but this way one can also prompt the hesitant into getting started. Take *One word reductions* (p. 46), for example, in which students select, and learn, one word per line or per speech and then attach to that word, an appropriate action. I have known some pairs agonise for ages over their first choice, while other pairs race ahead. Saying to everyone that in one minute we shall all, simultaneously, perform just the first two of our words and actions, one for each pair, will put the subsequent work on a good footing. There will be a much higher level of understanding and learning and no anxiety from particular pairs about whether they're on the right track.

With large classes, especially with language exercises involving individuals receiving particular phrases or lines to speak or learn, instructions should be given which minimise boredom, time-wasting and confusion. Sometimes it's appropriate to photocopy a speech and highlight lines before distributing them, or to have a single, enlarged copy already cut up into numbered lines, though on most occasions one will be working with a class in which individuals use their own texts. Say one wishes to do a group rendition of Friar Laurence's advice to the Capulet household, after Juliet has been found, apparently dead (*Romeo and Juliet* IV.v.65), giving a line or so to each student, and allocating two speakers to the same line, should the size of the group make that necessary. Avoid, as teacher, pointing to the first student and saying, 'Jenny, you say: "Peace, ho, for shame!",' then, turning to the second, 'and you go on with: "Confusion's cure lives not/In these confusions",' then, to Bill, 'and you say: "Heaven and yourself/Had part in this fair maid",' then, to the fourth, 'and you: "now heaven hath all".' One may enjoy speaking the whole speech oneself, but by the end someone will be asking 'what was my line?' or 'did you say I should just do half of Line 15?' etc. It's better to ask the class to stand in a circle and then say, 'you're each going to get a phrase or a line; Jenny, you begin reading aloud,' indicating with your hand, as she gets to *'shame'*, that that's her phrase and that the next student should take over reading. This 'indicating with your hand' is worth remembering, for it allows the words of the text to predominate in the minds of participants.

Good, clear instructions, with a minimum of words and repetition, then, will sharpen up the feeling of a workshop and can make a great difference to the class's confidence and their trust in you as teacher. They can also be used to overcome all sorts of incidental problems. If a class, especially a large class, is noisy, lowering one's voice, so that people listen, is a better way of being heard than shouting. In introducing practical work, one is performing the first stage of the event, creating focus and establishing an appropriate atmosphere. So, the way you deliver instructions can help to determine the quality of the work that follows. The way instructions were delivered played a part in solving a problem I had when teaching forty students in a room with the most terrible acoustics. It was also furnished with extremely noisy chairs, so that changing the seating arrangements made an intolerable noise. For this particular course, it was appropriate to begin sitting on chairs in a large circle, and after fifteen or twenty minutes, to clear the room of chairs, note-pads and books, and start practical work. The crashing and scraping that accompanied this seemed to dissipate the concentration and focus built up in the opening part of the class. If these were very young children, I thought, I'd make a game of getting them to make the transition quietly: 'When I say the word, without making a sound, pick up your books and chairs, without a sound, mind you, carry them to the side of the room, put them down without any noise, then form a perfect circle, standing back in the middle of the room . . . I'm going to close my eyes and I don't want to be able to tell when you're back standing in a circle . . . I just want to hear you whisper, all together, "we're back . . .".' It is, of course, just as much fun and just as effective, for older students to do this sort of thing, as it is for younger ones – but it's important not to patronise. The instructions should be given straight, seriously, as an active group task (which it is, of course: a mundane task has clearly helped with group formation and focus), and not as though one is treating the class in a juvenile or patronising way.

Apart from the intrinsic value of giving clear instructions and demonstrations, clarity is also very important from the point of view of safety procedures. In the unfortunate event of an injury's occurring, one of the investigative questions would almost certainly be 'what did the teacher tell/show/ask the injured person to do?' In dealing with this question, syllabuses, lesson plans, standard procedures would probably need to be produced. In this way it would be possible for the school/college/department/teacher to show that they had planned with reasonable care. It is reasonable to accept that a creative subject like Drama will allow for a degree of open-endedness in student responses but specific instructions given by teachers should always make it clear that the teacher expects careful, reasonable behaviour – hence the use of adverbs and adverbial phrases, such as 'carefully', 'making sure you do not bump into others' or 'looking out for others around you'. Such usage helps to create the sympathetic, caring, 'safety aware' culture that we all desire in our classrooms and workshops

The circle

This is the most basic form in practical work – efficient (for seeing, listening to and speaking to others), non-hierarchical, fluid, secure, yet full of anticipation, social charge and the possibility of drama. People in a circle can quickly become performers and as quickly return to being spectators, or the whole area can be transformed, in a moment, into an active performance space, as games like *Fruit bowl* (p. 184) and *Cat and mouse* (p. 179) neatly illustrate.

When making a circle, it's easiest to join hands until the shape is perfectly round. Always insist on a proper (round!) circle, explaining that everyone needs to be able to communicate with everyone else effectively and on an equal basis. Instead of joining hands, you may ask everyone to look down at the group's feet, when forming a circle. This makes for better circles.

Moving around: the speedometer

Some exercises, such as *Walking the grid* (p. 152), start with participants moving around the space, more or less filling it evenly, and return to this general movement in between other set activities. But asking students to just 'move around' in a directionless fashion, can be unnerving for them at first, in spite of encouraging comments from the teacher, such as 'weave in and out' or 'go against the flow' (general movement has a tendency to quickly become a dogged and depressing circling). It helps to use the idea of a speedometer, with seven walking speeds. You explain that 1 is dead-slow, 7 is fast walk and 4 is regular walking speed. The command 'move off at 1' (or 4 perhaps) will be followed eagerly, as the class will know what it's doing, and it's somehow easier now to respond to further commands, such as 'visit all parts of the room' or 'turn from people as you meet them'.

Countdown

There should always be time enough for a particular activity, but it is useful to be able to crystallise the moment at which choices must finally be made or actions carried out. For instance, 'After the countdown, move to a space away from everyone else in the room: 3–2–1 . . .', or, 'After 3, take up positions in your tableau and hold them motionless: 1–2–3 . . .', or, 'After 3, move to make a group of four or five people: 1–2–3 . . .'.

Side-coaching

This is Viola Spolin's term for discreetly coaching performers in rehearsal, giving 'assists' as she says, while they are actually working and without calling for their direct attention (Spolin 1973: 392). It allows work to proceed fluently and to improve, without interruptions breaking in. It is important, even though one may be using active methods purely for teaching purposes, to give performers encouragement, feed-back and advice on what they are doing.

Showing

It isn't always necessary for all work to be shown to the rest of the class. Sometimes you can ask who would like to show their work and sometimes you can ask for a particular piece to be shown, so that you can draw out a particular point. The more the class is focused on the workshop's objectives, the easier it is for students to tolerate not being asked to show work, when others, perhaps, are. As a rule, however, I do not single out 'a perfect example of what we're getting at . . .', though in commenting on the work of a whole class I would certainly highlight good qualities in particular groups. Generally, a 'strengths and weaknesses' approach, for all groups, works well. Often the most sensitive critics, who can praise fully without making others feel put down, are the students themselves.

If you have a very large class or if you are dealing with work which is particularly intimate, you may ask groups or individuals to show material in pairs, A to B and B to A, or in threes, C to D and E, D to C and E, E to C and D. This is particularly useful when individuals are working alone (e.g. Juliet preparing to take the contents of the vial which will make it seem that she has died, the night before she is supposed to be marrying Paris, or Lady Macbeth sleep-walking), and it would not be possible, or desirable, to make every piece public.

When an exercise has been set that involves a final showing, or 'sharing' (as in the language workshop example 'Macbeth's soliloquies', p. 139 below), it's good to set up a procedure which allows the unimpeded flow of presentations. Again, the circle is often a good performance form for this, especially if one has divided up a play or long extract of text into sections to be presented by groups in sequence. I first did this with a large class that was working on the *Agamemnon* of Aeschylus. Groups, of appropriate sizes, were allocated sections of text and, with everyone being required to speak roughly equal amounts, were asked to extract key lines from the beginning, middle and end of their extracts, to be presented as tableaux, each with a Brechtian title. In a morning's work, we collectively staged a dramatisation of the play, which aimed to instill both an understanding of the play's structure of scenes and tragic choral songs, and an enthusiasm for Aeschylus, in the students, at the start of their Classical Drama course.

The same technique, except with improvisations instead of tableaux and original text, worked extremely well with sequences of medieval mystery plays. Examples of the technique using Shakespeare's texts, are given in Chapter 3 on narrative. To achieve a continuous performance, a 'cue to cue' rehearsal is needed, then, when the whole sequence is run, groups know when to get up from their place in the audience, on cue, play their part and return to their places, before being replaced, in an unbroken flow, by the next performance group. Agree at the start that, for this kind of event, there will be no applause until the end, when everyone can join in to applaud each other.

With all 'showings', it's essential that participants are prepared and calm. There's nothing worse than a group still anxiously whispering together, planning final refinements to their presentations, when they are supposed to be watching others. It's also important that audiences know what they are looking for, why they are having presentations. They are always in recognition, and celebration, of students' achievements, but they should always be set up, within the framework of objectives for the session, to deliver particular substantive teaching objectives too.

Active discussion

In the example of 'Workshop planning' that follows (p. 139), the last section of the suggested programme includes 'discussion'. Active work on Shakespeare does not mean silent work, or work without comment. On the contrary, it should take place in a context of discussion and comment, so that students make links and draw conclusions for themselves. This does not mean, of course, that the teacher should just return to static, teacher-centred monologues. Active work is open-ended and exploratory and when discussion follows it needs to maintain this approach: what did we see or notice or feel in the scene or section of text, what was 'going on', how did it 'work' and why?

More specifically, when setting up discussions or class responses, there are many simple ways of ensuring that active processes, involving every-one, continue. These techniques are well-known: brain-storming ideas in a large group, using large sheets and felt-pen for comments and responses, snowballing (see p. 164), giving buzz groups limited tasks (e.g. three points to be put forward) in a limited time, going round the circle with everyone identifying one strength and one weakness, asking everyone in turn to complete non-judgemental sentences such as 'I was interested by . . .' or 'I didn't understand . . .', etc.

More dramatically, perhaps, you can use the class to promote discus-sion of an issue. In *The diagonal*, they can be asked to stand on a diagonal line across the room, Level 10 (very strong agreement) at one end, Level 1 at the other end, or, at a signal, they can be asked to raise a hand showing their response on a 5-point scale, by the number of fingers they hold up, though care needs to be taken with these techniques, as it's easy for people's views to become polarised and fixed.

Active discussion is particularly useful if you have taken students to a Shakespeare production and want to begin your class with a critical discussion of it. *Reconstruction* is a good opener, especially if a little time has elapsed between the visit and the discussion and you want to sharpen memories of it, or if the production was disappointing and you wish to put the emphasis on what it was trying to do, instead of allowing the discussion to be submerged in negative opinion, or if a number of people in the class missed the production and you want an evocative way of telling them a little about it. In a circle sitting on the floor, eyes closed, students are invited to recreate some aspect of the production in their imaginations for a minute or so, in silence. Then, eyes open, they are invited to 'float' comments, which must be short and descriptive, into the circle, on the chosen aspect, e.g. the design, or the way certain actors seemed to create their characters. Explain that if several students start to speak at once, they should just give way, taking turns, in their own time – don't, as teacher, try and 'chair'. The mood required is of thoughtful, precise evocation and reconstruction coming from the whole group. It is often remarkable how much detail can be recalled (if they are to write about the production and have not made their own notes in sufficient detail at the time, you could, after five or ten minutes of *Reconstruction*, allow people to go to chairs or desks and make notes on what they've just said and heard). Apart from other benefits, this exercise will call students back to the evidence which they need to support their views – and it is a way of bringing in quieter students, who are often overwhelmed in a free-for-all discussion. Make sure that the rules of *Reconstruction* are followed: no argument is permitted (that might come later after the exercise) and statements should not be developed or phrased as opinions. A good reconstruction, on the topic of a production's design, might sound like this (with each comment coming from a different speaker): '. . . a bare acting area, enclosed by high wooden walls . . . like a palisade boxing the actors in . . . white-washed wood, with mud-stains . . . rough materials – wood and stone . . . bright light, white, harsh . . . a pit of sand opening up in the middle for some scenes . . . the costumes were rough, ragged . . . as though home-made, woven . . ., etc.' Anyone starting out 'I liked the set, it was . . .' or 'I don't agree, the lighting was quite dim at times . . .' has not got the point and must be gently drawn back to the conventions – 'just say what you saw, a phrase or two describing what you saw'.

In *Meet and part discussion*, students move all around the room and, on a signal, speak to the person next to them for a short set time on an announced topic, e.g. how effective were the comic roles in the produc-tion? This is good for covering a range of topics fairly quickly and, of course, ensuring that everyone is involved. If you want to draw out some main points at the end, you can ask what comments on a particular topic especially struck people, and use what is volunteered to focus the class's ideas. Instead of free movement, one can use a formal seating arrangement for discussion, e.g. an initial circle is changed simply into a circle of pairs or threes. After a set time, chairs are then easily moved a few feet to make a large circle again, for plenary discussion.

Another variation of *Meet and part discussion* is to use a 'progressive barn dance' structure (an inner circle of people does not move, while an outer circle, at a given signal, moves on to join a new partner; to make things more interesting, you can suddenly say 'move on three places this time'.

Another, quieter way of circulating opinion, is to have everyone sit in a circle and make *Written critical comments* on one or more of several questions raised by you, or suggested by the class as being interesting for that production. When they've finished writing, they place their sheets in the middle of the circle and then take someone else's sheet back to their place. Now they comment on anything they read, with which they agree or disagree, before returning the sheet to the middle again, and so on.

In all *Active discussion*, note-books and texts should be close at hand and opportunities to save ideas and insights should be given to students.

Workshop objectives and the use of warm-ups and preparation exercises

Often, the mistake we tend to make once we start to really use active techniques in workshops, is the mistake of prolonging games and other warm-up exercises, and failing to test them for relevance to the objectives we have set down for a particular workshop.

There are so many drama games and activities, and they seem to go so well, that it's easy to forget they must justify their claim on precious time. It's not enough that they seem broadly relevant. How, instead, does each develop the work and contribute to the delivery of your objectives? Remember, too, that one initial game can do several things at once. It can simultaneously develop speed of thinking and reaction, warm up the body, further social interaction, and introduce the theme of the workshop. One also needs to think about the transition from one activity to the next. If, for instance, one has planned an individualised session (e.g. on Hamlet's isolation and feigned madness) it could be appropriate to start with individual movement warm-up exercises, carried out all together, leading into further individualised work on text. Working on one's own, though surrounded by others, is still socially interactive and exhilarating. Twenty-five Macbeths following the air-drawn dagger, each in their own trance, but weaving in and out of their fellow students as though they were not there, encourages a highly cohesive atmosphere, just as all copying 'Simon' in *Simon says* (p. 181) is an individual process in a very strong social context. Working on a crowd scene, on the other hand, might mean making the transition from an obviously collective opening game, such as *Boom coming over* (p. 152), to further whole group work on the text of *Coriolanus* or *Julius Caesar*.

Good timing, as in the theatre, is a basic requirement for a successful drama workshop. It's easy to underestimate the time it takes to carry out practical exercises and for groups to discuss tasks and prepare them. Often one has far too much material, particularly by way of warm-ups or preparatory activities, so it's best to limit these strictly and keep the focus strongly on the main teaching objectives for the session. Active work also throws up all kinds of opportunities for learning and the temptation to side-track or change direction will frequently be strong, so workshops need to be planned and executed to a firm time-scale. It's especially important, if one is aiming for a final sustained activity, for adequate time to be left for its rehearsal and presentation. It's very demoralising, and usually counter-productive, if one of the groups has to 'wait until next time' to do its presentation. It is bad practice to set any task which cannot be carried out satisfactorily in the time given, perhaps because it's too ambitious or it has too much new material in it. Something has gone awry when you hear a teacher shouting: 'Five minutes left! Come on, you should be on your feet doing it, not still talking about it . . .'.

Planning a workshop, as with planning a journey, means envisaging the end of the process – what you want the students to have learnt or what you want them to be able to do, by the end of the session. With Shakespeare workshops, however, as with Drama and Literature gener-ally, the stimulation of interest, or the open-ended exploration of text, may be the chief objective, but this will be hard to achieve, paradoxically, without breaking it down into more specific objectives, which will, in turn, result in particular sequences of activities on selected substantive material. This process is illustrated below with an example of a workshop plan for *Macbeth*.

Workshop planning: an example of a language workshop – 'Macbeth's soliloquies'

Aims and objectives for the workshop

The specific objectives of this 90-minute workshop (a double period) are that the students, who might be any age from 13 or 14 upwards, should:

- speak, and understand, selected soliloquies;
- experience through acting, and be able to comment on, the dramatic significance of those speeches;
- devise, with others, an imaginative presentation of a section of text, showing an understanding of its theatricality.

For students, the aim of the session is the creation of an effective and lively presentation to the rest of the class.

For the teacher the aim is to run a well-timed workshop that will equip the students with the skills to deliver their presentations. At the same time, the teacher will be following both the specific objectives and also longer-term objectives, to do with teaching the play, and teaching about its period and context. From time to time, for example, explanation or comment will relate to these objectives, e.g. when Macbeth speaks of 'the deep damnation of his taking-off', one might speak briefly of the Christian framework of the play, and exactly what personal price Macbeth is willing to pay in murdering King Duncan.

Workshop plan

A full session of active Shakespeare (using Macbeth's soliloquies as an example) might be thought of as normally occupying four sections of work:

(i) **Warm-ups and preparation activities.**   Thematic introduction to the subject of the workshop. Includes games and/or exercises to do with group formation, physically and mentally warming-up.

  Example: Opening game of *Stepping in and out* (p. 148) for group formation, followed by *Sword and shield* (p. 177), using *The speedometer* (p. 134) initially, but concluding with a 'murder focus', using stealthy slow motion. The lines '. . . with his stealthy pace,/ with Tarquin's ravishing strides, towards his design/ Moves like a ghost' (*Macbeth* II.i.54–6) can be given as an 'action' prompt.

10 minutes

(ii) **Exercises on the subject of the workshop.**   Deriving from formal aspects of the text, whether on language, narrative, character or a mixture of the three. These exercises may be individualised or they may be for pairs, groups or the whole class, but they will move the students more deeply into the subject matter, both in terms of knowledge about it and in terms of the performance skills involved in treating it practically.

  Example:
  EITHER
  Follow my leader speech (p. 25), with 'Two truths are told . . .' (*Macbeth* I.iii.126–41), Macbeth's first soliloquy. The speech is excellent for introducing the idea of equivocation ('Cannot be ill, cannot be good.

If ill . . . If good . . .' and '. . . nothing is but what is not . . .' – the lines to be spoken by the teacher, perhaps using a mixture of shifty eye movements, and hand movements indicating scales, and then repeated by the class) – and the idea of the enormity and the terror of the crime of murder, of regicide. Each student should experience, imaginatively and bodily, the physical effects of the fear of the act and the physical/spiritual disintegration which Macbeth seems to realise it entails.

OR

Reading round the circle (p. 34), using 'If it were done . . .' (*Macbeth* I.vii.1–28) one line each, with each student giving an action to accompany their line. Whole group performance 'for our own delight'.

15 minutes

(iii) **Student exercise or task.**   Requiring a response, critical and creative, to the subject matter of the workshop. For this to be successful, it is vital that the preparatory activities of the first two sections of work should have 'launched' the students into their own task, so they immediately work independently and effectively. Groups may contain up to eight or nine people. Usually concludes with some form of showing or sharing.

Example: Groups are asked to present 'Is this a dagger . . .' (*Macbeth* II.i.33–64), collectively, in the form of a deadly serious dispute or debate. Start with *Reading together* (p. 34). Next groups must decide, without telling the other groups, who they are going to be, as they speak the speech (a gang planning a robbery; philosophers making learned points in a seminar; workers preparing to strike; footballers debating strategy?). If necessary, the teacher can allocate situations, or present a choice to the students. Further conditions as to preparation may be laid down e.g. all must read roughly equal amounts; the argument must contain certain moments, such as a moment of silence or a time when all speak together; contrasting levels of delivery must be included; the piece must end with collective movement (though it might be done with movement throughout, of course). Conclude with showing to other groups.

45 minutes

(iv) **Discussion and 'winding down'.**

Example: A circle discussion is held on the theatricality of the presentations. Who were the (at first undisclosed) groups (guesses addressed to the groups) and what difference did their identities make to the theatrical qualities that emerged in the presentations of the different groups? What 'worked' especially well, as theatre?

'Winding down' might be a breathing or relaxation exercise, or, as suggested here, a reading by the teacher, with the students lying on the floor, eyes closed. 'This is what Macbeth says near the end of the play when he hears that his wife is dead and his enemies are closing in . . .' Read 'She should have died hereafter . . .' (*Macbeth* V.v.17–28). You could ask the students to 'echo whisper', like sighing, any words that they feel express regret.

20 minutes

When you've made your workshop plan, check it through, identifying and noting potential hazards, students who will need special help or attention (see the section 'Safety: physical and emotional' above pp. 122–8) and the measures you plan to take to reduce risk. Record these points succinctly.

The origins of the workshop activities in the following chapters

Many of the activities and exercises described in the last three chapters of this book, Chapters 6, 7 and 8, have traditional origins. Others go back to the burst of workshop activity that took place in the 1960s and early 1970s. Companies like Ed Berman's 'Interaction' and Keith Johnstone's 'Theatre Machine' devised many activities, while directors like Charles Marowitz took up drama games and developed specifically theatrical versions of them. It's impossible to acknowledge all the inventors and first users and it's no doubt also true that the same activities will sometimes have been 'invented' by practitioners simultaneously in different places. For example, I 'discovered' *Zodiac* (p. 159) and *The human map* (p. 163) and the breathing exercise I call *The sea-shore* (p. 201) for myself, but would not be surprised to hear that others have invented them too. Also, one's first encounter with an activity is probably not where that activity actually started. For example, I first came across *Electric shock* (p. 154) in a Saturday morning workshop on Buzz Goodbody's *Hamlet* at The Other Place in Stratford in 1975, but I don't suppose that activity originated there.

Chapter 6

Warm-ups and preparation

Group formation activities

Group formation

If you are planning a full active session, with a whole sequence of practical work, you will need to think about preparing the group and about its particular dynamics. Practical work makes special use of the social energy of the group and it is vital to use this energy productively. Classes unaccustomed to practical work, especially older students, may be nervous. Social inhibition may cause us to fear being forced to our feet, exposed, made to speak, relate, join in. Other groups, familiar with practical work, or already well-formed, may have no misgivings about taking to their feet, but may have rigid, pre-existing social alignments. Using these alignments in workshops may lead to good work from friends who enjoy playing or spending time together, but can mean that others are left out or abandoned to form awkward groups, not of their own choosing. The request to 'get into pairs' or 'get into groups' will be welcomed by some and dreaded by others. Some Drama teachers habitually allow almost complete 'freedom of association' to their students. Their classes may be such that good and satisfying work is produced by everyone, but as a general rule, the teacher should be responsible for the make-up of groups and should determine carefully who works with whom, and for how long.

Group Formation Activities function as ice-breakers between people and contribute to social relaxation and the development of 'bonding', a feeling of shared confidence, ease and belonging. They should lead to the removal of anxiety about participation and to freedom from embarrassment and inhibition. They promote friendly co-operation and a positive inclination to work and explore together in an open, trusting manner. They are also fun: many include imaginative pleasures and many are likely to make people laugh. All of the activities in the six categories included in this chapter will remind participants of the pleasures of association and the value of having the resources, support and encouragement that accompany membership of a group. 'Moving together' (pp. 147–53) and 'Mixing and meeting' (pp. 159–62) activities also often emphasise alertness and speed of reaction, while 'Introductions' (pp. 162–66) and 'Names' (pp. 166–69), both of which may be played by classes that already know each other, concentrate on opportunities for students to get to know each other better in active and involving ways. The categories 'Working together' (pp. 153–59) and 'Trust' (pp. 169–72) include different kinds of tasks and require various skills, in their paired, small group and whole class activities, which will be useful later in exercises on texts.

A number of Group Formation Activities involve techniques which are used in the teaching approaches described in Chapters 2, 3 and 4 in Section I. Many of the activities may be directly adapted and developed further, to play substantive roles in Shakespeare workshops. Some activities are followed by suggestions for such adaptation.

At the start of all my practical sessions, even with classes very well-known to each other and to me, group formation figures strongly. Neither familiarity nor unfamiliarity obviates the need to prepare everyone to interact quickly and responsively, so that all are treated equally as fellow actors, with no searching out of friends, or special people with whom to work. Even young children and highly cohesive groups of all ages will work in a different way because of the impact of preparatory activities. These can enable group members, starting a workshop, to think of their group freshly and openly. Good group preparation results in fluidity and cohesion in the class, minds and bodies working together smoothly in an atmosphere of easy social exchange. I like to include plenty of moving around and mixing. Ideally, everyone will have worked with, or encountered in some way, everyone else in the room, within the first ten minutes or so. One may then expect the class to engage with the main workshop topic rapidly and enthusiastically, and a good standard of work to be maintained. Very occasionally, in spite of skilful 'setting up' on the part of the workshop leader, individuals will not want to join in. I was once asked to take a Drama workshop for seventy mature students doing a Foundation Humanities course, which integrated Literature (several novels), History and Geography. Two students, both of whom had just spent ten or fifteen years in Wolverhampton factories before joining the university, were appalled at my first request to the class, which was to move all the chairs, arranged in the hall for a lecture, to the edge of the room, and then, leaving their pens and note-books behind, to come into the yawning space that had appeared. They asked if they could sit out. I readily agreed. They sat watching and at the end, they asked if they could speak to me. We went off for a coffee and they explained that they had come to the university, after many years of grinding labour, to work hard and in properly academic ways, not to fool about. Had this been a private conversation, I would probably have argued my corner furiously, with diminishing returns, but because it was a professional situation, with the students at the centre of concern, I just listened, trying to recognise 'where they were'. Their experiences were not to be denied. After a time they became open to other ways of learning, joining, in the following year, an active course on 'Contemporary British Theatre', but at the time of that first class, practical work was just too distant from their experience and expectations.

Although group formation exercises can do much to make a class feel unified, flexible and responsive to each other, differences in gender, culture, ethnicity, sexual orientation and belief are obviously fundamental to people's sense of themselves, and for all the drive towards cohesion that practical work entails, it is well never to forget these personal differences, many of which may be 'hot' – areas of great sensitivity for individuals. Sometimes, where differences are relatively 'cool' and uncontroversial, we can acknowledge and work with them directly: in many, but clearly not all, groupings, gender is a source of such difference. A more detailed look at how we might work with it, follows.

A simple opening request to a class, such as 'form two large groups' will immediately reveal much about the dynamics of that class. Younger students might immediately divide into boys and girls, while older students would only adopt this division if specifically asked to. The point is that we, as teachers, should anticipate the effect that a particular group composition will have on the objectives for our work, and we must be ready to set up groups accordingly, or, if we require a particular kind of grouping for a particular workshop, we may need to reconfigure the social *status quo*. Same sex work, for example, can be enormously liberating, especially if one is dealing with gender politics (the situations of Desdemona or Katherina or Ophelia) or a matter such as 'cross-dressing' in Shakespearian comedy. For a workshop on the latter, one might take prompts for action suggested in the text, as when Rosalind and Celia in *As You Like It*, typical Shakespearian cross-dressers, plan to disguise themselves as men and enter the male world:

> We'll have a swashing and a martial outside,
> As many other mannish cowards have
> That do outface it with their semblances.
> *As You Like It* I.iii.122–4

If the objective for a female group, here, were to explore the physical comedy of Rosalind and Celia's situation when they are dressed as men, the objective for a male group might be the opposite: how male actors, as in Renaissance England, can play as women, in order to *avoid* comic effect. When we first meet Rosalind and Celia, the text insists that we accept them immediately as women, as original audiences would have done, even though their roles would have been played by boys or young men. Preparation for a workshop on these themes would, then, begin with the teacher thinking about the class's general attitude to working in same sex groups; preparatory exercises would be designed to move from the 'given' social dynamics of the class, through an appropriate game or activity, into the unfamiliar territory of the workshop – with the advantage that though in unfamiliar territory, students will feel a secure, 'custom-designed' social basis for the exploration to follow. The final aim of the workshop might be a group presentation for the other half of the class, or, perhaps better, the devising of an activity for the other half, so that there is a sense of a shared understanding of the complete subject-matter of the workshop.

Before moving on to the Group Formation Activities themselves, we need to go back a step, to the moment before the workshop begins. It's as though we are standing around the edge of a swimming-pool or retreating up a beach as chilly waves lap in towards our feet. We have come into the room where the workshop will take place, but have not yet taken the floor.

Getting started

The class is expectant, but nervous. The teacher outlines, with growing verbal facility, what will happen in the workshop and how everything will be active and practical, but time is passing, there seems to be just talking, and hearts are sinking. When, and how, will it all begin? It's preferable to get activities going with the minimum of talk and introduction, though the class must always know where they are going. To start with, this can be done with brief 'headline' introductions, followed by activity, and then more detailed information. But even if such a procedure is followed, students still have to get from their places into the empty space. Getting people on their feet is something that is often uncomfortable but that must happen, even before your opening workshop activity, though it may only be an issue when groups are starting practical work together for the first time. Nevertheless, a good start, as in many fields of activity, may make a big difference to the way things continue, so it's worth considering it for a moment.

I recall attending a training day, which had been set up to encourage English teachers to teach more actively. Not everyone was there by choice and as we sat round waiting for the day to begin, the empty floor of the studio probably looked a cold and hostile place to some. The workshop leader bounced in, said 'good morning' and with no opportunity offered to any of us to express reservations about the day, simply said 'take hold of someone near you and bring them down onto the floor'. She had judged the mood well, for the reluctant ones were getting help, instead of criticism or exposure, and a certain surprised good humour seemed to fill the room. It was rather pleasant for those who were led down, to feel that their presence was actually desired by others. All this is similar to the art of being a good hostess or host – making guests feel welcome and at ease.

Other strategies to get people on their feet, divert attention from initial awkwardness. 'Take a deep breath and hold it', said to those sitting nervously around the edge of the open working space, can be followed by 'now, still holding your breath, come and stand as close together as you can in the middle of the room . . . now', when they've gathered, 'let out your breath slowly, like air from a punctured tyre . . .'. And the workshop has begun.

Finding the circle is another way of getting started. Everyone is sitting or standing around the outside of the room, waiting for the workshop to begin. 'Close your eyes everyone, and slowly move into the space'. When they've moved in a little way, the leader says: 'Now, eyes still closed, stop. Turn around once and move off again. Now, eyes still closed, join hands with everyone else and try to make a perfect circle.' (*Safety note*: although this activity is taken slowly, the leader will need to be alert to the possibility of any collisions.)

The more you work with a group, the easier starting practical work will become. Classes like intriguing openings, without any introduction, and your immediate assumption of energy and purpose will be infectious – for example, 'this half of the class, go and sit in the middle of the room, while this half stay standing, but with eyes closed . . .' or 'all of you, make a tight bunch together in the middle . . .' though such openings, of course, must obviously fit with the first activity you have planned for the workshop.

GROUP FORMATION ACTIVITIES

Moving together

Follow my leader

This is an excellent, traditional, free-flowing activity, open to all kinds of variation and development. *Follow my leader down the room* works well. Everyone stands, backs to the wall, at one end and the leader sets off down the room with the class following behind, repeating everything the leader does and every sound they make. It's good, after a little while, to hand over leadership to a volunteer, or even just to tag someone (who can always tag someone else straightaway if they don't want to lead). A useful variation is to put the class into two halves, one at each end of the room, each with a leader. As the two groups move through each other, there is a pleasing sense of unity, especially if the leaders are sensitive to each other's movements. Accompany the activity with music, if you wish.

You can use *Follow my leader* as a structure for movement and exercises of all kinds, including vocal work, on the text. Its principle of co-ordinated, organized movement, is useful, for instance, if your workshop is aiming to explore a play through movement (perhaps for battles or fights, perhaps to form a dance-drama of the narrative or the conflicts in the play, or perhaps for the free illustration of text). Whereas Dance teachers are able to move from structured exercises into such movement, and so into group exercises, English and Drama teachers may not have the training and experience to lead such work. With *Follow my leader*, however, they can still work effectively towards their movement objectives (perhaps using sounds made by the group, too), provided they feel confident enough to lead their class on an imaginative journey. A short while spent in this way exploring, for example, the storm in *King Lear*, can be a rich prelude to a group choral speech task. See, also, *Follow my leader speech*, p. 25.

Runabout

This is also a good, free-flowing starter. Begin with everyone spread out in the room. When you call 'Action!' everyone must dart about without bumping into each other, until 'Freeze!' is called, when all must immediately keep absolutely still. Then, when 'Action!' is called, everyone runs about again, but in slow motion backwards this time. The sequence is repeated a number of times, forwards and slow motion backwards in turn. Variations may be introduced, such as 'Action sideways!' or 'Slow motion for all actions'. Ensure that participants don't treat this as a race or engineer collisions. Stress that the exercise is about the success of the whole group in moving together without touching each other.

Stepping in and out

Make a large circle, with plenty of space between people. As you say 'With me . . .', step off with your left foot first into the circle and clap once, bringing your right foot to join your left, before stepping back again, left foot first, finishing up with your feet together. It's important to keep the 'left, right, left, right' sequence going throughout the exercise. Now, with your left foot leading again, take two steps in, clapping on each, again with your feet coming together before you take the two steps back again (it will be your right foot starting back first this time). In effect, claps mark the steps into the circle and a stamping sound seems to echo them as you step back. The short 'unstressed' steps as one foot joins the other in the middle of the circle, and again back at the starting position, act as missed beats, which actually keep the rhythm going regularly. The class will pick up the rhythm and the circle will contract and expand in unison, with the rhythm getting a little faster as the game goes on. So it continues, an extra clap being added each time for each extra step in and back, until it becomes impossible to add any more steps because the centre of the circle is packed full. Remember to always lead off with your left foot first into the circle, from the starting position. Try this activity on your own, or with a friend, before you attempt to teach it.

Crossing the circle

Stand in a circle and designate one half 'red' and the other half 'blue'. Ask the class to cross the circle in different roles, e.g. 'reds are dogs, blues are cats'. Other pairings might be: police and football fans; tourists and busy milkmen or women; parents and runaway toddlers; arrogant people and shy people. You can also use characters from the plays, e.g. 'Reds are Prince Hal, blues are Falstaff'. As a change, you can ask everyone to belong to the same group, e.g. say 'Everyone is tired/late/aggressive etc.' or 'You're all walking on tight-ropes across the circle/on stepping-stones across a brook/in your sleep, etc.'

Liberty horses

This activity is more suitable for older students and it requires a large room – too small a running circle might cause a participant to feel giddy.

It's satisfying to simply run, quite slowly, in a circle or oval, round the room, as a way of starting a workshop, particularly if you're going on to concentrated individual work, e.g. on characters. Start with: 'Follow me, we're going for a little run, but in complete silence . . . and stay behind the person in front.' You set a very gentle pace. As the class falls in behind and circles the room, the group seems to gel – like 'Liberty horses' in a circus, trotting round the ring. The sound of feet, with everyone naturally leaning in slightly towards the centre as they circle, creates, after a little while, a strong corporate feeling, but it's important to do the exercise for long enough, at least until you sense the group is really working as one.

Take a walk

Allow plenty of time between your commands in this exercise, so that students have time to get into the different moods. What you actually decide to say, and the length of time you leave them doing something will depend partly on how they are working. Your instructions do not have to be in narrative form, as in the example below: you can deliberately alter the mood by changing from one environment to another, without making any connections. You can either ask the class to walk in a circle (less exposing) or they can move freely.

'We're going for a walk. It's early morning and you're still a bit sleepy. You stretch . . . you saunter along the street . . . you stop and look at a bird in a tree. You jump to touch a branch above your head. Now you set off across the park to catch your bus . . . you've plenty of time. . . . You look at your watch . . . it's stopped . . . you're late . . . you need to hurry. . . . ' Or, 'it's night-time and you can't see much as you walk . . . it starts to rain . . . ' etc.

Take a walk offers a structure for teachers to give students an imaginative entry into the world of a play. You can go directly from this exercise, into work on particular characters, settings or dramatic situations (e.g. armies before a battle; households preparing a welcoming feast), bringing in text, too, when you judge the moment to be right. For an example of a workshop development, see p. 91.

The good moment

Tell the class that they will decide on 'the good moment', when, without any discussion, they will all leap into the air as one, shouting 'Yes!' Everyone will move around, meeting and making eye contact, until they will collectively gather themselves and jump into the air, shouting in unison. Repeat a few times.

Moving as one

Form groups of about eight people and ask them to sit together in their own space in the room. When they feel the moment is right, each group gets up and moves off together, in its own time, slowly at first, but faster as members become more attuned to each other. An unspoken consensus should develop, with direction emerging from everyone picking up on tiny, silent impulses. Now the group should begin to move fluidly, changing direction unbidden and, finally, in its own time, returning to the spot from where it began, to sit down again, perfectly as one. Remind the group that they will find it easy to move as one, if everyone is constantly aware of everyone around them. You can help groups to develop this awareness right at the start, when everyone's sitting down, with a word or two of side-coaching. This exercise is more easily done in smaller groups, so if your class has difficulty in groups of eight, you could work in smaller groups for a short while, until students are attuned to each other.

A variation is to give some set instructions at the start (e.g. 'visit two different walls, making three turns and crawling for part of the way'). Some Drama teachers follow up *Moving as one* with *Speaking as one*, in which groups meet and converse chorally, each group taking it in turns to speak a line together, but with no pre-determination about what their common 'voice' will come out with.

Princess Eugenie's circle

This exercise follows on well from *Moving as one*, as groups carrying it out need first to have already reached a good standard of co-operative work together. It is based on the slow, deliberate, co-ordinated action of everyone sitting down at precisely the same moment – but on each other's knees, rather than on chairs. Form a circle and all turn to the left. When you, in the magisterial tones of Princess Eugenie, say 'Please sit', everyone, very slowly, and perfectly together, sits on the knees of the person behind them. Repeat this a few times, before mixing the circle up (you can say 'Everyone cross the circle to a new place, wherever you like'), so people are now standing in a new order. Now repeat the command to sit. Continue, mixing up the order of the circle and encouraging everyone to become more and more expert at sitting, all perfectly together. They should be able to do this activity with comic precision

Moving in threes

In threes, hold hands and move around the room, gaining in speed, changing direction and circling round other threes. Try different ways of moving, each taking it in turns to provide the direction, but with no discussion, so leadership flows around the group. Now drop hands, and still in threes, take it in turns to lead. *A* might scurry off, bent low, and then kneel on one knee. When *A* stops, *B* and *C* follow, copying what *A* has done. They join *A*, before *B* sets off in a new direction and in the manner they choose, to be followed by *A* and *C*. Now let the movement flow freely, so the group goes where it likes and stops when it likes, all with no discussion. Side-coach speed and inventiveness. The objective is to move as one unit. *Moving in threes* is useful preparation when you want to go on to set a choral speech exercise. See also p. 141.

Copycat

Half the group watches, while the other half moves around the room, instructed perhaps, to go for a stroll along the sea-front, or to walk purposefully towards the bus stop. The watchers follow at a discreet distance, copying anyone who takes their interest, as accurately as possible. After a while, call 'Open House': from now on, anyone may copy anyone else, changing their subject as often as they like, but without drawing attention to the one who's being copied. Finally, on 'All together', ask the class to settle on the same copying action, but without any discussion or communication – just by unspoken consent. Now let the copied action change, whenever anyone starts a new action, with the whole class picking this up immediately and fluidly, moving as one organism.

Copycat dancing

This is a kind of *Follow my leader*, except the leader puts on some music and everyone dances wherever they like in the room, but they must follow the actions of the leader. Dancing, a very personal and potentially embarrassing activity, especially for those in their teens and twenties, suddenly turns into an amusing and exhilarating way of warming up – mostly because the responsibility for one's style and action is removed completely. Those called on to lead recognise the mood of pastiche and fun immediately, and are often very inventive in their leadership.

Keep still

Form a circle. Everyone silently chooses two people to watch, across the circle. Everyone must stay absolutely motionless. If anyone catches sight of any movement, however tiny, they must repeat it, making it very slightly 'bigger'. If the exercise is done with real control, it should be quite a while before the circle becomes a writhing mass of movement.

Walking the grid

This can be started from wherever students are in the room. 'Fix your eyes on a point on the wall across the room (or a spot on the floor, if you like). Now, slowly walk straight to that point, ignoring everyone around you, but giving way if you need to, in order to avoid collisions.' Everyone sets off. 'When you arrive, turn and fix on another point. Now walk on that in the same way.' Soon the class will be moving fluidly, getting a good sense of space and relationship to others. You can gradually speed up the pace, or you can use *The speedometer* (p. 134).

You can vary your commands, asking the class to travel on tip-toe/in as few steps as possible/with tiny steps/backwards/in circles/fearfully/suspiciously/proudly, etc. *Walking the grid* is good preparation for focused individual work on character (p. 93) and also for introducing language from the text, e.g. phrases or greetings delivered to others in passing (pp. 101–2).

Boom coming over (also known as Captain's salute)

This activity requires a large, suitable space, preferably a Drama studio. It's quite energetic and it's a good idea to practise all the moves in slow-motion first, pointing out where players need to be especially careful – the command 'Man Overboard', for example, which is certainly not suitable for every class in any case. 'Sharko' is fun, but should not be used if there's any danger of the mats slipping or your class pushing or shoving. If you're in any doubt about a particular move, leave it out.

'We're all sailors onboard ship (the ship is the whole room) and must do what the Captain says immediately.' Now you run through the commands and the accompanying actions, with the class practising, in slow motion first of all, as suggested above. On 'Port', everyone hurries to the left side of the boat; on 'Starboard' to the right; on 'Bows' to the front; on 'Stern' to the rear; on 'Man Overboard' they quickly form pairs with one holding the other so they're off the floor; on 'Boom Coming Over' everyone hits the deck so they don't get knocked over by the boom as it swings across; and, if you like, on 'Sharko!' they have to make for the life-boats floating on the sea – little non-slip mats. You only put out a few of these, and the Captain may choose to reduce their number further, so that the sailors have to pile on to the ones that are left, clinging to each other to avoid falling into the sea. You can invent other commands: one other I have heard of is 'Submarines', which means everyone has to lie on their backs on the floor with one leg sticking up in the air like a periscope.

On 'Captain's salute' the class hurriedly lines up on deck, down the length of the room, standing to attention and saluting, while the Captain takes the salute by walking from one end of the line to the other. Rather like *Simon says*, it's only when the Captain says 'At ease!' that anyone may move. So if the Captain says 'Port' before saying 'At ease', no one should move. Anyone who does move, can be asked to sit on the floor until 'At ease' has been spoken.

This is one of those gloriously absurd warm-up games that people immediately seem happy to join in. There are no winners and losers, just amusing collective movement. *Boom coming over* may be used to prepare for whole group work on the text – before working on a crowd scene from *Julius Caesar*, say, or the opening storm from *The Tempest*. It may be adapted accordingly, and appropriate language added in.

Working together

Knots

The usual way of starting *Knots*, is for everyone, standing in a circle, to hold out one hand high and one hand low and then to join each of their hands with another hand, but avoiding immediate neighbours and making sure they take hands with two different people. Now, without breaking hands, the group must try and disentangle the knot. More often than not, there's a final snag that can't be unpicked. The group should just get as far as it can.

The other way of starting *Knots* is less interesting, but can act as a useful precursor to the method described above. In this approach, the group starts off holding hands in a circle and then, without breaking hands, ties itself up in the tightest knot it can, before unravelling itself again. For this version, try suggesting to the tangled knot, before they begin their unravelling, that they carry out the whole process in one smooth, slow-motion movement, like sea-weed on a rock, waving in the current below the waves.

Zip zap pow

Form an expanded circle. To demonstrate the game, put your hands together, as though in prayer. Point to the person on your left and say 'zip', telling them to pass the 'zip' on in the same way, until it's gone all round the circle. Let this continue, getting faster, for a few rounds. Now introduce 'zap', the command that reverses the direction of the current: point your hands back at the person on your right (who has just 'zipped' you) and say 'zap'. Now 'zap' goes all the way round and back to you. Now you point, at random, across the circle and say 'pow'. By now the three commands will be understood and the game can be played freely. No one is ever 'out'. The idea is just that the group should become extremely fast and efficient, changing the direction of the current according to the whims of the players.

Clap on

Play in the same way as *Zip zap pow*, except you begin by clapping at the person on your left, instead of pointing and saying 'zip'. That person claps at the person on their left. Now the clap is sent round the circle for a few rounds. Then you introduce 'clap back', when someone sends the clap straight back the other way, by turning and clapping at the person who's just clapped at them. (There is no equivalent to the use of 'pow', across the circle.) Encourage students to start slowly and not to change the direction of the clap very often, until the circle is really working as one, with complete fluidity.

Electric shock

This is another 'sending round the circle' game, very good for developing group concentration and solidarity. This time everyone holds hands. The leader demonstrates by sending a little squeeze, the electric current, to the person on their left, who then gives a little hand-squeeze to the one on their left, and so on round the circle. Once everyone has the hang of the game, and the current has been round the circle fast several times, you can introduce the 'reverse squeeze'. Demonstrate this slowly to the group, by showing that you are squeezing the hand that has just squeezed your hand, so sending the current back the way it has come. As with *Clap on*, ask the students to only change direction occasionally at first, so the continuity is not broken. The objective is to build up speed, with all working together, and with no breaks in transmission.

Tick tock

This is a cumulative game, played standing in a circle. Someone starts by handing a pen to the person on their right, saying 'This is a tick', to which the reply is 'A what?' The starter reaffirms with 'A tick'. Now the one who's received the pen, No. 2, turns to the person on their right, No. 3, and hands the pen on, saying 'This is a tick', only when the reply 'A what?' comes back, No. 2 turns back to No. 1, repeating 'A what?' The reply from No.1, 'A tick', is now passed back round to No.3, and so on, all the way round the circle. Each time a new person is brought in, the question 'A what?' must go all the way back to No.1 and then the answer 'A tick' must be passed all the way on to the new person. So it goes on, until all in the circle are involved. After a little practice, introduce another pen, going round the other way, in the same manner, except with the words 'This is a tock'. Encourage the group to maintain their rhythm, even though people will sometimes get both pens at once.

On your marks

Before beginning, practise the 'on your marks' position with the whole class, first slowly and then at normal speed. This position is kneeling on one knee, as though getting ready to race, hands on the floor keeping the player balanced.

Now stand in a circle. The starter points at another person and then immediately takes up the 'on your marks' position down on the floor. That person does the same, and so on until all are on the floor. Now you time the class to see what their 'record' will be. Instead of kneeling down, or as well as kneeling down, you might invent some other action e.g. making a half turn (whole turns carried out several times in succession might lead some players to become dizzy), changing places with the person on your left etc. You could also add in a very short piece of text if you like.

Arm raise

Everyone stands in a close circle, arms hanging down by their sides. Explain that no one will lead, but that all our arms will gradually rise together. The class looks down at everyone's hands and, for a while, nothing happens. Then, gradually, everyone starts to raise their arms all together. Side-coach the group to maintain a perfectly level circle of rising hands – no one's hands should be above or below those of the group. Occasionally, I've come across a few individuals who find this very difficult, but generally classes find they can raise and lower and pause, all perfectly together, with no one person leading. As expected, if a group is warmed up and working well together, they will find this exercise much easier to do than if they attempt it 'cold'.

People to people

All move around and the leader calls out various instructions, to be carried out in random pairs, e.g. 'arm to leg'. Now pairs must form, and freeze, with one person's arm touching their partner's leg. The last pair to achieve this is identified. When 'people to people' is called out, everyone moves around again. The next command might be 'knee to shoulder'. Watch carefully that your class is working safely and avoid dangerous instructions, such as 'head to head'.

Silent counting

In a circle, eyes closed, the leader announces a final number, say it's 14, and begins counting at a regular pace, with everyone else silently counting to themselves. After about 7 or 8, the leader falls silent and everyone concentrates on counting silently to themselves, maintaining the pace set. When people reach 14, they say this number out loud. If all have kept the pace well, then the whole class will come in on 14 together. All kinds of speeds and final numbers can be used and leadership can be passed around the group, but remind the class that they should only progress to something more difficult if they are working really well together, with everyone coming in, eyes closed, on cue.

Beating the floor

Sit in a circle on the floor. The starter beats out a slow, simple rhythm, of one or two beats. After a few repetitions, the person on their left adds in a further beat or two, and so on, round the circle, until everyone is in and the whole circle is making a collective, rhythmic sound. Encourage students to listen carefully before making their own addition. Anyone who wishes, may simply reinforce existing beats instead of making the rhythm more complex.

The exercise may be done as *Clapping rhythm*, with the class standing and clapping instead of beating the floor.

Flowing pairs

I learnt this at a workshop led by Augusto Boal. *A* begins by offering a 'freeze frame' greeting, such as a hand-shake or open arms, to *B*, who takes up a position in relation to that offer. *A* now 'unfreezes' and observes *B*'s freeze frame position, before taking up a new position in relation to *B*. Now *B* breaks, observes and 'relates' in a fresh way to *A*. Encourage the 'relating' to be inventive; use different levels; if the students are working confidently, develop the sequence into a free-flowing dance. (For workshop developments: see p. 47.)

Hypnosis

This is another excellent Augusto Boal activity, originally invented as a 'disjunctive exercise', designed to force actors 'to assume bodily positions that he (*sic*) never takes in his daily life, thus reforming permanently his muscular structures' (Boal 1979: 129. See, also, Boal 1992: 63). An important element of Boal's theory is that work shapes us physically, as well as mentally, into its own forms and, for many, especially for those whose labour is exploited, this process literally deforms our bodies and imprisons us. *Hypnosis* used with students works in a parallel way. It allows participants to free themselves from convention and the rigid movement of our habitual, self-conscious lives, and it is a perfect preparation for some kinds of work in pairs.

In *Hypnosis*, A puts a hand about 6 inches away from B's nose and begins to move it slowly around. B must focus only on that hand, keeping their nose at the same distance away from it, following it wherever it goes. As with *Mirrors*, this is a co-operative activity and the aim is to work together, not for A to catch B out – so, while speed and direction and level will be varied, both should concentrate on maintaining a constant distance between hand and nose. (For workshop developments: see p. 37.)

Mirrors

This familiar activity is done in pairs. It is co-operative, so stress that the object is not to catch your partner out. A begins by making slow movements and B, the mirror, copies them perfectly, as though A's mirror image. Introduce the idea of using different levels, from high up, down to working at floor level. Different distances from the mirror, and different speeds, but only if synchronisation remains perfect, can also be introduced. Movement may be abstract or naturalistic mime. After a while, pairs switch roles. Finally, they can change roles, backwards and forwards, by mutual, silent understanding, without interrupting the flow of movement. If you have a threesome, B can mirror A and C can mirror B.

Mirrors develops well into substantive work on texts, e.g. for language work in pairs (see pp. 37–8) and character work on the twins in *Twelfth Night* and *The Comedy of Errors* or on close friends or lovers in a whole range of plays. The sonnet that Romeo and Juliet speak at their first meeting at the Capulet feast at I.v.92 invariably, on stage, is accompanied by symmetry and mirroring ('And palm to palm is holy palmer's kiss'), as the lovers instinctively harmonise their hearts, minds and bodies through sharing the speaking of a formal sonnet, but *Mirrors* is just as revealing when used, for example, to explore Viola/Cesario's love for Orsino, or the grim love of Macbeth and Lady Macbeth.

Marionettes

In pairs, one is puppeteer, the other marionette. The marionette's movements are controlled by strings worked by the puppeteer. Start with the
marionette lying on the floor face upwards and get the puppeteers to
'check' that all the strings are working. Then go on to the marionette
being set on its feet, moving around, doing simple actions and, finally,
encountering other marionettes.

As the exercise progresses, speech can be brought in and the puppeteers
can take over responsibility for all the commands from the workshop
leader, e.g. 'Tell this person over here (another marionette) about what
happened to you at breakfast this morning'.

Marionettes could almost have been the inspiration behind Shakespearian
scenes in which characters are led like puppets – as they are by Puck in *A
Midsummer Night's Dream* and Ariel in *The Tempest*. Less directly, the
manipulation of Othello by Iago or the humiliation of Shylock at the end
of the trial, when he must submit to all demands, may be explored
through developing *Marionettes*. (An interesting use of 'human puppetry',
imitating *Ventriloquism* rather than *Marionettes*, occurred in the 2002 RSC
Academy production of *King Lear*, when Lear, with the Fool sitting on his
knee like a ventriloquist's dummy, and picking up on two different
'voices' within his speech, spoke some of his lines as himself, and some as
though he was himself the fool, with the Fool baring his teeth like a
dummy and providing the actions.)

The machine game

This is similar to *Shapes* (p. 161), but it involves the whole class cumul-
atively. Ask someone to go into the centre of the circle and begin a
simple, sustainable action as though part of a machine. Now the next
person joins them, relating to what is being done by adding another
piece of the machine, and so on, until all are involved. You can ask
people to make a noise appropriate to their action, if they wish, or
(because it can be a bit tiring to keep noises going while everyone is
gradually brought in) you can wait until the machine is completely
assembled and working away, before asking everyone to add a noise in
turn, starting with the first person who went in to begin making the
machine. Now, if you like, you yourself can mime working a giant lever,
which, you explain, goes from 'dead-slow' to 'full-steam ahead'. To
finish, the machine can blow up.

A variation is *Moving machines*. Small groups (five to eight) number off,
and members are called in, one after the other, by the leader. So, when
you say 'No. 1', all the 'Number Ones' go in to start up their group's
machine. The way in which the machines move, and their speed, is entirely
up to the individual groups. *The machine game* may also be adapted for

choral speech. Small groups can be given text out of which to make, for example, machines representing that text's theme – justice, mercy, war, death or love, for example.

Who me?

This is a verbal warm-up drill, using a short dialogue. Form a circle and number off around it. Teach the dialogue, which goes like this, started, say, by No.12 in the circle addressing No. 3:

No. 12:   Number 3.
No. 3:   Who me?
No. 12:   Yes, you.
No. 3:   Not me.
No. 12:   Then who?
No. 3:   Number 15.
No. 15:   Who me? etc. etc.

It's important that everyone learns the dialogue well, at the start, otherwise the drill will have an irritating broken rhythm to it. Practise as a whole class first, all saying the whole drill together.

You can encourage variation in the way the piece is spoken, and you can ask for pregnant pauses or for inventive movement to accompany the words.

Mixing and meeting

Zodiac

'Do you all know your birth-signs? Then as quickly as you can, make a group with your fellows.' After a pause, people begin calling for other Sagittarians and Taureans etc. This seems to appeal because even the totally unsuperstitious want to find their fellows, if only out of curiosity to see what they happen to have in common. When the groups are nearly formed, I usually say 'Arrange yourselves in the right order, as you appear in the Zodiac.' This often results in two groups of the same sign realizing that they need to combine and, eventually, a circle of groups by birth-sign. If you like, you can then ask the groups to find out what personality features they might share (which certainly gets people laughing and talking to each other). This is obviously a very light-hearted 'ice-breaking' exercise, though I remember an occasion when a student was offended by it, on religious grounds.

You may follow up *Zodiac* with the request that people move around the room and then, on a hand-clap, stop and hear what groups they should form next. You might ask them to group by what they had for breakfast, the last drink they had the previous night, their favourite childhood pet, the colour of their socks or 'tops', the kind of shoes they're wearing, their favourite meal or band or football club or soap-opera. All this should be done fast and lightly, so that everyone mixes and interacts easily and naturally.

A variation is for the leader to call out some interest or feature people might share, e.g. stamp-collectors; skate-boarders; clubbers; beer-drinkers; or anyone who's had a waiting or waitressing job. Those in that category form a tight group sitting on the floor in the middle of the room. Move around between calls, but sometimes you may have to allow a moment or two for people to swap experiences! The variation may be played, using things characters from a play have in common – this can give rise to considerable discussion.

It's not my fault

Form a circle. *A* must cross the circle and address any chosen person, *B*, using a given tag, e.g. 'It's not my fault.' Now *B* sets out across the circle and addresses the words to a new person and so on. Leader coaches a sense of context, approach and address in the class, encouraging variety of delivery and changing the tag every so often, e.g. 'You said you'd be here early', 'Why are you looking at me like that?' 'Have you seen a small brown dog with a red collar?'. The focus on the interaction and the address naturalises the language. *It's not my fault* is custom-made as a warm-up for the language activity *Language across the circle* (p. 28).

Walking the line

If you happen to be working in a hall with a badminton court marked out, you can use that, but otherwise chalk out a rectangle or polygon on the floor. Pairs stand back to back on the line and then everyone sets off to follow the line, until they meet their partners again, face to face – only they must not fall off the line, so passing others, especially on sharp corners, requires careful co-operation.

Spot challenges

Start with general movement. Each time you stop the class, set a challenge, e.g. 'touch everything blue in the room', 'two people help a third to jump', 'groups of four make a flower arrangement out of their hands'. Every so often you can shout out 'Down!' Everyone has to immediately drop to the floor as one, as though under fire.

Sizes

Starting from 'moving around', the class is asked to make groups of various sizes, e.g. if you have thirty-three students, you can call for 'Pairs, with just one threesome' or 'Groups of three' or 'Elevens' or 'Fours with just one fivesome'. As soon as groups are the correct size, they should join hands and raise them in the air.

Shapes

This is similar to *Sizes*, but you ask the whole class to make various shapes, e.g. 'Make me a multiplication sign . . . in five seconds . . . it shouldn't be lopsided . . .'. As well as other mathematical symbols and letters, you can ask for other shapes, such as a coach party, an orchestra, a dentist's waiting-room, a football crowd, or a theatre audience. Side-coach to get people moving into position as swiftly and smoothly as possible.

A variation of *Shapes* is to say, for example, 'Make four equal groups and give me an aeroplane . . .' or a space-ship, a fire-engine, a cat, a street accident, a house, a snake, a rock, etc.

Lost voices

A suitable space, preferably a Drama studio, is needed for this activity (eyes are closed, so there must be no danger of bumping into furniture or obstacles). If you have any concerns about the safety of the room, divide the class into two halves and ask students to take it in turns to either take part in the activity or to act as 'safety guards' around the playing space. The job of the safety guards is to gently keep participants, who have eyes closed, from bumping into any obstacles there may be around the edge of the room. The activity requires good concentration and listening skills and is probably only suitable for classes which have been working well together for some time.

Pairs choose one of the vowels a, e, i, o or u and develop a call signal, which they sing together. Now everyone forms a tight group in the middle of the room, closes their eyes and turns round once a few times, before setting off for where they think the nearest wall is. On 'Begin', they all, eyes firmly shut, try to find their partner by singing their call signal. When pairs have found each other, they stand still. This game can be a little embarrassing for the last few pairs to find each other, especially if anyone's hearing is not too good; sometimes, without drawing attention to it, I have gently steered such pairs towards each other.

A variation is for everyone to stand in a circle, make a different noise in turn and remember the noises from the people to their right and left. Now, eyes closed, everyone moves around and, at a signal, begins to make their noise, listening, at the same time, for the noises made by their neighbours. The objective is for the group to reform the circle, still with eyes closed.

Knees

Touch as many knees in the room as you can, without your own knees being touched. Played in pairs, this becomes Chinese Boxing.

Coin behind your back

Everyone places a coin on one of their upturned palms behind their backs. Now they try to knock the coins off other people's palms, while simultaneously avoiding the same thing happening to them. No contact, except with the hands holding the coins is allowed, and palms must remain fully open.

A variation, which should only be played by groups which are used to working together co-operatively and well, is for everyone to tuck a handkerchief or scarf behind their backs. Now everyone tries to collect as many trophies as they can. Or, but again only with a good co-operative group, you can simply say that people should try and touch others gently in the small of the back, while avoiding that happening to themselves.

Introductions

Almost every activity in this category may be adapted to introduce, or work with, characters from the plays. Sometimes the workshop leader can give out names or character information, and sometimes students can be left to choose for themselves. See also pp. 56, 90 and 99.

This is my neighbour

If a class does not know the names of everyone present, you may want to get all the names in circulation as quickly as possible. One way is to form a circle and use the drill 'this is . . . and I am . . .'. The starter (say this is Ahmed) needs to know the name of the person on their left (say this is Natasha): Ahmed turns to Natasha and says 'this is Natasha and I am Ahmed'. The next one, on Ahmed's right, of course, says 'this is Ahmed and I am John'. So it goes on round the circle, with Natasha the last one to announce 'this is . . . and I am . . .'. Note that they are not being asked to accumulate names, 'Persian market' style. The idea is to get all the names announced quickly, with everyone getting to hear all the names twice.

To reinforce all the names, have a final round, when the whole class speaks everyone's name in turn, all together. Begin by pointing to yourself and saying 'All together, with me . . .' and speak your name. Then, nod to the person on your left or your right, and so on round the circle.

An alternative is for everyone to step into the circle, in turn, speak their name and perform a gesture; the whole class, all together, then repeats both name and gesture. This continues, for every individual in turn. Demonstrate, using your own name first. Or, try *Singing introductions*. Ask the class to mill around in a fairly tight group, then, in turn, one person leaps out from the group, everyone freezes, and that person sings their name in any style they like. The whole class then sings it back at them and the person rejoins the group. If more than one person should jump out at the same time, they simply stay out and take it in turns to sing their names.

Another variation is *Shake hands*: tell everyone to shake hands with everyone in the room as quickly as possible, exchanging names as they go. This can be usefully extended by saying 'if you can't remember a name, go back to that person and repeat the same routine – i.e. exchange names again'. Keep doing this till everyone has every name.

Singing introductions is good for reinforcing the names of the characters in a play. Each student may only sing one name and they should try to bring in a new name until the whole cast has been announced. If anyone can't think of a new character, they must sing the repeated name in a new way. Singing styles should, of course, be appropriate to the characters. A form of words to follow the character's name, and its repetition by the class, may be introduced, e.g. someone sings 'I am Claudius'; the class copies the singing of 'Claudius' and then Claudius adds 'and I like to . . .' (with appropriate words supplied) or 'and I'm important because . . .' with the class repeating the last few words Claudius adds in.

The human map

This is best played with large groups of students who are not all from the immediate area (and when there are no particular sensitivities about where people live), though you can easily make an imaginary version based, for example, on regions or cities participants would like to visit, or where they have friends or relatives. Begin by pointing to all four walls of the room: 'This end of the room is north, this south, this side is east, this west. Imagine, for a moment, where you would stand to show where you live (or come from). When I snap my fingers, go straight to that spot.' When they're settled (a good deal of talking will have gone on to achieve this), ask them what towns and cities they are 'in'. Small groups (all from one town or city perhaps) should still follow the NSEW rule. Encourage the class to rearrange itself a bit. Ask them to get the map 'right'.

Now you can make various 'introductory' requests, e.g. 'From where you are on the map, shake hands and introduce yourself to five or six people around you. Say something about where you live (e.g. one good thing and one bad thing), but keep moving on quickly.' Or, 'Make a group of four and go and meet another group of four from a different part of the map.' Or, 'From where you're standing, wave to someone on the other side of the room. Now meet, shake hands and then discover three precise things you have in common.' Side-coach ('only three things and they must be precise'), if it looks as though they are getting into conversation. Instead of the 'three things in common', you might announce one topic, such as 'people', 'places', 'activities' or 'animals': the pair that gets the 'oddest' and 'closest' match wins, e.g. 'we've each got an uncle in Portsmouth, called Bill' or 'both of our cats can open the back door'.

A quiet, and rather intense variation on such 'meeting activities', is to ask pairs to look into the pupils of each other's eyes until they can make out their own reflection there; at this point, they say whom they can see reflected – themselves, and give their own name, before moving on to another partner – but only after both have seen their own reflections in each other's eyes.

Paired introductions

Ask students to turn to the person next to them. In pairs, each speaks for a minute about themselves, as informatively as possible – or you can specify three or four topics. Next, two pairs join up ('snowball'), but partners must introduce, and speak for, each other. You can leave it there, or have fours snowball to become eights. Alternatively, after the first paired discussion, you can reconvene the whole group, if it's not too large and you're keen for everyone to encounter everyone else. This can also be played using character briefs from a play – such as those given on pp. 57 and 99–101. See also *Active discussion* (p. 136).

Two true, one false

Either using the structure of *Paired introductions* or with everyone sitting in a circle and taking it in turns to speak to the whole class, participants give two true facts about themselves, and one false. Others must guess which is which. This can also be played using characters from the plays – particularly when students know the text well.

About me

Everyone writes down responses to two or three questions (e.g. what is one of your hobbies, or one of your favourite expressions, what pets have you kept, what's unusual about you, or what you're good at, or bad at, or what's the dish you most like to cook), and also invents an 'alias' for themselves, which they write on their sheet. Now put all their papers in the middle of the room and everyone picks one up at random. Everyone moves around and when two meet, they try to find out if they have their partner's sheet by asking open questions, i.e. without directly quoting the response on the sheet. For example, for the response 'I am good at playing the recorder', you could ask 'Are you good at playing any musical instruments?', but you could not ask a question directly quoting the information on the sheet, such as 'Are you good at playing the recorder?' Also, everyone must speak the truth! If you haven't found the person whose sheet you have, you move on to someone else in the room and ask them a question, using the same sheet. If you think you have found the owner of the sheet you have, you may check their alias and, if you're right, return the sheet to the middle of the room and pick up a new one, before going searching again. The objective is to identify, from the sheets alone, as many of the aliases of the people in the room as you can in the time allowed.

A variation is to ask people to write down several personal things about themselves, but these should only be things about which they don't feel too sensitive, e.g. 'I talk too much about my dog' or 'I'm really grumpy at breakfast' or 'I'm shy at parties'. Now repeat the procedure as above, with everyone picking up a sheet from the central pile. Again, when pairs encounter each other, they try to find out if they have their partner's sheet by asking open questions, i.e. without directly quoting the question on the sheet. For example, you cannot say 'Are you grumpy at breakfast?' but you could ask the open question 'What are you like at breakfast?' Again, you must speak the truth about yourself at all times. The game goes on, just as described above. *About me* may be adapted by giving students given characters to research from the text (in strict secrecy, so that no one knows who has which characters), prior to playing the game in the same way as the warm-up activity.

What we share

Pairs are given one or two minutes to discover as much as they can about what they have in common. Then proceed as in *Paired introductions* (p. 164), with the proviso that they must speak 'as one'– as twins sometimes do, not speaking together, but each taking over seamlessly from the other as they recognise what the other is talking about.

Why is that?

In this game, the speaker wants to stick to the subject and the interrupter wishes to distract them. 'Look across the room and find someone you've not yet talked to today. Go across, shake hands and introduce yourself. One must begin speaking, using the opening "I'm interested in (they name their topic) because . . .". As they speak on their topic, the other asks "Why is that?" whenever they wish. An answer must then be given.'

A variation is *Never mind that*. In pairs, *A* begins telling *B* about something that happened to them. At any time, *B* may interrupt with 'Never mind that, tell me about . . .' (picking up a word or two from *A*'s speech), so it might be 'Never mind that, tell me about the person in the pub'. *A* must then switch to that topic. Numerous other 'conversational changers' may be invented as the rule of the game, such as 'No it wasn't . . .', with the proviso that the speaker must accept the new direction.

Status cards

Give everyone a playing-card, using only the numbered cards 2 to 10, and then ask them, without looking at the card they've got, to hold it on their forehead so others can see it. As they move around, they should greet people appropriately, according to the value of the card they can see displayed, exchanging names and shaking hands. Soon everyone will have a sense of how they are being perceived and judged in terms of status. You can ask them to arrange themselves, without giving away what people's numbers actually are, in a line, ranged from low to high. (See Chapter 4, pp. 97–9, for more on status work as it applies to teaching 'Character' in Shakespeare.)

Presents

Several people in the circle 'give' (suggest) a present that someone in the group would like to receive. The person then says which present they would actually like best. Extremely simple, but present-giving can create a strong sense of well-being in the group! *Presents* may be played, as a light-hearted warm-up, using characters from the plays.

Names

As with the previous category, almost every 'Names' activity may be adapted to introduce, or work with, characters from the plays. Sometimes the workshop leader can give out names or character information, and sometimes students can be left to choose for themselves, as in the first activity that follows. See also pp. 56–8 and 90.

Names across the circle (also known as Jack to Jill)

'Form a circle. I'm going to speak my name across the circle to someone and then move across to take their place. As I arrive, that person then moves to take the place of the one they choose to name next. Try and name a new person each time. Right. James to Kelly.' I go across towards her. Kelly looks surprised and then catches on. She says 'Kelly to Rhiannon.' Rhiannon responds quickly, 'Rhiannon to Gary.' Make sure everyone's name is called: when you sense that there are only four or five people left who haven't been called, ask who hasn't yet been called and ensure that they're now brought in. Continue, playing the game freely. If you like (perhaps you just want to speedily reinforce names), you can play the game just with pointing, without anyone moving across the circle. If the person 'on' doesn't know someone's name, they can ask for it as they set off across the circle.

I believe that *Names across the circle* originated as a throwing and catching game. Instead of moving across the circle, you can play it using tennis-balls (or bean-bags, for a more continuous game – tennis-balls have a tendency to roll all over the place), though these versions are obviously less active than the standard one and any continuity will be broken if the ball or bag is dropped.

If this is played using characters from the text, students can 'impose' a name on someone across the circle, i.e. I might start the game off 'I am Romeo. Romeo to my father Montague' (and I walk towards someone, who then becomes Montague).

Name chain

Start as for *Names across the circle* above, but now you must insist on students naming a new person each time, so that after one round, everyone will have been named once, and once only. Now: 'That was a practice. We're going to do that again. We'll make a new name chain, and as soon as we've spoken it once, we'll repeat the same order, only faster. Lorraine, you start this time.' If anyone chooses someone next to them, say 'choose someone across the circle, remember, not next to you'. As the work speeds up, make sure the 'naming drill' keeps going: you must say your own name first, 'Shaun to Vicki'.

When the group is speaking and moving really swiftly and smoothly, repeating the chain continuously, you can ask Lorraine, who started the chain, to start a second one (using exactly the same order of names), before the first one has run round. Suddenly two people are crossing the circle at once and it becomes tricky to see where your 'nominee' has moved to. As you cross the circle, you also have to avoid banging into the person from the second chain, who is also on the move. If the group masters two chains at once, you may ask Lorraine to start a third or even a fourth chain, before the first and second have come round. This is excellent for alertness and speed of response and it has the effect of totally emptying people's minds of everything except the co-operative game. One's awareness of others in the space seems to move into another dimension and a kind of harmony comes about. *Name chain* is good for reinforcing the names of the characters in a play.

Chain killer

This is like *Name chain*, above, except that it's an elimination game, which immediately makes it more problematic. I only play it with small groups, so no one is out for long. It's worth walking through this game, and even rehearsing the speaking part all together, before you begin, as it can be quite tricky to get it going quickly and easily.

The one who is 'on', the killer, must not move until they have finished saying their line, e.g. 'Marco to Sue'. Then, at a fast walk, or a run, if one wishes, once the game is thoroughly understood, Marco tries to reach Sue and 'tag' her before she can say 'Sue to Maria' and so save herself. If she manages to say this, then Marco takes her place in the circle and Sue takes over as the killer. Sue, of course, must not begin to move towards Maria until she's completed saying her line. This is the thing that everyone finds hard. You must not move until you have finished speaking. If you do, you count as 'dead' and your intended victim will immediately become killer. You're also 'dead' if the killer reaches you and tags you before you can say your line. (Those 'killed' can drop back two or three yards, rather than leaving the space altogether; this maintains their interest and helps to build tension as the game progresses). If you 'kill' someone, you stay 'on'. You go into the place of the one you've just killed, who's now on their way out of the circle, then you turn and announce your next victim. But remember not to 'travel' while still speaking! If you say your line before you're tagged, you are safe and you become the killer, though obviously the more quickly you set off on your target, the better.

The object of the game is to stay on as killer, as long as you can, eliminating everyone in the circle, if possible. When the game gets down to just two players, the killer will have won, as there is no longer any sanctuary for the victim. The game is complicated at first, but it is good for quick thinking and warming up. An efficient killer may knock out the whole circle in one sequence.

Chain killer may be played using the cast of plays for participants' names, with the 'villain' of the play as Killer – Richard III and Macbeth are obvious candidates, but Claudius and Iago may be called upon too.

Name killer

Stand in a circle. One person goes into the middle and says 'One, two, three . . .' and then the name of someone, repeated quickly three times. That person has to shout out their own name once, before 'It' can finish saying it three times. Anyone who succeeds becomes 'It'.

Name fruit bowl

This is similar to *Fruit bowl* (see below, p. 184). Both activities were traditionally played with chairs, but accidents might happen with students diving to sit down first on the same chair, so instead of using a circle of chairs, ask everyone to stand shoulder to shoulder in a circle. 'It' stands in the middle of the circle and calls out the names of the people who are to swap places, e.g. 'Simon and Navinder'. As soon as It moves, Navinder and Simon must try and reach each other's places, before It does. You can call out as many names as you like so that, for example, five people compete for four spaces. The old instruction, 'All change', when everyone had to move, worked well in the days when chairs could be used. To make 'All change' workable nowadays, instead of using chairs to define places for the whole group, you could mark places on the floor with tape or chalk crosses.

Trust

Trust activities can generate a powerful shared focus and a strongly supportive and sensitive climate for active work on texts, but special care must be taken with trust activities. The whole point about trust work is that it can only succeed in its objectives if genuine trust is present, and genuine trust develops gradually. So, you should be taking this work slowly and you will need to feel confident that you can implement it without confronting anybody either with any kind of unacceptable risk, or with some challenge for which they are not ready. As leader of a trust activity, you will need to be sure that all those involved have sufficient strength, co-ordination and confidence to carry out the work, as well as the right attitude. The teacher's own experience is especially important in trust work, so if you are new to it, take time to build up your own ability, perhaps starting with *Trust leading*, which will allow you to develop your ability to observe students closely and to side-coach appropriately.

Trust leading

In pairs, *A* closes their eyes and B leads them anywhere in the room. *B* must trust *A* implicitly, so side-coaching should establish early on, that absolutely no bumping, whether into others or into objects, should occur. Start everyone slowly, so from the beginning, movement in the room is fluid and aware. The contact point for leading may be the arm or the elbow, or the shoulders (lightly held from behind) or, the hardest contact point to use, the small of the back – in that case, while directions can easily be suggested through your fingers, the only way you can stop your partner, is by taking your hand off them. There must be no talking – unless you are doing the sound version in which *A* goes just ahead and *B* follows purely by following the sound of *A*'s voice. Pairs can switch roles after a while, so each experiences being led. Side-coaching is needed to build the whole class, all working in their pairs, into an integrated whole of smooth and flowing movement. This most easily comes about when you're using arms or elbows as contact points. Now you can introduce 'parking', which means the leader leaves their charge and someone else picks them up and continues to work with them, or 'exchanging', when two leaders agree, just by eye contact with each other, to exchange their charges, with no pause or interruption.

Trust leading is very suitable for Edgar and Gloucester approaching Dover Cliff in *King Lear* (see *Poor Tom shall lead me*, p. 103), but it is also very effective in paired speech work, in which *A*, reading from the text, leads *B*, who repeats the words given, following with eyes closed. Either touch, or voice alone, may be used for guiding. Susan Dransfield has pointed out to me that (as this activity is based on the idea of the sighted leading the blind) the led person should take the leaders's arm, as happens in reality, rather than being 'steered'. This is now the way she always does the exercise.

Fall-guy

As with all trust activities, everyone must understand that the objective is to develop absolute trust in participants. Stand in a tight circle, shoulders almost touching, with both palms facing inwards at chest level. Eight is a good number for the circle of supporters. The 'fall-guy', eyes closed, head up, feet firmly together, stands in the middle, hands straight down by their side, but relaxed. All gently place their hands on the fall-guy and begin, very gently, to rock them backwards and forwards and side to side. The fall-guy's feet should act like a pivot and their body should be rigid, but relaxed. It's important to side-coach groups in the early stages. The first rocking movements should be small, only increasing as the group feels the complete confidence and trust of the fall-guy. Everyone takes a turn.

Pendulums is a variation done in much the same way as *Fall-guy*, but in three's, with A and B facing each other and C standing, and then gently being rocked, like a pendulum, between them. Side-coach groups to maintain 'the pendulum' in a perfectly erect position. How far backwards and forwards the pendulum moves is not important – only that the activity should be done with complete trust, so the pendulum is relaxed, but standing absolutely vertical, trusting the two supporters implicitly.

I'm falling

This exercise is only suitable for older students who are used to working together and also have a good understanding of the responsibilities and seriousness of trust work, and for workshop leaders who are experienced teachers of trust activities. It should only be done with classes that have already carried out *Fall-guy*, with complete competence and understanding. It is an excellent activity for trust and group formation, but it does require special care in the way it's set up. In addition to the conditions stipulated above, I only do *I'm falling* with classes that are already warmed up and moving and working well together. Demonstrate it with yourself as the faller, first, and be sure that the class is absolutely serious about its responsibility for those falling. Take the exercise slowly, insisting on a period of movement and concentration in between each 'falling'.

All walk around at random in a relaxed way, but keeping alert and on the look-out for anyone who may stop and announce that they are falling. After a little while, when the workshop leader is satisfied that the class is moving around together with good concentration, they can quietly say 'From now on . . .', which is the signal for anyone who wishes, to stop, stand still and call out 'I'm falling'. Then they let themselves fall towards the floor. Those around must immediately move to catch and support that person and restore them to an upright position. Ensure that alertness and concentration are maintained as the group moves around between each 'fall'.

Bridges

A suitable floor and suitable non-slip foot-wear are essential for this exercise. Pairs face each other, hands on each other's shoulders, or hands clasped to make an arch between them. Now each gradually inches their feet backwards, making a bridge with an arch that slowly becomes flatter. The exercise is best done with people of similar build, but uneven partners working well together easily compensate for physical differences.

If a class is working easily and well with *Bridges*, you can ask pairs to try helping each other to stand up, from a starting position, sitting back to back with elbows interlocked. First they should lean back onto each other's shoulders and then, as they feel supported by their partner, gradually rise to their feet. There should be no undue straining – it all depends on feeling your partner's weight and using each other's weight co-operatively, to rise. You may find that some pairs have difficulty with this exercise: ensure that everyone proceeds at their own pace and, if a pair is only able to rise a little way off the floor, give them credit for this. Side-coaching is important in this exercise.

Body lift

This is only suitable for older students, familiar with trust work. It is basically like the kind of stage-lift called for by Shakespeare at the end of *Hamlet*: 'Let four captains/ Bear Hamlet, like a soldier, to the stage;' though I recommend eight captains to do the lifting. When I have done this exercise with Drama students, they have usually commented how easily and smoothly 'the body' can be lifted, and what a reassuring and pleasurable sensation it is to be lifted in this way.

One person lies completely still on the floor and the rest of the group (8 or so people) bend down, with hands beneath the person to be lifted. When absolutely ready, they all simultaneously lift the person smoothly off the floor, keeping them parallel to the floor and without any unevenness or loss of trust. Groups of this size will be able to lift individuals to shoulder height with perfect safety, but work carefully, with only one group active at a time, and ensure that the return to the floor is just as even and smooth as the lift. Uncertain groups should only lift the person a little way off the floor, until they are able to operate perfectly smoothly and efficiently together.

Chapter 7

Warm-ups and preparation
Games

Games, like the specific Group Formation Activities of Chapter 6 are often useful, too, for group formation, warming-up socially, while the physicality and mental effort and absorption involved in playing games make them excellent as warm-ups for body and mind. Games are strongly focused and tightly organised social activities and, for the most part they are literally play, not real, and so provide a 'safe area' in which we may enjoy the emotions of our uncertain lives outside that space and, something which is especially important for the young, a place where we may practise and experiment, with impunity. However, not all games are inclusive and benign, necessary qualities of games used as warm-ups. Some are based on elimination or exposure, with isolation and penalties and forfeits, and, of course, any game can be made sinister by the intrusion of forces from the world outside its bounds. Harold Pinter's plays, most notably *The Birthday Party*, with its cruel game of *Blind Man's Buff*, come first to mind, but the dramatic tension of Shakespeare's Richard III owes much to Richard's sudden turning of game and play into vicious reality.

Games insist that we act in role, according to their rules, and participants in drama workshops know that this connects games with the substantive workshop activities to follow. For all their fun, there is a seriousness of application about teenagers and adults playing games in a drama workshop, although they may not have played such games since childhood.

A further dimension of games is their frequent potential to connect directly with the subject of your workshop, as in the example of the workshop plan in Chapter 5 on pp. 139–42, when *Sword and shield* is suggested as a game to play before work on Macbeth's soliloquies. Games have an integral relationship to social situations and relationships (they emerge from them), and so to Drama. For any play, and almost any situation in any play, there seems to be a game of some kind (often traditional and familiar, sometimes waiting to be articulated or invented) that will act like a dumb show or riddling 'argument' for what is to follow. Games, and developments and variations of them, can lead directly into the text and help to clarify the action of the drama and involve students in that action. This seems to be especially true of Shakespeare, partly, perhaps, because of his frequent adaptation of strongly-defined popular narratives: ambitious men wanting to be king at any cost, lovers blocked by families, the exposure of a murderer, the corruption of an unsuspecting mind, as well as a host of historical episodes, and comedic narratives made up of disguising, trickery, mistakes, chases, separations and reunions. It is also true because of the extremely sharp definition he brings to even the most fleeting of exchanges. Take the brief episode involving the Nurse in I.iii of *Romeo and Juliet*. The 'game' is that the Nurse wants to gossip and reminisce, taking all the time in the world, while her powerful mistress, Lady Capulet, is impatient to raise the matter of Paris's offer of marriage to Juliet, but seems to find it hard to interrupt the Nurse. The status of the 'players' sharpens the effect: the Nurse is a lowly servant, but of the most intimate and trusted kind, respected, too, because of her age. Lady Capulet cannot immediately use her authority to halt the Nurse's repetitious reminiscences, and even her stern line 'Enough of this; I pray thee, hold thy peace' fails to stem the tide. I cannot think of a traditional game for this scene, so, if I wanted a 'thematic game' to start the workshop, I might invent an '*Interruptions*' game, such as one person telling an involved anecdote to a semi-circle of listeners, who may only try and interrupt when the teller is looking directly at them. Every time they seem to have succeeded, the teller simply looks away, or at someone else, and continues with their rambling. Work might then go on using the speech itself, in a large group, or, perhaps, in pairs or small groups. There are extensive possibilities for using, adapting, modifying or inventing games directly relevant to Shakespeare's texts, once one has identified the dynamics of a particular scene or passage.

The games included in this chapter are formal and almost all are traditional. They are divided into nine categories, according to the main impulse driving each: Games testing authority, Straight-face games, Hunting, chasing and catching games, Tricking games, Victim games, Guarding games, Racing games, Mime games and Improvisation games.

The majority of the games listed are energetic, especially Hunting, chasing and catching games and Racing games and are useful as straight-forward warm-ups, but be extra careful about safety when using such games (see pp. 122–8 on 'Safety: physical and emotional'). Many of the games may be directly adapted and developed further to play substantive roles in Shakespeare workshops, especially to explore gaming situations in the plays and for language work. Some specific suggestions for such adapt-ations, follow some of the descriptions.

Games testing authority

Grandmother's footsteps

Perhaps the best-known of all traditional children's games, *Grandmother's footsteps* is based on a large group (the people) daring to approach 'Grandmother' (authority). 'Grandmother' stands facing the wall at one end of the room, with everyone else standing in a line, backs to the wall, at the other end. The aim is to creep up on Grandmother and touch her back, without her seeing you move. If, when she turns round, she sees you moving, she points at you and you must return to base. Anyone who successfully reaches her, then takes over as Grandmother and the game begins again. *Grandmother's footsteps*, because of its subversive attitude to authority, acts as good preparation for work on *King Lear* (see p. 27) and other plays.

Crust or crumb?

This is a more energetic version of *Grandmother's footsteps*. It's similar in the way you set it up, but when Grandmother turns round, she either says 'Crust' or 'Crumb'. If she says 'Crust', then no one must move; if they do move, they are sent back to the base-line. If she chooses 'Crumb', then all must race back to the base-line before being tagged by Grandmother. Anyone tagged is 'out' (which means, immediately, it may not be suitable for all classes), though you can keep those who are 'out' involved by sitting them on the floor in a 'time-out' box half-way up the room. If any players can tag them, without being seen by Grandmother, they may return to the base-line and rejoin the game.

Elephant ears

Form a circle with everyone cupping their palms round their ears. The 'Spotter' stands in the middle. Whenever their back is turned, everyone flaps their ears, like elephants. If you're seen flapping, however, you become the Spotter.

What's the time Mr Wolf?

Mr Wolf stands facing the wall at one end of the room and the rest of the class, the sheep, wait in their safe 'home' at the other end. When Mr. Wolf turns round and begins to prowl up and down near his wall, the sheep must leave their home. Now they chant 'What's the time, Mr Wolf?' Mr Wolf replies, for example, 'Five o'clock'. Again they chant their question 'What's the time, Mr. Wolf?' He might reply 'Two o'clock' (it's traditional, and more exciting if the time moves unpredictably, according to the whim of the wolf!). Suddenly Mr Wolf answers 'Twelve o'clock, dinner-time' and he runs to tag as many sheep as he can before they regain their home. Any sheep caught join Mr Wolf's end of the room and help him catch (but only Mr Wolf announces the time). The structure of the old game *What's the time Mr Wolf?*, with the fearful figure of Mr Wolf and tension rising as the game goes on, is often echoed in dramas in which an unpredictable tyrant turns on their own people. Interestingly, Shakespeare seems to play on something very like this when, in *Richard III*, the Duke of Buckingham inopportunely asks Richard for the 'the earldom of Hereford and the moveables', promised to him for earlier favours, only it is the King who asks the question 'What is't o'clock?' in reply – a very sinister reversal of the question in *Mr Wolf*.

Straight-face games

The 'Straight-face games' that follow are excellent for introducing comic work. Playing comedy 'straight' is half the battle and in order to release the comedy of Malvolio or Benedick and Beatrice, those characters must first take themselves absolutely seriously. Their faces remain straight: they simply don't, or can't, see the joke.

Hagoo

There are various games requiring everyone not to smile or laugh – such as Clive Barker's famous *Holy Dido*, which involves ritual and invention (Barker 1977) and this one, *Hagoo*, played by the Tlingit Indians of Alaska and described by Andrew Fluegelman (1976), in which two lines face each other and pairs of players, one from each side, starting from opposite ends, take it in turns to 'run the gauntlet'. The opposing side tries to make the one who is 'on' smile or laugh, as they walk down the line, looking everyone in the eye. Anyone 'on' who fails to keep a straight face, joins the other line.

The bears are coming

Chris Johnston gives an amusing account of this game (Johnston 1998: 249). Two or three bears, who eat people, are appointed and they leave the room. The rest of the class are lumberjacks, and they sing songs and chop down trees. As soon as the bears are heard growling outside the door, everyone runs around in a panic, shouting 'the bears are coming'. As the bears come in, still growling, everyone 'plays possum', keeping completely still and quiet, and pretending to be stones or trees, so that the bears will not eat them. Without touching anyone, the bears check out that the stones and trees are real – and not people. Any giggling or tiny movement means that that lumberjack is caught and eaten – which means joining the bears for the next round. So it goes on until everyone is a bear, except for one victorious lumberjack.

Poor pussy

This is a traditional game, similar to *Hagoo*. Groups probably need to feel very relaxed with each other in order to play it, as there is, potentially, more embarrassment than with most other games collected in this book.

Two equal lines face each other. The first player goes across to their opposite number, kneels down and miaows like a cat, several times. The opposite number must now also kneel down, stroke the head of the 'cat' and say 'Poor pussy, poor pussy', without smiling or laughing. If either smiles or laughs, the other line scores a point (or, in a long version of the game, which goes on until only one 'sour puss' is left, they are 'out'). Now the 'stroker' becomes 'pussy' for the second person in line opposite, and so on. So that everyone has a turn playing both roles, the last person in line will need to play pussy to the person who first began the whole sequence.

I first saw this game at a children's party, when it was played the other way round, with children taking it in turns to be pussy in the middle of a circle of all the others, who stroked and cooed, trying to make the pussy laugh. A similar game is called *Dead Lion*, in which the lion must feign dead, eyes open, while everyone else sees (no prodding!) if there is any sign of life there.

Hunting, chasing and catching games

Sword and shield

Everyone, without giving away their choices, secretly selects one person as their 'sword' and another person as their 'shield'. The person you have chosen as your sword is a threat to you, so you must keep away from them and you must also try and keep the person who is your shield between you and your sword. All move around. Vary the pace of the game.

Tag

Maybe this is the oldest and best-known children's game of all. The one who is 'On' must tag someone else, who then becomes 'It' until they manage to tag another person. Or, in *Chain tag*, they join hands with the tagger (as in *Fox and geese* p. 178). A variation of *Chain tag* is *Snake killer*: the 'snake' is on and must hiss and wiggle their hands together as they catch people, who then become part of their lengthening body, until all are caught. *Chain tag*, and variations of it, are banned in many schools because of the danger of people travelling at high speeds hanging on to the ends of chains. Always watch out for, and stop, such high speeds. *Chain tag* is, in any case, much better if played with cunning and deception. Also, be absolutely sure that there are no obstructions that end people might collide with.

Stick in the mud tag

Once you are tagged, you have to freeze, legs apart. You can only be released when someone crawls between your legs. 'It' tries to tag everyone in the room, while the others frantically try to release everyone 'stuck in the mud'. Another way to 'release' people is to have two join hands around them.

Stick in the mud tag can be played with language added to the 'release' activity of crawling between victims' legs. Certain words or phrases from the text must be spoken, by the victim or the releaser, or by both (with two different phrases), before the caught person is free.

Hug tag

You cannot be tagged if you are hugging someone else, but you can only hug if 'It' is within six feet of you. Anyone tagged becomes 'It'.

Bronco tag

One person is the 'Rider' and everyone else stands in lines of three, one behind the other, with the second and third in each group holding the waist of the person in front to form a 'bronco'. Now the Rider tries to catch the waist of the third person in one of the broncos. If they succeed, the one at the head of the bronco becomes the new Rider. You can have several Riders loose at once.

Circle tag

Form circles of three or more players, holding hands, with another player outside each circle as Catcher. The game begins when the circle nominates one of its number as the target for the Catcher to try and tag. If they're successful, the tagged person becomes the new Catcher.

Fox and geese

This is basically a tag game. The fox, the catcher, stands at one end of the room and the rest of the class, the geese, at the other end. The geese must reach the fox's end, without being tagged. If they are tagged, they join hands with the fox. The game is played from one end of the room to the other, so the geese have a brief 'home' or resting-place. Gradually a chain of foxes is formed, but the chain has only two 'catching hands', one at either end. The geese may be able to slip through the middle of the chain. You can also play this without a home base, i.e. the fox simply chases the geese round the room and the geese who are caught are added to the chain. If the group is large, you can break the chain into two halves, or into fours, or whatever you wish, but note the comments on *Chain tag* on p. 178 above.

Cat and mouse

Everyone except the cat, who is in the middle of the circle, and the mouse, who is outside it, stands in a circle with about an arm's length between people. The cat tries to tag the mouse. If the mouse stops just behind anyone in the circle, then that person becomes the new mouse and the old mouse stays in their place in the circle. If the cat catches the mouse, then they switch roles and the chase goes on, but in reverse. Remind everyone that any pause just behind someone, by the mouse, will result in a new mouse setting off. (At first, you often get two mice running at once, because the mouse forgets that their pausing behind someone will turn that person into the mouse – so the leader has to rule who goes back into the circle and who stays on, as mouse.) Encourage the mouse to switch roles fast, so that everyone is involved.

The game can also be played with a double circle of people, i.e. with pairs standing in two circles, one in front of the other. In this case, it is the one at the front who becomes detached and turns into the new mouse, should the old mouse stop behind the pair. Another version of the game has the class standing in equal lines, side by side, making up a square of people, rather like a square made up made up of dots drawn on a piece of paper. Everyone hold hands laterally and the cat and mouse begin their chase up and down the corridors. On the command or signal 'Turn left' (or right), the class drops hands, turns to the left and then rejoins hands. Every time turns are called, it's very confusing for both the cat and the mouse.

Cat and mouse might be played, and then modified, as part of work-shops on fugitives or escapees, such as Edgar or Coriolanus, Prince Hal, Celia and Rosalind, Juliet or Hermia, most of them sons or daughters escaping the anger or control of fathers.

Wizards, giants and elves

This is a dramatic version of the old *Paper, scissors, stone* game and I learnt it from my Wolverhampton colleague Jeremy Brown. Divide the class into two groups, one on each side of the room. Each group huddles together, making muttering sounds, and secretly decides whether it will be wizards (who mime piano-playing and go 'Hoooo!'), giants (who stretch their arms up high and go 'Aaaah!') or elves (who crouch down, using their fingers and thumbs to mime chattering and squeak 'Eeeee!'). Giants 'take' elves, elves take wizards and wizards take giants. On the signal, the groups approach the centre of the room and, exactly together, enact who they are. The losing group must run back to their base wall before any members are tagged by the winners. Instead of keeping score, or having the caught people change sides, it's easier just to say 'Who was caught? OK five of you' before moving on to the next round. Choosing three 'plays' in advance works well.

We are from

The West Midlands company Theatre Foundry first introduced me to this excellent 'mime and chase' game. Form two equal groups of people and allocate them suitable places to which to belong; for example, if you're in the West Midlands, you might use two local towns, such as Walsall and Dudley. Now the teams meet in a huddle and each secretly decides on an occupation (e.g. Personal Assistant for one team, and Judge for the other). Tell them that the first round is only a practice. Start with the teams standing in two lines facing each other, about 10 or 12 yards apart, their base-line defined by a wall, line of chairs or chalk line. One side goes first: altogether they march up towards the centre line, chanting 'We are from Walsall.' Now they stand still and the other team, all in line, marches forward chanting 'And what do you do?', coming to a standstill about 3 or 4 feet away. Now the Walsall line mimes their occupation, each individual doing their own version of a PA's work, watched intently by those in the Dudley line, who try to guess what the occupation is. Note that guesses must use exactly the right words, e.g. 'Personal Assistant', not 'Secretary' or 'Admin. Assistant'. As soon as anyone in the Walsall team hears someone from the Dudley line guess correctly, they turn and run back to their base-line. This is the signal for all the others in the Walsall line to run for home and for those in the Dudley line to give chase, trying to tag the person opposite them, before they reach 'home'. Remember that the whole line should take flight as soon as any one of them hears the correct words. Next, roles are reversed and the Dudley line comes forward, chanting 'We are from Dudley', and so on. Iron out any problems in these first two dummy runs and then set each team to huddle together again to choose three occupations each, so the game can progress smoothly for a while.

Snake by the tail

Form one long line, each person holding the waist or shoulders of the person in front, with both hands (or split the class into two or more snakes, if it's very large) and give the last person a scarf to tuck behind their back. Now the 'head' of the snake tries to catch its 'tail' (the scarf), but the snake will die if anyone breaks their hold on the person in front. The tail person tries to stay tail as long as possible. This can be played with no scarf: the head just catches the tail.

A variation is to have two or more snakes chasing each other's tails. Another is to play the game in pairs, with one having a 'tail' which the other tries to catch, but note the comments on *Chain tag* on p. 178 above. Stop the game if the end of a snake begins to whip dangerously from side to side.

Tricking games

Simon says

Simon stands facing the whole class, who are spaced out before him. He gives all kinds of instructions, but the class only carries them out if they're prefixed with 'Simon says . . .', otherwise they must remain motionless. This used to be an elimination game, but you can play it with anyone caught out becoming the new Simon, or you can give everyone three lives, before they are either 'out' or become the new Simon. Commands might be 'Simon says do this . . .' (Simon demonstrates and all follow) or 'Simon says do that . . .' or he might say 'Simon says, at a fast walk, touch all four walls of the room . . .'. The game can also provide, as by-product, a lot of physical work, so it often functions as a useful warm-up too. Side coach to ensure that Simon does not set any tasks that could lead to injury.

A variation is to say 'Do this' for all commands that must be carried out, and 'Do that' for the remainder. This game also used to be known as *O'Grady*, with O'Grady giving the commands.

Simon says can be played as a playful test, a 'Shakespearian warm-up'. Using *Macbeth*, say, make announcements, accompanied by actions, which the class must do, but only so long as they occur in the play: 'Macduff flees his castle' (with gesture of running), 'The Porter lets Macduff and Lennox into the castle' (gesture of opening a door), 'Lady Macbeth speaks to the witches' (gesture of hands to your mouth). On the last, inaccurate announcement, anyone who raises their hands to their mouth, has been caught out.

Stretch and bend

This is like *Simon says*, but you follow what the leader does, not what they say. Use just two commands and actions, 'Bend' and 'Stretch'.

Matthew, Mark, Luke and John

Form a circle and number off, though the first four people are named (Matthew, Mark, Luke and John) rather than numbered. The rest of the circle is numbered from '1' onwards, with the last person, who has the lowest number, standing next to Matthew. The object of the game is to get to heaven (by becoming one of the four apostles), preferably to the top spot, occupied by Matthew. Say you are No. 8 and you are asked to start. You say '8 to . . .' and then add a number or one of the four names. Perhaps you choose '4'. No. 4 must now respond quickly and accurately (e.g. by saying '4 to Mark'), or they will be demoted to the very bottom position and everyone who was below them will move up one. The tricky thing is that there is no re-numbering out loud: everyone has to quickly calculate for themselves what their new number or name is. Although you may like to use a 'snap fingers, slap thighs' rhythm, this isn't necessary. Just set the rhythm going and it will be maintained. You can side-coach the class to up the tempo, as they become more successful at the game.

Body parts

In pairs, *A* points to a part of their body, say their knee, and says 'This is my knee, 1, 2, 3.' *B* must point to their own knee, before *A* can finish counting to 3. After taking turns for a round or two, players may trick each other by pointing to one part of their body and saying another – but it is what they say that counts.

Victim games

Vampires

This game, a modified version of Boal's *The vampire of Strasbourg* (Boal 1992: 110) is only suitable for older classes used to Drama who are also used to working well together. You also need a suitable space (eyes are closed, so there must be no danger of bumping into furniture or obstacles). You need to practice with your class the correct (i.e. safe and disciplined) way in which 'vampires' will be acting during the game. You could start by saying something like this:

> 'If we're to play this game, we all need to show that we can work carefully and safely together and we need to practise how we act the vampire's touch. In pairs, A, the vampire, stands behind B, the victim, whose eyes are closed. To make B into a vampire, A very gently places their hands on B's shoulders, like so.' You demonstrate, your fingers resting on the top of B's shoulders, thumbs together gently resting on B's spine. 'Can you all do that? B's, as soon as you feel those hands on your shoulders, you will become a vampire. Good! Now,

change places and the B's show me that you can make the A's into vampires just as carefully . . . good, we can play the game, but remember that we're all actors in this game: we're not really being vampires! I'm your audience . . . act this game for me . . .'

All circulate, with eyes closed, within a safe, confined area. Explain that one person, whose arm the leader squeezes briefly, is to be the vampire. Once that has been done the vampire is 'active' and tries to change others into vampires, as described above. Victims may not struggle, but they must let out a cry as they realize what is happening to them. Once 'bitten' in this way, victims become vampires themselves and join the original vampire in hunting for more victims. Should a vampire encounter another vampire, that person ceases to be a vampire. To mark this, they let out a sigh of pleasure. Once the game is in motion, cries and sighs fill the room.

Vampires may be played with appropriate phrases from the text substituted for the cries and sighs (*Macbeth* fits best, but any text may be used and it's entertaining to find the most suitable phrases).

Witches

This is similar to *Vampires*. All stand in a circle, hands behind backs, eyes closed. The leader squeezes one person's hand as a signal that they will be the witch. Now, eyes open, everyone scatters. Anyone may pretend to be the witch, but only the real witch may squeeze anyone's hand (the more surreptitiously, the better) and when they do, that person, having counted slowly to 5, still moving around, must sink to the floor at the side of the room, until eventually there is only one non-witch left standing.

Guarding games

Keeper of the keys

Special care must be taken when playing this game, as it involves blindfolded players. The rest of the class, however, act as a 'safety wall' and it is worth practising how people in this wall will gently stop blindfolded players from bumping into anything. Everyone stands in a square, within which the game will take place. Two players, blindfolded, or with eyes closed, are guided into opposite corners, and a bunch of keys is placed on the floor. One person is the Keeper of the keys and the other is the Thief. To win, the Thief must find the keys and steal them, while the Keeper must catch the Thief. Should the Keeper find the keys, they must leave them where they are and continue searching for the Thief. Everyone else must keep absolutely quiet and only intervene to turn either player gently back in towards the space, should they stray into the surrounding 'safety wall' of people. This is a tense, quiet and stealthy game.

It can also be played, however, as a faster game, still using just two players, and with the remainder of the class still surrounding them like a 'safety wall'. Now only the Thief is blindfolded. When the Thief calls out 'where are the keys?', the Keeper, who keeps hold of the keys, must immediately jangle them for a second, moving away as quickly as they can before they're tagged by the Thief. Allow half a minute for a winner to emerge. There's also a version without keys, called *Adam and Eve*, played with only Adam blindfolded and using the question 'Where are you, Eve?' Eve must immediately reply 'Here I am, Adam.'

Sometimes, the rules of games can be changed to reflect, say, the power some characters hold over others. *Keeper of the keys* might be played for a while, and then modified into Prospero as Keeper and Caliban as Thief, except Prospero's blindfold is removed without Caliban's knowledge. What is the nature of the dramatic interest in *The Tempest*, when so many things are 'rigged' in this way?

Hunter and hunted

Both Hunter and Hunted are blindfolded, or have eyes closed. They start from opposite ends of the room and the Hunted person must get to the other end without being caught. Like *Keeper of the keys*, this is a game of stealth and absolute silence, so the Hunter can hear any movement from the Hunted. The rest of the class lines the walls to make sure neither player crashes into anything.

Giant's treasure

While the other *Guarding games* have only two main players (though they are fun, for a short while for a whole class, especially if you're playing the versions where silence is essential), *Giant's treasure* involves everyone very actively. A suitably sized 'lair' for the Giant is chalked or roped off in the middle of the room. Everyone else places a shoe a couple of feet inside the Giant's lair. On the word to start, everyone tries to steal the Giant's treasure, the shoes, without being tagged by the Giant. If tagged, they are 'dead' and must fall back away from the lair. The Giant may not hold or touch the treasure.

Racing games

Fruit bowl

This is like the old game *Musical chairs*, which was played with two lines of chairs back to back, around which everyone circled until the music stopped, when everyone had to try and sit down – but there was always one chair too few. As people diving to sit on the same chair might result in an accident, *Musical chairs* is no longer considered a safe game to play with students. In addition, it is an elimination game and so would probably, in any case, be unsuitable as a workshop activity.

In *Fruit bowl*, everyone stands in a circle, shoulder to shoulder, on a taped mark or chalked cross on the floor. Everyone is given a name, either grapefruit, orange or lemon. One person is 'It' and stands in the middle. When they call out the name of one of the fruits, 'lemons', for example, all the lemons must change places and 'It' tries to occupy one of their marked places in the circle. If they succeed, they become that kind of fruit and the displaced person becomes 'It'. If 'Fruit bowl' is called, everyone must change places. I remember playing this game, as a child, but it was called *Stations*: the stations were London stations, and instead of the command 'Fruit bowl', we had 'All change'.

Relays

Relay races of all kinds were once immensely popular, but they do tend to slow things up. If you want to do one, however, *Shoe relay* is fun. Everyone takes off a shoe and a pile of them (or separate piles for each team, if you prefer) is made at one end of the room. On the word, the first person runs to get their shoe, put it on and return to their team. Only then can the second person set off to retrieve their shoe.

Another kind of relay is *Amoebas*. Groups form circles, holding hands, and practise moving like amoebas, circular fashion. Now races can be held, but the rule is that everyone in the amoeba must lead at least once (i.e. to keep the amoeba revolving), or perhaps twice for a longer race, before reaching the finishing line, still all holding hands.

Skin the snake relay, in spite of its dreadful name, is also fun. Teams stand in line, with everyone putting their left hand between their legs and clasping the right hand of the person behind. On the word, the last person in each line lies down flat on the floor and the whole line, without breaking hands, must shuffle backwards over them, until all are lying flat. As soon as this is achieved, the person who started at the front, and who is now at the end of the line, gets back on their feet and shuffles forwards, pulling the whole line up in turn, still without loosing hands, to finish in the same state as they began.

Mime games

'Mime games' allow students to practise particular skills, after, perhaps, appropriate 'Mime Exercises' (pp. 196–8) and whenever you have decided to use mime in your Shakespeare workshop.

Changing the object

This exercise normally uses an object, such as the cardboard tube inside paper towels or cling-film (though it can be played purely through mime), and starts with the leader indicating, with a basic mime, what they are imagining that object to be, e.g. a telescope held up to one eye, or a toothbrush. They now hand on the object, taking care to keep the illusion going, to the next person, who must receive it as it has been imagined, before 'changing it' into something else, e.g. a pen or an umbrella.

A variation is to take it in turns to go into the middle of the circle where there is an imaginary 'rummage box', from which you take out a mimed object. You take this to someone else in the circle, who receives it and replaces it back in the box again.

Another variation is to throw imaginary objects across the circle. Someone begins by miming an object. People try to guess what it is, and when someone guesses correctly, the mimer immediately 'throws' the object across the circle for someone else to 'catch'. Now the object is thrown about for a while (with the leader encouraging mimetic faithfulness to its dimensions and weight), until someone chooses to put it down on the floor and mime a new object of their own. The same procedure is then repeated with the new object.

Changing the scene

This is best done without any language, though sounds may be used. Two people go into the middle of the space and one begins a mimed action. The other watches, picks up what is happening and joins in. Now a third person may enter, but as they do so, they change the mime. The two already in must immediately pick up on the new scene. A fourth person enters and changes the scene again. So it goes on, until everyone is in. I find myself coaching most groups to 'watch for the newcomer', as students often become so absorbed in their scenes that they fail to pick up the entrance of the newcomer.

This is not, perhaps, a game to play with groups that are unused to working together practically, as you may find some students towards the end left painfully exposed as they try to decide on what new mime to introduce. With such groups, it's better to use a 'roll-over' variation, in which the first person leaves the mime, as soon as the fifth person enters – and so on, with the second person leaving as the sixth person enters, so there are only ever four people involved.

Liars

Someone mimes an activity, e.g. channel-switching while watching TV. Another says to them: 'What are you doing?' The one miming must lie (e.g. 'I'm taking the dog for a walk') and that lie must now be mimed by the one who asked the question. The next person repeats the drill, asking 'What are you doing?' and receiving an answer which will cue what they, in turn, must mime.

Improvisation games

'Improvisation games' allow students to practise particular skills, after, perhaps, playing *Offer/block/accept* as a warm-up (p. 199) and whenever you have decided to use improvisation in your Shakespeare workshop.

Fortunately/unfortunately

In this group story-telling game, the narrative is passed round the circle, the words 'fortunately' or 'unfortunately' alternating and so influencing the way the story develops. It starts 'Once upon a time . . .' and everyone takes a turn, signalling that they've finished their contribution by saying 'fortunately' or 'unfortunately' and then turning to the person on their left to continue the tale.

Fill the gap

The story-teller goes into the middle of the circle and begins a story, but they leave gaps wherever they wish, pointing as they do so at random, to someone in the circle, who must then supply an appropriate word, phrase or, maybe, a whole sentence or two.

Why?

Someone goes into the middle of the circle and the rest fire questions at them. The responder in the middle must turn and answer the questioner as rapidly as possible, trying to keep on top of the questioners all the time. The questions may be about anything, real or imaginary, but must all begin 'Why . . .', e.g. 'Why did you get up late?' or 'Why are you wearing that T-shirt?' This is a suitable warm-up for *Victimisation* (pp. 107–8).

Judge and lawyers

This is only suitable for small groups, because it involves elimination. Someone in the circle volunteers to be Judge. A chair is brought and the Judge sits. Everyone else stands. The Judge begins their investigation (whatever their imagination conjures up) and every so often points at someone in the circle and asks them a direct question – however, the person to that one's right must answer 'for my client'. Don't forget that you are the lawyer for the person to your left. Anyone who answers for themselves, or fails to answer for their 'client', is out and must sit down on the floor.

Hand puppets conversation

In pairs, hold conversations with each person using one hand as a puppet. You can use a 'speak and move on' method here, announcing the topic to be discussed for a minute or two and then asking everyone to move around again, until your next announcement.

Paired encounters

This is a more developed version of *Crossing the circle* (p. 149). Have half the class, 'Blues', moving around the middle of the room, while the 'Reds' move around the outside. Now announce roles for paired encounters, e.g. 'In pairs, Blues are cathedral guides and Reds are tourists'. There are endless options, some co-operative, some confrontational: people needing a coin for a phone-box (or needing to borrow a mobile) and others who have money, or a mobile, but are not keen to help; old people shopping, or crossing the road, and helpful children; smokers in a non-smoking carriage; difficult diners and waiters for whom nothing is too much trouble; people lying on prohibited grass and park-keepers; neighbours with a disputed fence or hedge, etc.

Chapter 8

Warm-ups and preparation
Drama exercises

This chapter includes individual activities and physical exercises appropriate for particular kinds of workshop – as in the example of individualised work on Hamlet's isolation and feigned madness, *Hamlet demands* (p. 110). Some kinds of movement work benefit from specific movement warm-ups, most obviously stage-fighting exercises as preparation for work on battles, duels and scuffles. It is salutary to remember that Elizabethan scripts were performed by actors who often had an armoury of skills, like the famous stage clown of extempore from the 1580s, Richard Tarlton, who was also 'a maker of plays and ballads, a drummer, tumbler and qualified Master of Fencing'.[1] Modern actors know well that the skills of clowning, mime, playing musical instruments, stage-fighting, dancing, tumbling and acrobatics are often vital to them, as they were to their Elizabethan forebears, in securing work. Modern Shakespearian production has been greatly enlivened and enriched by recognition of the part these skills have to play. The same is true of the workshop. Workshop leaders cannot be experts in all these things, but we need to be open to their use. Even without special expertise, one can become confident in using the simple physical, relaxation and breathing exercises included in this chapter, though you must always be certain that anyone teaching a particular skill is competent to do so safely. You are fortunate indeed, of course, if you have developed some expertise in any one of a whole range of other activities, from yoga, martial arts and dance to exercise routines and keep-fit, for you can often use these, too, in your workshops. We can also recognise that our students often have unknown talents, skills and resources for us to tap and develop. Their qualities, fused with the dramatic and poetic power of Shakespearian language, can bring about vital theatre within the concrete or brick-built 'O' of the classroom or drama studio.

The six categories of drama exercises in this chapter are: Movement warm-ups, Stage-fighting, Mime exercises, Voice warm-ups, Improvisation and Breathing.

Movement warm-ups and Mime exercises can both add enormously to the richness of Shakespeare workshops. Movement suggests character and emotion before any words are spoken and the creative delight of suggesting imagined objects immediately gives power and density to enactment. While simple props or items of costume, such as hats, are sometimes essential to what one is doing, the staple of mime also brings freedom and ease into the workshop. Using a few basic mime techniques, such as those given here, can help us to refine our own and our students' ability to mime, so that it plays a fuller part in work on Shakespeare's texts. We all enjoy copying and imitation, giving, for example, a sense of how someone moved their head and shoulders as they talked, or how they walked. There is a place, without any specific teaching, for natural ability to be expressed and incorporated. When Michael Jackson did his famous 'moon walk', for example (his version of appearing to be moving forwards on a conveyor belt that is taking you backwards), or when body-poppers and break-dancers started using extraordinarily sharp, isolated movement, apparently turning their bodies into robots, admirers in every school-yard in the country soon followed suit, some producing amazing results. We may not be able to teach the movement required for Lady Macbeth's sleep-walking or Titania and Oberon's dance, but this should not stop us from making opportunities available to our students to explore and refine what they can do. Even simple responses from teachers can be helpful, for example, to make their students' Calibans and Oberons flat-footed and 'grounded', with low centres of gravity, and their Ariels and Titanias the opposite, rising on their toes and pressing their centres of gravity upwards. Such contrasting terms for exploring spatial zones, as high and low, before and behind, are readily understood, as are 'high voltage' and 'low voltage' to refer to the power movement contains, and 'attraction' and 'repulsion' to the degree of magnetism, or its opposite, experienced by individuals or groups moving together. You can encourage students to focus through and beyond where their movement is taking them, so that the movement's impulse seems to travel on even after the body or part of the body affected, has come to rest, giving a sense of clarity and definition. Try this with a simple action like picking up a pen or settling into a chair. Another approach to movement for characterisation, is to use Laban's *Eight basic efforts* (p. 194).

As with teaching movement and mime, teaching voice is obviously a highly-skilled professional matter, but we can still use non-specialised Voice warm-ups, to sharpen and improve our own and our students' performance and, more to the point here, our, and their understanding and appreciation of Shakespeare's use of language, speech and sound. Cicely Berry teaches that the individual's sense of their own distinctive voice ('The need to be at home in your own voice. Sitting down in it – whatever language, dialect, you may be using . . .' Berry 2001: 63) is paramount in voice work. It is one of the chief aims of active Shakespeare teaching that students locate their own voices within the rhythms and sounds of the language and the way to do this, is through speaking (experiencing) that language. To help with this, voice warm-ups have two main aims – the physical aim of loosening up the areas of the upper body concerned with the production of sound and the mental aim of freeing the mind to allow sound and language to flow. Again, as with movement and mime, one can achieve this preparation through games and integrated activities, but there is also a place for exercises that allow one to develop more specific aims in speech and language work.

As individual teachers wanting to use voice warm-ups, we can prepare ourselves by exploring our own breathing and voices. *The Teaching Voice* (Martin and Darnley 1996) includes a most helpful account of the voice and how it works, and at the end of *The Actor and the Text* (1987: 276–84), Cicely Berry provides an excellent sequence of exercises that can be carried out alone. There are many others in that book, especially in Chapter 6, that are suitable for doing on one's own, as well as in a group. Doing these greatly increases one's confidence to use voice warm-ups and breathing exercises with students.

The last two categories of drama exercises included in this chapter are Improvisation and Breathing. The breathing exercises included are for relaxation and recuperation, and for 'winding down' at the end of workshops. The improvisation exercises recognise, although the book is committed to working with the original language of texts and to beginning with text, that there are times when improvisation, silent or spoken, is needed in Shakespeare workshops. It can be useful in two main ways. One, *Improvisation using the text*, is for reinforcement and further exploration, using existing knowledge of the text (as in *Hot-seating*, p. 118), or for collectively telling a play's narrative in contemporary language, perhaps in a particular contemporary genre (*Hamlet* as film-noir, *Romeo and Juliet* as romantic novelette). The other main way is *Personal improvisation*, asking students to imagine characters and situations as if they are themselves those characters in those particular situations, so using their own lives and experience, and improvising their own language, to realise and intensify the drama. We need to be clear about our use of *Personal improvisation*, if our objectives are primarily about texts, rather than about texts as the inspiration for creative drama – a perfectly legitimate use of them, but one using a different discipline.

In the late 1960s, improvisation was a key element in the relatively new subject of Drama – which was very much a creative, predominantly non-text based subject. Drama was valued as an aid to children's self-expression and personal and imaginative development, and the work of Peter Slade and Brian Way was crucial in the struggle to extend this kind of drama in schools. For many newly qualified English and Drama teachers at that time, the School Play, with its system of stars and also-rans, was only tolerable if transformed into a structure with a role for every child. It was also often felt that improvisation had greater potential to connect with children's minds and imaginations, than work on scripted plays, but for many, including myself, commitment to the educational ideals of the new subject was matched by an equal commitment to the power and richness of literature (which, in the case of English Literature, meant literature in its original language) and to its place in the curriculum. So improvisation within texts was problematic: there was something worrying about distilling roles and situations from Shakespearian texts and presenting them to students in scenarios for improvisation, when one also felt that the particularity of the language itself was the true scenario. Anything less felt selective and arbitrary, as though interpretive assumptions had replaced the intricacies of the actual drama. This was true, I feel, of an introductory session I once taught on *Othello* – an improvised 'prequel' in which Desdemona confronted her father's racism. The Desdemonas, instead of using personal experience and ideas, for motivation to play their role, seemed, often, to be replacing the role with their experience and ideas, largely because, at that time, they had little knowledge of the play. Since then, I have used *Personal improvisation* in Shakespeare workshops within tighter textual frameworks. For example, in an improvisation on Ophelia's bewilderment at Hamlet's rejection of her, students would still improvise using their personal resources and their own language, but with a close knowledge of how the text defines the situation and steers the action.

One of the most important things to learn, before improvisation can be used effectively, is that accepting and working with what is offered to you, often leads to a better quality of work than constantly resisting or confronting others. After all, Drama is about co-operative creation, not competition. Once students have learnt this, and the activity *Offer/block/ accept* given in this chapter (p. 199), supplemented by the Mime games in Chapter 7 (p. 185) should be helpful, students' early improvisations, which might simply involve escalating arguments, begin to turn into much more subtle, and 'life-like' episodes.

Movement warm-ups

Safety, of course, is crucial and you should be sure about the safety of any exercise before you ask students to do it. In general, start slowly, with small, easy movements and be especially wary of anything involving twisting movements or lifting.

Many workshop leaders have their own sequences of movement warm-ups, starting gently and slowly and moving through *Isolations*, during which particular parts of the body are warmed-up in turn. A typical sequence follows.

Standing in a relaxed position, feet apart and arms loosely by your side, start by loosening the head and neck with small, slow circular movements, mouth open and jaw relaxed, leading to larger head circles, then moving on to small shoulder rolls (hunching and dropping the shoulders in a circular movement) or lifting and dropping the shoulders together or separately through three positions, up, middle, down. Next might come arms, hands and fingers (reaching upwards or sideways, making small and large circles with arms outstretched, shaking out hands and fingers) and then torso turns and rolls, with fingers on the back of the neck or arms akimbo – again, gently and slowly, working up gradually to slightly broader turns, followed by hip pushes (pushing out to each side in turn and returning to the middle position each time), and pelvic circles, arms akimbo. Now, arms still akimbo, straighten your back and lean forward, head up, sweeping slowly from side to side as though searching, keeping the lower body still. Follow this with free swinging, circular movements of your arms and body in any direction you choose, feet firm and knees bent, arms and shoulders loose. Next drop your head and arms forward and down and gently bounce up and down towards the toes, knees bent. Stand up straight again and shake out each leg and foot in turn, then make small circles in the air, leg outstretched, with your toes. You might, at this point, ask people to put their arms straight out on each other's shoulders, in pairs or in lines, in order to give support while they swing their legs backwards and forwards or make figures-of-eight in the air with knee and lower leg. Finally, *Stand up straight*, which means, in the memorable drill I learnt from an American dance teacher: 'head up, shoulders back, stomach in, buns together'. Then relax with a general loose body-shake.

You can go on to *Walking on the spot*. This is a good, safe way of limbering up the tendons and muscles of the feet. Everyone stands on their own spot and follows the leader's demonstration. To begin with, the feet remain flat while the knees are bent, in turn, as though walking, with accompanying arm movements. Very gradually, the heels start to lift a few millimeters off the floor, until, after a little while, one is walking on the spot, going right up on one's toes, at a robust pace. Continue until well warmed-up. This work could be followed with a breathing exercise (pp. 200–2 below).

A simpler movement warm-up is *Reach and bounce*. Stand in a relaxed position, legs apart. Now reach up as though grasping an apple high above your head, eight times (four stretches with each hand) and then loosely drop down, arms and head hanging towards your toes, knees slightly bent, 'bouncing' eight times towards the floor. Now repeat the arm stretching, except counting out six stretches this time, followed by 6 bounces, then four of each, two of each and, finally, one of each, with both hands stretching up at once for the final time. Another movement warm-up exercise is *Swing and catch*. Stand flat-footed and swing your arms loosely backwards and forwards, with knees slightly bent and giving. After a little while, gradually increasing the size of your arcs, swing your hands up high, both together and 'catch' an imaginary bar above your head, balancing with heels just raised off the floor and holding it a moment, before dropping down again, and repeating the sequence.

To explore the movement and nature of particular characters, Drama teachers often use Rudolf Laban's *Eight basic efforts*, his way of analysing actions as either direct or indirect in their use of space, quick or slow (sometimes also described as sudden or sustained) in their use of time, and heavy or light, in their use of weight. The indirect movements are light and slow (*floating*, like a sleep-walker); light and quick (*flicking*, like horses' tails at flies); heavy and slow (*wringing*, like a defensive karate stance); heavy and quick (*slashing*, like flailing arms). The direct movements are light and slow (*gliding*, like a snake); light and quick (*dabbing*, like brushing bits of grass off your clothes); heavy and slow (*pressing*, like turning a difficult door-handle) and heavy and quick (*thrusting*, like punching or stabbing with a sword). Preparatory exercises will familiarise students with each of these basic efforts. It may help to move from the indirect to the direct form for each, so that the indirect effort of floating, light and slow, turns into the direct, light and slow effort of gliding, and so on. Next, apply the efforts to characters moving and speaking. Rather than arbitrarily deciding which effort seems to dominate a certain character (slashing for Tybalt, floating for Romeo, perhaps), try, with students working individually, exploring the effect of different efforts on the same character and passage of text. For instance, the Laban efforts can be used to determine the nature of Hamlet or Macbeth's mental disposition as they speak 'To be or not to be' or 'If it were done when 'tis done', and this can be accompanied by movement. This exercise is a good prelude to discussion of how the language of the soliloquies works, both to map thought processes and to suggest moral or philosophical contexts.

Keith Johnstone's activity *Fast-food Laban* (1999: 283–4) puts students into families, whose behaviour is governed by a chosen effort (e.g. the Punch family). When they've decided their family relationships, they are given a scene, coming down to breakfast, for example, which they all play in a punchy manner. Other Laban-based exercises include different types improvising scenes, e.g. between a punchy landlord and a stroking (Johnstone's 'character equivalent' for 'floating') tenant or a slashing pupil and a smoothing (Johnstone's 'character' equivalent for 'gliding') teacher.

Stage-fighting

I am much indebted to Peter Cann, in whose workshops at Wolverhampton I learnt the following basic movements in stage-fighting, though I have not attempted to incorporate any of his expert work with weaponry. That is very much an area for professional tuition. Peter stresses the importance of eye-contact in all stage-fighting, both to ensure safety and so that actors know that their partners are ready. This reinforces the notion of co-operation and collaboration. Stage-fighting is, in fact, a dance being performed. When dealing, in workshops, with duels or such climactic encounters as those between Hal and Hotspur, Edgar and Edmund, Romeo and Tybalt or Macbeth and Macduff, I normally ask students to mime weapons and to accompany the sequences of blows which they work out, with words or phrases from the text.

There are a few simple stage-fighting techniques that can be safely used in Shakespeare workshops. Hair-pulling is one: *A* places a fist on *B*'s head, and *B* takes it, or their wrist, in both their hands, pulling the fist down onto their head. Now it is *B* who provides all the movement, with *A* simply keeping their fist on *B*'s head. *B* makes appropriate movements, as though their hair is being pulled. The impetus is reversed: the victim actually provides the movement and the aggressor merely follows. This technique works for ears and noses too!

To punch, and make the sound of a punch, the victim, preferably with back to the audience, and standing just out of range of the aggressor strikes their own shoulder with the palm of their other hand at the moment of mimed impact, reeling backwards at the same time. In this way, the punch can be made to sound and look real and full-blooded, but it cannot reach the victim – which is safer than the technique of 'pulling punches', within range. Making the sound of a smack on the face is similar. The one miming being smacked turns their face as the other's open palm approaches, and claps their hands together, following this, perhaps, with their own open hand going up to their face as though to soothe the pain. The aggressor must reverse what happens in reality, so keeping their weight well on their back foot.

Kicking can also be safely done, but you should practise it with someone yourself first. For a kick in the face, the victim holds their hands in front of them, palms down, so only their hands are kicked – again, the illusion requires the victim to have their back to the spectators. For a kick at someone lying on the floor, put one foot next to the person's stomach and aim at the floor well in front of them, with your other foot – which makes a kicking sound as you strike the floor. Alternatively, the kicker can make a realistic sound by slapping their own thigh (on the other side to their kicking leg), as they kick. This is one occasion when students will cheerfully judge who's 'doing it best' – and get a lot of pleasure from doing so. Needless to say, all this requires absolutely safe procedures, which depend on discipline and care, and such work may not be for every class.

The action and reaction fight

This fighting game is done in pairs, in slow motion, with no sound effects. It's a series of actions and reactions, starting with *A* either kicking, punching or stabbing at *B*, who reacts, recovers and retaliates. So it goes on, in strict alternation.

Mime exercises

Understanding, and being able to apply, a few basic principles of mime will give students a great deal of added pleasure and will allow them to develop the quality of their work. Introducing the idea of *Definition* is helpful. To achieve good definition, encourage students to think of the space and time before and after it. First comes preparation, mental focus – something is about to happen or to be shown. Next comes the definition itself, sharply held, clear and strong, and then comes relaxation, leaving the illusion, returning to neutrality. To illustrate this, rehearse the class in a weight-lifting mime – preparing for lifting the weights by loosening up, shaking the body and limbs (preparation), gripping the bar in a sharply focused act of concentration and carrying out the lift (definition) and then stepping away from the weights and shaking out again (relaxation). Or, you might 'parade' the class, beginning with everyone standing at ease (preparation), calling them to attention (the moment of definition) and then returning them to standing at ease (relaxation). Now repeat the exercise with a specified mime.

Another way of 'defining' movement clearly, is to ask several students in turn to pick up an object, any object will do, look at it and put it down again. Now ask them to repeat this, but quietly brief them to use this framework: turn, see the object, breathe in, pick it up, look at it, put it down again, breathe out. Ask the rest of the class, who have not heard the brief, what differences they see. Now let everyone try for themselves.

Accuracy is also essential. You might ask students to carry out *Finger mimes* individually, e.g. threading a needle, sewing on a button, picking up pins, removing a splinter, changing a plug, using a mobile phone. Next, ask them to devise their own finger mimes in pairs.

You can introduce size and shape and weight with *Individual mime* exercises – asking students to pick up a heavy box (perhaps failing to get it off the ground at first) or unpack and put away their shopping ('You take out a large box of cereal – where will you put it in your kitchen, but first, what's that written on the back? Next comes a packet of biscuits – you can't resist trying one . . .'). *Eating and drinking mimes* are very popular (ice-cream, fish and chips, spaghetti, juicy peaches, bananas, crumbly biscuits, cream cakes, hot coffee, Coke, lager, wine-tasting . . . alcopops), with refined manners or bad, eagerness or boredom, no time or plenty of time, keen appreciation or preoccupation with reading a magazine or speaking on the phone. Other *Individual mime* ideas might be packing a suit-case, preparing a meal, dusting a room or settling down with a TV dinner to watch your favourite programme. (The latter works well as an *Interruptions mime*: things keep happening that prevent you from settling down – the phone rings, you've forgotten the pepper, the cat wants to be let in, someone comes to the door.) An 'uncoached' mime, in which everyone works in their own way and in their own time to recreate as accurately as possible what they actually do in their own lives, without any ongoing instructions, might be 'Getting ready to go out' or 'Having breakfast'. Try, too, a *Fixed point exercise*, such as opening a door and entering a room. Ask students to turn the door-knob, open the door and then, still holding the knob in a static or fixed position, enter the room by walking round that fixed point. They can then change hands, still concentrating on the unmoving fixed point of the door-knob, to close the door. Ask them, now, in pairs, to devise a mime of their own using the idea of the fixed point.

Group mimes, in which a variety of roles and activities have to be shared and mimed, provide a challenging context for development. No preparation or planning is allowed. 'In groups of four, move across the street and get into your family car' or 'In fours, clear the table and wash up' or 'You're two teams having a tug o' war; the rope is lying on the floor diagonally across the room . . .' or 'In groups of eight, move a grand piano across the room/through a doorway/down a flight of stairs . . .', or, 'Let's all take a look at this elephant/these ants/this hole in the ground/ the stars . . .'.

A more imaginative kind of *Group mime* is *People as objects*, described by Keith Johnstone in *Impro for Storytellers* (1999: 303): 'Improvisers become chairs, tables, telephones (or whatever else is needed) for the players in a scene.' This exercise can be done as a whole class activity or in small groups – for instance, in groups of 6 or 7, with one person acting as narrator or 'voice over', ask for 'a silent film' of a particular event, e.g. 'Buying a new pair of shoes' or 'The lovers' picnic'. Things, such as shoes and the contents of the picnic basket, should all be played by people. It's important to keep up the pace of the activity: an actor should say 'I'll just sit on this chair for a minute', whereupon an improviser should instantly behave as a chair, but should certainly not say 'you, you're a chair, and you two, you're a table'. Side-coach to avoid accidents.

Paired mime can be used just as effectively to produce a shared imaginative focus, especially as other pairs in the room also have to be allowed for, for example, pairs carrying a ladder or plank or a large plate of glass, or using a tape measure to mark out a plot of land or carrying out a short narrative mime, such as searching for, and finding, someone's contact lenses.

In all this mime work, side-coaching and showing or sharing, are essential. What works, what is convincing, what is sharp and clear? We are not producing mime artists (almost all of us will not be qualified to do so anyway). Instead, we are carrying out exercises which will allow our students, when the same concentration and pleasure and effort are transferred into their practical work on Shakespeare, to work in greater depth and make richer discoveries.

Voice warm-ups

First, it is easy to strain the vocal chords.[2] Workshop leaders should beware of shouting and strain: our voices are not designed, without long and arduous training, to produce loud noise and it is best to resist the temptation to create dramatic effects by encouraging students to turn up the volume. (In the theatre it's often the sign of a directionless production when the actors constantly raise their voices, as though to compel the audience's attention with noise, rather than drama.)

Every Drama teacher uses, whatever they call it, some version of the *Resonance exercise*, which is based on the whole group developing resonant sound from the exhalation of breath. Begin with *Breathing for relaxation: lying down* (p. 201), and after five or six exhalations, ask the class to breathe out with a humming 'mmm' sound, starting quietly, lips together, the sound growing and vibrating in the head, and then, opening the mouth, change the sound to 'aaah!'. As the mouth opens wider and wider, so increase the volume, filling the head, thorax and chest with sound and the whole room with a strong, easy buzz. The floor acts as an additional resonator and students will both hear the power of the sound they are making and feel the vibration too. The exercise may be done in a 'bicycle wheel' circle (see *Group relaxation*, p. 202) or standing in a circle. After a few rounds of this, if you wish, you can ask the group to 'wind down' again, so that the 'aaah!' gradually diminishes into silence.

Another exercise, good for raising awareness of the production of sound through the three main areas of resonance in the body, is *Violin, viola, cello*, which I learnt in a workshop run by Foursight Theatre Company. Standing in a circle (see *Stand up straight*, p. 193), ask the class to take a breath and exhale on the word 'violin', hanging on to the last syllable, which will resonate in the nasal cavity. Did everyone know they had a hollow chamber there, like the box of a violin? Now do the same with the word 'viola', hanging on to 'la', which will resonate in the throat and upper thorax. Lastly comes 'cello', which will resonate lower down in the chest cavity. Everyone will naturally find they are singing. Next you can repeat the exercise, nominating individuals, while everyone is singing together, to change the pitch and asking the group to pick up and join in on the new note. Recap for everyone, reminding them that they have this powerful instrument – their voice, with its range of tones and sounds. Later, mention of 'violin' or 'viola' or 'cello' may serve to prompt students to locate what they are speaking within a particular part of their upper body.

Call and response

This traditional technique is useful before Listen and Speak language work (pp. 24–33). The leader claps a brief rhythm, or sings a vowel sound or chants an improvised phrase (such as 'way-a way-a hee-ha') at the class, who then clap, or sing/chant it back. The leader may vary the chant, add to it, change it or build on it, while the response follows whatever is given. Leadership can be passed around the class.

In terms of verbal facility, *Tongue-twisters* are sometimes useful. In pairs ask people to take it in turns to say 'Bad Blood' quickly, ten times, or 'Red lorry, yellow lorry' quickly, five times. Alternatively, form a circle and ask people to take it in turns to speak the tongue-twister. Only one person may speak at a time, and, to be able to speak, they must jump into the circle, in random order. If they succeed in completing the tongue-twister, or if they fail to complete it without making a mistake, someone else may jump in to the circle to replace them. Keep this exercise going as quickly as possible. Who's fastest at saying the tongue-twister? *Peter Piper* is a good one to do all together:

> Peter Piper picked a peck of pickled pepper;
> A peck of pickled pepper Peter Piper picked;
> If Peter Piper picked a peck of pickled pepper,
> Where's the peck of pickled pepper Peter Piper picked?

The class will know other brief tongue-twisters, so volunteers may be asked to start a new one. Also, take Shakespearian text and treat it as tongue-twister, encouraging speed and repetition. It's interesting, and revealing, that it's quite hard to make tongue-twisters out of many famous opening phrases, such as 'To be or not to be . . .' or 'Is this a dagger . . .' or 'It is the cause, it is the cause, my soul . . .' or 'Blow winds, and crack your cheeks . . .').

Improvisation

Offer/block/accept

This activity, played in fours (two pairs), helps to develop understanding of the basic co-operative principle underlying improvisation.

Each pair nominates one person to speak and one, standing or sitting behind the speaker, to prompt. Begin with the prompter of Pair A instructing their speaker to make a conversational offer, e.g. 'I think you're so lucky to be going to London for the week-end'. The prompter of Pair B now whispers 'offer', 'block' or 'accept' to their speaker. Blocking means obstructing or denying, e.g. in response to the offer 'Are you lost – can I help you?' a block might be 'I'm quite alright, thank you'. An 'accept' might be 'oh thank you, I was hoping to find a pub'. Students will soon realise that improvisation is about co-operation and that the pleasure of improvisation lies in uncovering drama in the shared space before all the participants.

It's fun to play this activity using *Alien arms*. The speaker folds their arms behind their back and the prompter puts their arms, from behind, under the speaker's arm-pits. Now the 'alien arms and hands' literally have a mind of their own, carrying out all kinds of actions (from drumming fingers irritably to stroking the side of the speaker's nose), as the conversation with the other pair progresses.

Students might go on to try, in pairs (i.e. without the speaker/prompter structure), sections of Shakespearian dialogue, choosing, for example, one blocking everything and the other accepting, or both offering, or each ending their line with a whispered instruction to their partner opposite, to offer, block or accept with their reply.

Marionettes (p. 158) also develops students' ability to relax and improvise, because it removes most of the responsibility for making choices and so frees them from the fear of failing or seeming pretentious. It, too, can be continued into work on passages of Shakespearian dialogue.

Breathing

Breathing for relaxation: standing up

'Winding down' at the end of a workshop is often best achieved by a simple breathing exercise. There may also be times in a workshop when you want the class to calm down, relax or re-focus and, again, breathing exercises can achieve this. The exercise *Breathing for relaxation: standing up*, however, is best done when people are not at all out of breath – maybe before speech-work, for example. (If they are out of breath, straightforward deep breathing, in through the nose and out through the mouth, is more suitable.)

Stand in a relaxed position, legs a shoulder's width apart. Put your right index finger on the bridge of your nose and gently close your right nostril with your right thumb. Breathe in slowly and deeply through your left nostril. Now place your middle finger on your left nostril and remove your thumb from your right nostril. Breathe out slowly through your right nostril. Now breathe in again through your right nostril and out through your left, continuing to close one nostril at a time. Repeat for as long as desired.

Another *Breathing for relaxation* exercise, is to stand in a relaxed position, legs a shoulder's width apart, arms hanging down. Breathe in softly through the nose for a count of 6; hold your breath, pulling in your stomach muscles for a further count of 6; breathe out softly through your mouth for a count of 6 and then relax your stomach muscles for a count of 6. Repeat a number of times. This is especially good to calm nerves.

Another breathing exercise starts from a relaxed standing position, legs slightly bent, hands resting by your side. Breathe in slowly through your nose as you rise gently onto your toes, arms spreading out to the side and palms meeting above your head like a ballet-dancer. Hold it a short while and then gently exhale through your mouth, as you return to your starting position, arms to your sides. This may also be done with the extra movement of going down into a squatting position, sitting on your heels, as you breathe out, before returning to your starting position.

To increase the capacity to breathe deeply, ask students to breathe in fully through their noses to a count of 3, and out again, also through their noses, to a count of 3. Then ask them to breathe in and out to a count of 4, then 5, always through the nose. They can do this in their own time, stopping when they feel any difficulty and simply repeating the number they've reached (e.g. the count of 8), at which they feel stretched, but comfortable.

Breathing for relaxation: lying down

This is especially good as preparation for voice work, and also for winding down after vigorous activity. Lie on the floor, arms by your side, palms upwards, feet in a natural position with toes pointing very slightly outwards. Be aware of all the contact points your body has with the floor, starting with the back of your head and moving downwards. Feel completely settled as though you are merging with the earth. Now breathe in slowly through your nose, hold your breath for a few seconds and breathe out slowly through your mouth, with a gentle sigh. Repeat until you feel total relaxation has been achieved. With a class, I start by coaching the rhythm (though without counting it) and then, after a little while, leave them to continue in their own time.

A good variation is *The sea-shore*. (This, incidentally, is a very relaxing one to do yourself if you are over-tired and don't know where to put yourself.) Imagine you're lying on the sand at the edge of the sea. As you breathe slowly in through your nose, picture a very gentle wave coming towards you. As it breaks, you breathe out through your mouth, with a gentle sigh. You imagine your exhaled breath is the sea-water gently flooding out on the sand beside you. For your first exhalation, you think of the water miraculously flowing out from every part of your face and head. For the next exhalation, the water washes out through your neck and shoulders; then down inside your arms and out through your hands and fingers; then down your chest and out through your lower abdomen; then down through your legs and out through your feet and toes; finally, the sixth time you breathe out, with a long sigh, you imagine water flowing out from all these parts of your body and draining into the sand around you. Focus on that for a moment, and then, if you wish, repeat the exercise.

Group relaxation

Lying on the floor like the spokes of a bicycle wheel, with heads in the centre, ask the class to breathe in and out deeply and slowly, in their own time, thinking only of their own rhythm.

A more intimate arrangement is for all to lie on the floor on their backs, making a large circle, or polygon more strictly speaking, each with their head resting on the middle of another person. Again, this is a basis for slow, deep breathing in one's own time.

Notes

Introduction

1 True, there are some who are directed to teach Shakespeare, in spite of a lack of personal enthusiasm, and for these teachers the problem of making their Shakespeare teaching effective, is compounded. I hope that this book's focus on teaching methods designed to involve and interest even the most alienated of students, may also serve, for these teachers, to return some attention to the qualities and pleasures of the plays. The teaching activities assert little about the excellence or genius of Shakespeare, assertions that understandably goad Shakespeare sceptics into deeper entrenchment: they are simply about accessing the drama and the poetry which is in the texts.

2 There is a great amount of speech work that any English teacher may undertake without training, but experiencing workshops taken by the voice professional of one of the big theatre companies, or by actors who teach voice, is often a revelation and can take one's teaching into new regions. So it is with all the other performance skills that theatre involves, whether dance or movement, stage-fighting, mime or improvisation. The professional theatre, in addition to the stimulus it provides through creating new productions, and depending on the resources particular theatres are able to devote to education, can be a rich source of 'in-service training' for those who want to develop their work as teachers of active Shakespeare.

3 For those unfamiliar with higher education in Britain, the 'new universities' were mostly created in the early 1990s from existing colleges and polytechnics, which, up until then, had not possessed the authority to award their own degrees, although many of them, such as Wolverhampton where I worked, had been, for many years, large and varied providers of higher education. They had traditions of working closely with their local communities and often recruited substantial numbers of local, especially local mature students, and they offered all kinds of diploma and degree courses, from the original 'typically polytechnic' areas of Engineering, Technology and Science, to Art and Design, Business, Law, Education, Sport, Humanities, Languages and Social Sciences.

4 For the private process of reading, some writers talk of 'the theatre of the mind', though the kind of imagining that goes on here is multi-

dimensional, associative and anarchic. In a flash, when reading the opening lines of *Richard III*, for example, those brought up on Olivier's film
version, hear regal, celebratory music and crowds cheering; see, and
hear a door shut, so that the sounds beyond become muffled and low;
and watch a dark figure turn from the throne on which he is leaning and
limp down towards the camera, before clipping out 'Now is the winter of
our discontent . . .'. Their lips probably mime Olivier's delivery, as they
read, but in an instant they have moved into the role of Richard and are
also trying out their own way with the words. As they read on, hosts of
unbidden pictures and associations and echoes from plays, films, their
own lives and the wide world around, come tumbling in, at the same
time as their reader's conscience begins to insist they read notes, look
things up, cross-reference and check back.

In writing a critical essay, something less pictorial and vivid, but no
less intensely imagined, seems to be taking place. Now there is more
rigour and mental discipline: one is forensic, preparing a case, or, perhaps,
summing up and suggesting conclusions, like a judge. The theatre of the
mind has become a bare office, or a silent study, furnished with no dis-
tractions.

5 I believe we should encourage academic trespass: it is more important to
follow pedagogical values and learn something of related disciplines,
than to stay off academic territory where we are not completely at home.
As teachers, we are constantly challenged by our need for new knowledge
and expertise. Until recently, for example, the basic language of film
criticism seemed adequate to deal with new film versions of Shakespeare,
but films such as Baz Luhrmann's *William Shakespeare's Romeo+Juliet*
(1996), often use new and sophisticated computerised techniques. A
knowledge of how these techniques operate will provide particular critical
insights, yet we do not claim that without a knowledge of them, or
without a grounding in Film Theory, we should not be using Shakespeare
on film in our teaching. In the same way, training in Drama gives new
and rich dimensions to the traditional study and teaching of Shakespeare,
but approaches using drama can be employed both by those new to its
potential and by those with much experience of it.

6 Colleagues teaching other subjects on the modular degree and diploma
scheme at Wolverhampton have frequently commented to me that Drama
students are often a great asset in group work in these other subjects,
perhaps because they are used to producing work collectively to dead-
lines, with all the interaction and give-and-take that that entails – not
that the process is always smooth, democratic and harmonious!

1 Why use active methods to teach the plays?

1 In *Shakespeare For All Time*, Stanley Wells makes the following intriguing suggestion about the First Folio editors:

We don't know when the Folio was first planned, but my guess is that
Shakespeare discussed it with his colleagues during his last years...It seems

significant that the Folio was put together by the only colleagues named in Shakespeare's will except for Richard Burbage, who had died in 1619. Is it not possible, even likely, that they had earned their bequests by a promise to oversee the compilation of a volume which would preserve in print eighteen plays that had not previously been published, and to provide improved texts of those that had already appeared in print?

(Wells 2002: 97–9)

2 The *Shakespeare and Schools Newsletters* contain accounts of the work of Cambridge Experimental Theatre and The Cambridge Syllabus Players. There have been many other companies working on Shakespeare in Britain in the last twenty years, often with very little funding and extremely demanding schedules. At the time of writing, 2003, in the West Midlands area where I live, there are two companies, apart form the RSC, offering touring Shakespeare, together with workshops – Black Cat and Midland Actors Theatre.

3 Risk, of course, is involved. Teachers showing children a video or taking them to a theatre face a dilemma: if the children have not read the text first, then they may be overwhelmed by the production's version of it. The setting offered will probably, at least for a while, seem like the natural, the only setting for that play. We have all written a comment in the margin, at some time, saying 'no, that was just this production's view, not a fact about the text . . .'. If they have read the text first, they may be tempted to be dismissive of the performance setting and version offered to them.

Furthermore, some productions turn out to be muddled, badly performed and tedious and these can have a devastating effect on young audiences – but two things can reduce the risk of such an experience taking place. First, those taking theatre trips can familiarise themselves with the work of the companies, directors and actors involved in the productions to which they are taking students. You cannot always preview shows – often you have to book 'blind', but a close relationship with companies (and many now offer all kinds of contact and support for teachers) will reduce the likelihood of inflicting a disaster on students. Second, going to the theatre will always have, and should always have, some risk attached to it: sometimes audiences polarise and people disagree strongly about the same production. The point is that visits to the theatre should not be exceptional, one-off events, with everything staked on the show's being a hit. We need, though money is obviously a major issue in meeting this need, to take our students to the theatre regularly, so they learn to cope with the occasional, inevitable disappointment without feeling 'that's the last time I ever go to Shakespeare', or whomsoever – and, vitally, so they learn to get beyond their irritation or disapproval by developing their powers of critical analysis. In this context, see pp. 136–8, on active discussion.

4 Influences from their own education are always crucial too, one way or another, to the development of teachers. In my own case these included the influence of parents who loved theatre and poetry, especially that of Shakespeare and the Authorised Version of the Bible; a brother who became a teacher and performer; and dedicated teachers and lecturers – who made visits to the theatre part of the curriculum; who set us to learn and speak poetry and to act in plays; who asked us to write poems and ballads and, in one case, to fill a whole exercise book with a long story; who delighted us by reading poetry, novels and stories to us in their own distinctive voices and ways; who encouraged us to read other texts relevant to the one we were actually studying; who let us argue fiercely amongst ourselves about the meaning and merits of a poem chalked on the blackboard; who gave inspired lectures, which made us

feel the world was all before us and who discussed texts, and our essays, with us, as though our voices and opinions were as valid as their own, but without sparing the truth.

5 Rob Jeffcoate (2002:11) comments on Caldwell Cook and Finlay-Johnson: 'She was the headmistress of a village elementary school for "children of the labouring class" on the Sussex Downs; he was the English teacher of mostly middle-class boys aged ten to fourteen at a prestigious school in Cambridge. Although apparently unaware of one another's work, their approach to teaching Shakespeare's plays was almost identical. Their lessons resembled early theatrical rehearsals: reading and walking through the text, with homemade props and costumes, in order to devise a rough-and-ready performance whose only audience was normally the teacher and the children themselves. . . . Harriet Finlay-Johnson describes her Shakespeare work in Chapter 5 of *The Dramatic Method of Teaching*, which was published by Nisbet in 1911; Henry Caldwell Cook describes his in Chapter 7 of *The Play Way*, which was published by Heinemann in 1917. Both books are unfortunately long out-of-print and hard to obtain. Two later accounts of Cook's work are to be found in: D.A. Beacock (1943): *Play Way English for Today*, London: Nelson; and Christopher Parry (1972) *English Through Drama*. Cambridge University Press'.

6 These have been extensive, including Rex Gibson's own books on the teaching of Shakespeare (see References), the *Shakespeare and Schools Newsletter*, which he edited, and the *Cambridge Schools Shakespeare* (CUP), an edition of the plays in separate volumes, addressed to students themselves and with numerous suggestions for active work. The twenty-four beautifully produced editions of the *Newsletter*, full of useful and stimulating material, much of it from those teaching Shakespeare in schools of all kinds, were published between Autumn 1986 and Summer 1994. The *Newsletter* was distributed free to all secondary schools in Britain and for eight years, was an extraordinarily rich and democratic medium for the exchange of information and ideas.

7 Keith Johnstone makes the same sort of point when he remembers how: 'We were warned that Algebra was going to be really difficult, whereas Einstein was told that it was a hunt for a creature known as "X" and that when you caught it, it had to tell you its name' (Johnstone 1999: ix).

8 Rob Jeffcoate gives some good examples of this process in operation, when he describes the effect of working actively on *Hamlet* with mixed ability 7–10 year olds in a working-class area of Liverpool. 'One (parent) said her son had asked her what Shakespeare she had done at school. When she said, "*Macbeth*", he replied , "Well I'm doing *Hamlet*".' Jeffcoate's evaluative interviews with the children after the project 'confirmed that many children had taken their enthusiasm home with them. "My dad said 'very good' my mum said 'very good' too", "My mum said it was very good but I'm too young to act in plays," "I told my mum what I thought was going to happen and about the deaths and about my part"' (Jeffcoate 1992: 201–2).

9 The first question is actually, more often, the question of discipline, which depends on self-respect, the mutual respect of teachers and students, and good morale in the classroom. Active methods of teaching, as advocated here, can help to engender these things. Performance, even workshop performance in the classroom, requires high standards of concentration, co-operation and discipline.

10 I'd read the reviews of the 1986 RSC production we were going to see. Adrian Noble's 1995 forest of light bulbs, or Peter Brook's metal forest of 1970 would have required a different slant. (I remember how annoyed a school party

around me was, when Howard Davies's 1982 production of *Macbeth* distributed the witches' language round the cast and dispensed with the witches themselves!)

11 Having a stake in a text may be more personal and less dramatic than this: Hutchinson's *Shakespeare Made Easy* series, for example, with its modern version printed opposite the original text, allowed access and a sense of ownership to a friend's son, who was labouring through *Macbeth* for GCSE. Before a visit to *Romeo and Juliet*, instead of soft toys, I have used the Cartoon Shakespeare version published by Michael Joseph. Children know they have 'rights' over the picture language of cartoons and, with Von's illustrations, a great deal of original language, as well as my interpretative story-telling, was welcome. Though about reading rather than practical work, these last two examples have important elements of ownership. The same goes for the half-hour cartoon film versions of Shakespeare, the *Animated Tales*.

12 Sue Jennings (1986: 152) describes how students may be asked to create a representation of 'My life now', using any assorted small objects available in their bags or pockets: '. . . jewellery, watches, coins, keys, pens etc. may be used to represent people, places, objects, feelings, etc.' In pairs, students may then answer questions about the 'spectograms' they have just made, though there should be no comment or interpretation from the questioner. The technique may be varied to deal with the past or the future, and may be used as a starting-point for other kinds of work.

13 At the University of Central Lancashire Conference on 'Shakespeare and the Teaching of English' (April 1993), for example, one speaker caricatured workshops as 'rolling around on the floor'.

14 In work of this kind, students are like actors, discovering links between themselves and the impulses of language. For professional actors, however, critical theory is inevitably subordinated to the pressure of performance – needing to 'find' the part, to discover the emotions and experience of the character, and embody them. Articulating the search for the role in this personal way can sound exclusive or essentialist, but actors know, as students soon discover in workshops, that the parts they play are made from the meeting of themselves with texts and that stage history is an ever-changing record of such encounters. The 'definitive performance' is a competitive concept, 'definitive' for a generation only. In the last thirty or so years, the study of stage history (that is, the history of productions of a text) has paralleled the changes in literary criticism: both theatre audiences and readers of plays are acknowledged as active makers of meaning. We have come to see that the observation that, for example, David Garrick's Hamlet says more about the eighteenth century than it does about Shakespeare, applies equally, when eighteenth is swapped for twentieth or twenty-first, to the Hamlets of our own time.

15 Active techniques to teaching are essentially 'progressive' and 'student-centred', though there is a good deal of rote-learning and repetition, too, in many of the suggestions for teaching Shakespeare's language in Chapter 2. Both 'progressive' and 'student-centred', like the phrase 'politically correct', are frequently perceived now to be discredited or negative terms. Today's popular view is that student-centred and progressive ideas swept through education in Britain in the 1960s and 1970s, much as the Vandals and Goths swept through Europe in the Dark Ages. Critics were quick to diagnose sloppiness and the abrogation of teacher responsibility: the teacher who arrived with no plan, just a disingenuous eagerness to 'listen to the kids' and respond to their interests; the project work that entailed double periods of 'finding out for

yourself' in the library, and week-ends at home spent collecting leaflets, or copying out, or sending off for, masses of material to be included in bulky folders.

There was certainly, however, no inherent reason why progressive methods should not be structured, disciplined and purposeful. For the overwhelming majority of teachers committed to these methods, myself included, experience of them has always involved as much, or more, of the structure and discipline associated with traditional methods, as well as considerable managerial skill to implement them. My own recollections of the same period are, therefore, rather different. One introduced new methods in order to better children's education – and their exam results. For instance, in the early 1970s I took classes of School 'O' Level English Language failures for November and June re-sit exams. in a College of Further Education. These were well-motivated students enjoying their new independence in college and their re-sit results improved, sometimes dramatically, but I would partly attribute their success to the injection of life and interest brought to them by the stimulus of the new active and 'progressive' methods of teaching that they encountered. We used drama, creative writing and two new anthologies of prose, poetry and photographs, for all our work. The anthologies contained modern classics, as well as a range of contemporary items which were socially, and geographically, inclusive. The images and the writing were full of acute observation and of broad moral commitment completely in line both with the Leavisian tradition of 'seriousness' in nineteenth- and twentieth-century English Literature, and the idealism and social consciousness of the 1960s. They engaged the children's minds and imaginations and extended their sympathies. Used in conjunction with active methods (for example, for comprehension we used a variety of small working groups and 'in role' techniques to devise questions from the anthologies), they contributed greatly to the development of the children's literacy. I used all kinds of approaches for writing. One dark autumn morning (I think this was during the brief period in Britain when the clocks went forward two hours in March, instead of one hour, so it was still dark when classes started at 9 a.m.), we watched the sun rise, each individual noting down every rapid change in the shapes and colours of the clouds, and another time we experimented with automatic writing, which we then turned into conventional prose. I taught sentence structure and grammatical English without recourse to the traditional grammar lesson and marked, I hope, with tact, certainly not submerging work in red ink, but there was no sense of abandoning standards or that the new progressive methods were sloppy or undemanding. They just seemed to make it possible to connect more effectively and to achieve better results with students.

16 Companies such as Théâtre de Complicité, Cheek By Jowl and Volcano have shown how rich 'free exploration' of texts can be.

2 Shakespeare's language

1 It is true that those 'beginners' who seriously set about comprehending Shakespearian language will be surprised how much, at the first level of meaning, they actually know. A similar approach to 'perceived difficulty' is taken by the New York language teacher, Michel Thomas, when he is teaching French to beginners. One of his opening strategies is to demonstrate, with the full involvement of his pupils, how much French they already actually know – using the vast number of everyday words that are essentially the same in both

languages, though pronounced differently. However, the resistance I am discussing is more to do with the wholesale alienation of people from the total cultural event of Shakespeare's drama, of which language is the central part, but which is also to do with its history, theatricality, style, expansiveness, distance – its ways of seeing and its structures of feeling, in fact. It is the language that seems to circumscribe everything else, to keep it 'in bond'.

2 Debate about Elizabethan and Jacobean performance styles was once vigorous between the 'formalists', who saw Renaissance acting as highly stylised and restricted (and as emerging from the study of rhetoric and oratory in schools and universities), and the 'naturalists', who argued that acting styles were flexible and life-like. In some modern accounts, however, such as Peter Holland's in '*Hamlet* and the art of acting', there is recognition that all systems of acting are ultimately conventional:

> All acting is formalized to the extent that it observes and uses what it sees as constituting reality, formalizing it into patterns that imitate and represent that reality. Those formalized patterns are the only means by which the audience can understand the acting within the terms of the shared culture. Equally well, the audience may, and usually does, agree to accept this formalized pattern as a representation of reality for the purposes of the drama that is being performed . . . the claimed 'naturalism' is merely another set of conventions, a different claim for a representation of reality in a differently formalized pattern.
>
> (Holland 1984: 43–4)

Nevertheless, we know that there was a general movement in Elizabethan acting from formalised towards naturalistic styles and that exaggerated or pantomimic gestures were widely condemned in the late Elizabethan period. Andrew Gurr's chapter 'The Players,' in *The Shakespearean Stage, 1574–1642*, gathers together a wealth of detail on the whole question of Elizabethan acting styles, but although gesture is a rich source of techniques for Shakespeare workshops today, the apparent continuity between Elizabethan performance practice and modern workshop practice has been explored little as yet. Gurr, discussing *Chirologia* and *Chironomia* (1644) by the teacher of the deaf, John Bulwer, writes:

> The thoughtful man is shown scratching his head, threats are made with a shaking of the clenched fist, a finger on the lips asks for silence, and oaths are sworn with raised palm, much as one might expect today if one were to seek out gestures with which to mime such processes. Of Bulwer's illustrations, 120 in all, perhaps 20 would not still be readily recognisable to a modern audience.
>
> (Gurr 1980: 85)

Gesture, which may in the theatre seem to be more to do with mime, dumb-show or even (in Thomas Campion's words) 'childish observing of words', is important in the workshop, especially in helping students to express meaning physically, memorise sequences of actions and engage, as actors, with each other.

3 See also the Arden edition of *A Midsummer Night's Dream*, edited by Harold Brooks (Brooks 1979: xlv–xlviii).

4 Christine Way has written: 'I have always told my students that Shakespeare very often puts important words at the end of the line and therefore to take notice of them. I was fascinated recently when I discovered that the late Sir

Ralph Richardson's only advice to a group of drama students was "take a coloured pen and underline the word at the end of each line"' (Way 1994: 16).

5   'Natural', because the caesura reflects the way we pause, when speaking, to allow listeners to keep up with our train of thought. I like Cicely Berry's definition because it picks up on the relationship of the caesura to actual speech: 'Sometimes this break coincides with a full-stop or a colon, and so with a break in thought. But more often it . . . is simply a poise on a word – i.e., the word holds and lifts for a fraction of a moment before it plunges into the second half of the line. This poise is necessary for the ear of the listener in that it allows a space, a still moment, for us to clock the key word in the line, and so be ready for the information in the second half of the line – to throw it up as it were' (Berry 1987: 58).

6   The most extreme example of this that I remember seeing was Ian Bannen's Hamlet in Stratford in 1961. Bannen could certainly speak verse, but he did not believe that Hamlet always should. Sometimes words were deliberately lost in naturalistic mumbling, but these were times when dignified conventions and traditions were seen by many actors and directors, as stultifying and artificial. Bannen was thought to have brought the dignity of the Prince into disrepute by, among other things, speaking 'Oh what a rogue and peasant slave am I!' from within the players' costume trunk.

3 Narrative in Shakespeare

1   Two recent examples are Andrew Davies's TV re-working of *Othello* for ITV in 2001 and *10 Things I Hate About You*, the 1999 Hollywood film directed by Gil Junger, based on *The Taming of the Shrew*.

2   Most readily available in Boal 1992: 2–3.

3   See Tucker and Holden (1993) – or any of their editions of the plays in *The Shakespeare's Globe Acting Edition* – for an example of a reconstructed platt. This edition is a great source of ideas for practical work, especially when used in connection with a visit to Shakespeare's Globe Theatre in London.

4   At one of our Stratford Summer Schools, Ulla Mundil introduced an excellent empathic warm-up for developing appreciation of the feelings of love and revulsion in these lovers' scenes in *Dream*. She asked someone to approach another person across the circle and to say 'I love you . . . No, I don't', taking time to feel, and show, the establishment of love and the change to revulsion, before walking back to their place in the circle, thus signalling that the person just approached should carry the exercise on in the same way. This activity could be done in groups of four, after *Lovers' tag*, before starting on *Fond pageant*.

5   As a warm-up, you might use *Flowing pairs* (p. 156).

6   I was introduced to this particular version of 'uniting' many years ago by the West Midlands Theatre Company Pentabus, who used it as the first stage of all their rehearsals.

7   When directing *Richard II* for the RSC in 1973, John Barton divided up the play into sequentially numbered scenes, each with its own title, instead of following the Act and Scene divisions of the text. The prompt-book, now kept in the Shakespeare Centre Library in Stratford-upon-Avon, shows that these titles were brief and substantive, often reflecting the importance of particular characters (e.g. 'Duchess of Gloucester', 'Welsh Captains') or particular events or places (e.g. 'Banishment', 'Flint Castle', 'Deposition') at certain moments in the play.

8 The director Max Stafford-Clark's version of unit titles involves the idea of action. He calls for titles with transitive verbs, e.g. 'Hamlet taunts the King.'

9 Instead of these old continuous rolls of 'computer paper', one could now use end rolls of newsprint, sometimes obtainable from local newspapers, or several sheets of flip-chart paper stuck together.

10 The statements are:

- If any in Vienna be of worth it is Lord Angelo
- Lord Angelo scarce confesses/ That his blood flows, or that his appetite/ Is more to bread than snow
- A man whose blood/ Is very snow-broth, one who never feels/ The wanton stings and motions of the senses
- When he makes water his urine is congealed ice
- Most damned Angelo
- Murderer
- Adulterous thief
- An hypocrite, a virgin-violator
- Thou cruel Angelo
- I crave no other nor no better man
- One so learned and so wise.

4 Character in Shakeseare

1 John Philip Kemble first played Hamlet in 1793.

2 Different productions over time, for example, have seen the personal, moral responsibility of Lear rather differently. Charles Laughton's 1959 Lear was a snowy-haired, foolish, fond old man, very much 'more sinned against than sinning', in the Victorian tradition, while Paul Schofield's Lear in Peter Brook's 1962 production, was authoritarian, sclerotic, irascible, unreasonable, implicated in some way in the cruelty to which he himself fell victim. In 2002, Nonso Anozie's young Lear for the RSC Academy's production was powerful, but vulnerable, bewildered and unpredictable (after hugging Cordelia in the first scene, he hurled her to the floor). He seemed to stumble into his own destruction. What it took to exhaust and kill this Lear through madness and suffering became an agonising and terrifying spectacle.

3 The activity *How to tame Katherina* (pp. 78–9) uses the same section of text, but in a different way.

4 This brief was drawn up by my colleague, Rob Jeffcoate, for one of our Arena Theatre Summer Schools.

8 Warm-ups and preparation: drama exercises

1 This description is quoted by Andrew Gurr (1980: 85), from E. Nungezer (1929) *A Dictionary of Actors and of Other Persons Associated with the Public Representation of Plays in England before 1642* (New Haven: Yale University Press).

2 See Stephanie Martin and Lyn Darnley (1996) *The Teaching Voice* on the health and care of the voice.

References

Barker, Clive (1977) *Theatre Games*, London: Eyre Methuen.

Bate, Jonathan (1997) *The Genius of Shakespeare*, London: Picador.

Berry, Cicely (1987) *The Actor and the Text*, London: Harrap.

—— (2001) *Text in Action*, London: Virgin Publishing Ltd.

Boal, Augusto (1979; first published 1974) *Theatre of the Oppressed*, London: Pluto Press.

—— (1992) *Games for Actors and Non-Actors*, London: Routledge.

Brooks, Harold (ed.) (1979) *A Midsummer Night's Dream*, London: Arden.

Coles, Janet (1990) '"A" Level Workshops: Active Discoveries', in Rex Gibson (ed.) *Secondary School Shakespeare*, Cambridge: Cambridge Institute of Education.

Dale, Angela (1989) 'How to Have an Exciting Time Teaching Bored Third Years!' in Rex Gibson (ed.) *Shakespeare and Schools Newsletter* No. 8, Spring, Cambridge: Cambridge Institute of Education.

DES (1988) *Report of the Committee of Inquiry into the Teaching of English Language*, (the Kingman Report), London: HMSO.

Dollimore, Jonathan (1984) *Radical Tragedy*, Brighton: Harvester.

Elam, Keir (1984) *Shakespeare's Universe of Discourse*, Cambridge: Cambridge University Press.

Finch, Graham and Derek Marston, with acknowledgements to Dorothy Heathcote (1987) 'Focus on *Macbeth* . . . a Page of Ideas for Teachers – by Teachers', in Rex Gibson (ed.) *Shakespeare and Schools Newsletter* No. 2, Spring, Cambridge: Cambridge Institute of Education.

Fluegelman, Andrew (1976) *The New Games Book*, New York: Doubleday.

Gibson, Rex (ed.) (1986–94) *Shakespeare and Schools Newsletter* Nos. 1–24, Cambridge: Cambridge Institute of Education.

—— (1988) 'Teaching *The Tempest* . . . Active Explorations', in Rex Gibson (ed.) *Shakespeare and Schools Newsletter* No. 7, Autumn, Cambridge: Cambridge Institute of Education.

—— (1989a) 'RSC on Tour', in Rex Gibson (ed.) *Shakespeare and Schools Newsletter* No. 9, Summer, Cambridge: Cambridge Institute of Education.

—— (1989b) 'W.H. Smith Interact: A National Theatre *Twelfth Night* Workshop,' in Rex Gibson (ed.) *Shakespeare and Schools Newsletter* No. 10, Autumn, Cambridge: Cambridge Institute of Education.

—— (ed.) (1990) *Secondary School Shakespeare*, Cambridge: Cambridge Institute of Education.

—— (Series ed.) (1992) *Cambridge School Shakepeare*, Cambridge: Cambridge University.

—— (1997) *Shakespeare's Language*, Cambridge: Cambridge University Press.

—— (1998) *Teaching Shakespeare*, Cambridge: Cambridge University Press.

—— (2000a) *Stepping into Shakespeare*, Cambridge: Cambridge University Press.

—— (2000b) 'Narrative Approaches to Shakespeare: Active Storytelling in Schools', in (ed.) Peter Holland, *Shakespeare Survey No.53: Shakespeare and Narrative*, Cambridge: Cambridge University Press.

Gilmour, Maurice (ed.) (1997a) *Shakespeare for All in Primary Schools*, London: Cassell.

—— (ed.) (1997b) *Shakespeare for All in Secondary Schools*, London: Cassell.

Goldswain, Ralph (1990) 'Two Lessons on *Measure for Measure*: Sixth Form Shakespeare', in Rex Gibson (ed.) *Secondary School Shakespeare*, Cambridge: Cambridge Institute of Education.

Griffin, Malcolm (2001) *Everyday Safety for Secondary Schools*, London: Routledge.

Gurr, Andrew (1980) *The Shakespearean Stage, 1574–1642*, Cambridge: Cambridge University Press.

Hahlo, Richard and Peter Reynolds (2000) *Dramatic Events: How to Run a Successful Workshop*, London: Faber & Faber.

Holland, Peter (1984) '*Hamlet* and the Art of Acting', in James Redmond (ed.) *Themes in Drama 6: Drama and the Actor*, Cambridge: Cambridge University Press.

Hunt, Albert (1976) *Hopes for Great Happenings*, London: Eyre Methuen.

Jeffcoate, Robert (1992) *Starting English Teaching*, London: Routledge.

—— (2002) 'How Should We Teach Shakespeare's Plays?', in *Der Fremdsprachliche Unterricht Englisch* No. 56 *Shakespeare Kreativ*.

Jennings, Sue (1986) *Creative Drama in Groupwork*, Bicester: Winslow Press.

Johnston, Chris (1998) *House of Games*, London: Nick Hern Books.

Johnstone, Keith (1979) *Impro*, London: Eyre Methuen; new edition, 1979, London: Faber & Faber.

—— (1999) *Impro for Storytellers*, London: Faber & Faber.

Kermode, Frank (2002) *Shakespeare's Language*, London: Penguin.

Leach, Sue (1992) *Shakespeare in the Classroom: What's the Matter?* London: Open University Press

Leith, Dick and George Myerson (1989) *The Power of Address: Explorations in Rhetoric*, London: Routledge.

Lewis, Paul (1987) 'Boydell, the Shakespeare Gallery and National Identity', in *AD HOC: Art, Design and History of Culture* No. 1, Autumn, Wolverhampton: University of Wolverhampton.

Linklater, Kristin (1992) *Freeing Shakespeare's Voice*, New York: Theatre Communications Group.

Marowitz, Charles and Simon Trussler (1967) *Theatre at Work*, London: Methuen.

Martin, Stephanie and Lyn Darnley (1996) *The Teaching Voice*, London: Whurr Publishers.

McGregor, Lynn, Maggie Tate and Ken Robinson (1977) *Learning Through Drama*, London: Heinemann Educational Books for the Schools Council.

Neelands, Jonothan (1984) *Making Sense of Drama*, London: Heinemann Educational Books in association with 2D Magazine.

O'Brien, Veronica (1982) *Teaching Shakespeare*, London: Edward Arnold.

O'Neill, Cecily, Alan Lambert, Rosemary Linnell and Janet Warr-Wood (1977) *Drama Guidelines*, London: Heinemann Educational Books in association with London Drama.

Pinder, Brenda (1991) 'Inquests and Inquiries: Trials and Tribunals', in Rex Gibson (ed.) *Shakespeare and Schools Newsletter* No. 16, Autumn, Cambridge: Cambridge Institute of Education.

Poulter, Christine (1987) *Playing the Game*, Basingstoke: Macmillan

Reynolds, Peter (1991) *Practical Approaches to Teaching Shakespeare*, London: Oxford University Press.

Rodenburg, Patsy (2002) *Speaking Shakespeare*, London: Methuen.

Slade, Peter (1954) *Child Drama*, London: University of London Press.

Spolin, Viola (1973) *Improvisation for the Theatre*, London: Pitman; first published 1963, Evanston, Illinois: Northwestern University Press

Stanislavski, Constantin (1937) *An Actor Prepares*, London: Geoffrey Bles.

Thomas, Peter (1987) 'Shakespeare: Page to Stage: An A Level Approach to *Antony and Cleopatra*', in Rex Gibson (ed.) *Shakespeare and Schools Newsletter* No. 2, Spring, Cambridge: Cambridge Institute of Education.

Timm, Norbert (ed.) (2001) *Romeo and Juliet*, Paderborn: Schöningh.

Tucker, Patrick and Michael Holden (eds) (1993) *The Shakespeare's Globe Acting Edition: Measure for Measure*, London: MH Publications.

—— (2002) *Secrets of Acting Shakespeare*, London: Routledge.

Vickers, Brian (1971) 'Shakespeare's Use of Rhetoric', in K. Muir and S. Schoenbaum (eds) *A New Companion to Shakespeare Studies*, London: Cambridge University Press.

Way, Christine (1994) 'Line Endings', in Rex Gibson (ed.) *Shakespeare and Schools Newsletter* No. 24, Summer, Cambridge: Cambridge Institute of Education.

Wells, Stanley (2002) *Shakespeare For All Time*, London: Macmillan.

Index

Specific activities, exercises, games and teaching techniques are identified in the Index below, using brackets immediately after their titles. **Bold type** indicates where explanations of practical approaches and techniques may be found in the main text.

Comments or suggestions

If you have any comments or suggestions on any of the activities, games or exercises in this book, please send them to the author. They will be gratefully received and acknowledged.

Email address: james.stredder@btinternet.com
Postal address: Wincot Press, 42 Maidenhead Road, Stratford-Upon-Avon, Warwickshire, CV37 6XT.